HIT
WOMAN

HIT WOMAN

Adventures in Life and Love
during the Golden Age of American Pop Music

A Memoir

SUSAN HAMILTON

HIT WOMAN
*Adventures in Life and Love during the Golden
Age of American Pop Music / Susan Hamilton*

Copyright © Susan Hamilton 2013

Cover line drawing © Al Hirschfeld. Reproduced by arrangement with Hirschfeld's exclusive representative, the Margo Feiden Galleries Ltd., New York. www.alhirschfeld.com. All photographs are courtesy of the author, with the exception of *Not As a Stranger* courtesy of Metro-Goldwyn-Mayer Studios Inc.

ISBN 978-0-9894930-0-0

Library of Congress LCNN: 2013952660

Hit Woman may be purchased for business or promotional use. For information, please email the Special Markets Department at:
 SPsales@HitWomanBooks.com.

1. Biography & Autobiography: Entertainment & Performing Arts – General   2. Music: Business Aspects 3. Biography & Autobiography: Women 4. Biography & Autobiography: Personal Memoirs   5. Business & Economics – Advertising & Promotion 6. Biography & Autobiography – Composers & Musicians

First Edition

Hit Woman is also available in paperback and electronic formats

Published by Hitwoman Publishing

To my two muses: Michael and Alex

ACKNOWLEDGEMENTS:

I never thought I was a writer. My heartfelt thanks to all who contributed so generously — and changed my mind: James Patterson, Mary Jordan, Glenn Berger, Marvin Waldman, Bob and Loretta Cox, Sue Read and Michael Golub, Richard Benoit, Steve Sohmer, Lynne Lussier, Steve Smith, Ned White, John McCurry, Jim Wilkinson, Gerard McConville, Hunter Murtaugh, Rachel Margulies Smit, Doug Katsaros, Bryce Lee, John Nieman, Manny Perez, David Briggs, Gordon Grody, Don Hahn, Kevin Halpin, David Shostac, Connie Boylan, David Wolfert, David Lucas, Bernard Drayton, Arthur Schroeck, Linda November, Jumpsturdy Klieger, Jeannie Davis, Frank Denson, Bill Radice, Ben Lieberman and Pat Brewitt.

Table of Contents

PART III: BIG TIMES

PART IV: SOLO

PART V: REINVENTION

FOREWORD

Susan Hamilton is someone you don't know you already know — she has been the talent and brains behind many of the most successful commercials and popular songs that we have all heard for much of our lives on the radio and television. She has also run into, made music with, laughed with and yes, loved, many of the most famous and brilliant people in the world of music.

We knew she could compose and produce a song, but here is the surprise: she's also a writer.

— Judy Collins

Prologue

——

THE PHONE RANG late on a Friday afternoon. It was Sue Read, speaking in a deep-throated whisper.

"Are you alone in the office?"

I explained that a couple of us were just winding down from the week with a cocktail or two.

She rasped, "Frank and I are coming over now and we need complete privacy."

It didn't take them long. Their ad agency, Lintas, was a few blocks away. Frank DeVito, hunk honcho creative director, and Sue Read, senior writer on the Diet Coke account, were ushered up the stairs to Bernie Drayton's room for the total security evidently required for this meeting. They sat on the broken-down couch and I stood. Sue got control of her rapid breathing and announced, "We got Elton."

This was the late '80s, and HEA Productions, the music company I now owned outright, had become the largest jingle-production enterprise in the world. A few weeks before, I (with the help of arranger Doug Katsaros) had produced the winning re-arrangement of the Diet Coke "Just For The Taste of It" jingle — so I knew what they were talking about. All I could say was "wow."

A couple of weeks later I was working in L.A. when I got the next call from Sue Read. "Elton wants to meet with you tomorrow, so get your ass on a plane and be at Madison Square Garden at seven." For months, Sue, the creative genius behind the new campaign, had relentlessly fought both agency and client to overcome the unspoken homophobia. It was also true that her single-mindedness could be, at times, nerve-wracking...

The circus had just left. The huge underground corridors reeked of elephant dung and big cat piss.

Motherly Connie Hillman, one of Elton's people, showed me to the green room. It was just after 7 pm, and for almost an hour I sat there, trying to look nonchalant. Billie Jean King was there. Eric Clapton was there. Bernie Taupin, Elton's lyricist, popped in for a moment. There was a splendid overflowing cornucopia of gourmet delicacies and vintage wines arrayed across a broad table. I didn't move; I didn't speak; I watched the clock. At 7:55, only five minutes before show time, I had given up all hope of a meeting. Suddenly the door opened and Connie motioned me out. She led me into one of the radiating corridors that fed onto the stage. Elton was standing there, waiting for me.

Even in the florescent-lit, ugly gray surroundings, Elton looked fabulous in a sparkling all-white Versace three-piece suit. He got right down to business.

"I've checked you out and heard nothing but good things, so you can go ahead and produce the tracks. Where do you want to do them?"

I told him I would record them here in New York with my favorite people. He said fine, but wanted to overdub his piano track and vocals in Boston on the day before he started shooting. Our day-time session would fit nicely into his schedule. Of course I agreed.

All the while we had been talking, we'd also been walking closer and closer to the stage. He kept gesturing for me to follow him.

"If you have to reach me in Boston, call the hotel and ask for 'Yves Ho'." He did spell it out for me, with a smile.

I stopped dead at the edge of the darkened stage as the band started the intro to "Benny and the Jets," but he kept talking and waving me forward. I had to hear what he was saying so I moved right out onto the stage floor in the dark. I looked up.

The crowd was roaring and there were thousands upon thousands of lighters being held up high and swung back and forth. My knees buckled. Laughing at the panic in my face, he waved good-bye and said something like, "It's going to be fun working together!" With that, he spun on his heels and, timing it perfectly to the last four beats of the intro, strode over to the piano bench, sat and hit the first chord with full force. The lights slammed on. I fled.

A few weeks later Sue Read, Rick Kerr (my engineer), and I boarded the shuttle to fly up to Boston. The basic tracks had been recorded at Power Station. Dougie (Doug Katsaros) had done his usual terrific job of arranging, and I was proud of the production. All was well; I anticipated a quick, easy session with Elton. He was booked for noon, and although he had a concert in Massachusetts that night, we really didn't have that much to do. A couple of 60's, a couple of 30's — piece of cake. Setting up the amenities specified in a rider on Elton's contract was a tougher assignment than this little session was going to be. Sue had stressed and fussed for weeks about everything from the proper furniture in the waiting room, to setting up a private bathroom for Elton where there wasn't one, to finding the correct wines, gourmet foods, newspapers and selection of current popular movie videos. I kid you not — all for a session that was going to take an hour or two.

Our problems started early. There was thick fog; the plane couldn't take off. We had booked an extremely early flight on purpose, but as the time ticked by on the tarmac, Sue started to lose it. She threatened the airline by shouting at the stewardess. "Do you know who we're going to meet? Elton John, for God's sake! *ELTON JOHN!!* Do something, PLEASE!"

I tried to tell her there was nothing to do, but she grabbed my arm so tightly I had fingernail marks for days. Rick pretended to sleep next to the window.

When the plane finally did take off, it was pretty rough. "We're going to crash and we're all going to die. I just know it. I'll never get to work with Elton. Never. I might as well just kill myself now." Sue had a lot invested in this project, but then again, this behavior was not exactly new to me. She was fiercely passionate about her work.

We made it to the studio a little after eleven. Sue calmed herself by hassling every person who worked there. In the client lounge, she rearranged couches and little wrought iron cafe tables with chairs at least four times. She had the staff make a sign for the bathroom that read 'for use by Elton *ONLY!*' She refolded and restacked the newspapers three times. She engaged me in a discussion about which video should be on top of the pile. Rick and I escaped into the control room to set up, and then we all settled down to await Elton's arrival.

And we waited, and waited, and waited some more as we watched the big hand go 'round the clock.

Around two, John Reed, Elton's longtime manager, burst through the door and flung himself onto the middle of the couch, his arms spread wide across the back. He stared at Sue and me. "He's says he can't do it, Sue; he can't do the job." I had a sudden vision of the bottoms of Sue's perfect little black heels as I imagined her throwing herself through the sixth floor plate glass window.

John Reed continued, "He's telling me he's quitting the business, the whole business. He's never doing another concert; he's never entering another recording studio. He's done. Finished. Had it. It's over."

Sue stood, ashen, completely silent, swaying slightly. I thought she was going to keel over. My mind raced. *Who else could we get to do it? Billy Joel? Don Henley? Glenn Frey? Yes, the key would be fine.* Okay, we'd probably have to change the arrangement some but hey, what else was I going to think about? The show must go on.

It was then that John Reed delivered the final blow. The *coup de gras*. He sighed dramatically and said, "Do you know what he told me just now? He told me, 'John, I'm just not the Pinball Wizard anymore.'"

Suddenly I remembered. *Holy shit! – the convention!!* At that very moment, Coca-Cola was having its annual Bottlers' Convention in New Orleans, and it would be right about now that they were going to play a videotape of Elton himself announcing from a huge screen that he was going to be the celebrity spokesperson for Diet Coke.

I whispered to Sue and rushed over to the stupid beat-up pay phone on the wall. As I scrabbled in my purse for a quarter, she ticked off the names of the account guys I had to find. After some agonizing minutes, I located one of them and had him pull the tape. Bad for the agency and the convention — but better for Coca-Cola, in case the whole thing really did fall apart.

Then a very strange phenomenon occurred. It was as if the whole building started vibrating in a wave of energy that was coming toward us, and we knew. Elton had entered the building.

We all froze. Elton walked briskly into the room, looked at me, sat down at one of the red cafe tables, and asked politely if he could have a ham sandwich and a cup of coffee. He looked pretty bad. Nothing like the Elton I had met a few weeks earlier in the bowels of Madison Square Garden. He looked pasty and puffy; what little hair he had was cut very short and snow white. Dressed in khakis and a short-sleeved shirt, this Elton was a tired older man. I got the sandwich; I think Sue got the coffee, and Rick disappeared into the control room.

Elton ate steadily, sipped the coffee and patted his mouth delicately with a paper napkin. Didn't even glance at the glorious array of foods, wines, etc. He just looked directly at me again and said, "Well, let's get this done, shall we?"

I led Elton into the booth. We had set up an electric keyboard with a really good acoustic piano sample in the control room. That's what Elton had requested. I had Rick play the track a couple of times, first with Dougie's scratch piano track and then without — assuming all the time that Elton was already quite familiar with the music. I quickly realized he had never heard it before, despite the multiple copies the agency had sent all over the country.

When I put a basic chord chart next to him, he shook his head and asked to hear the track again. He started to play along. It was a complete disaster. My heart sank. The chords were wrong; he was out of sync with the track; I didn't know what to say. The volume of the music was deafening, and he didn't look once at the chart. He motioned me over to his side and screamed, "Just yell the changes into my ear." So I stood next to him and did just that, trying to anticipate correctly. Suddenly, one bar fell into place and was perfect; then another; then another. Within three or four takes, we had a brilliant performance.

I was greatly relieved — exhilarated, but exhausted. Just drained. Elton seemed fine. He was ready to sing.

The same astonishing transformation from nightmare to perfection happened with the vocals. As he stood in front of the microphone, alone in the big studio, the first few lines he sang sounded terrible. Strident, out of tune, making up his own melody. Without coaching, without comment from me, it began to happen. First there was one great phrase, then another, then another. We got three or four great takes on tape and I was delighted. At one point, Sue did lean over to me and whisper, "Is he lisping a bit on the 'just for the taste' part?" I looked at her and said, "Would you like to ask him that?" She shut up.

After I was sure we had it, I let her speak to Elton on the talkback. She was dying to. She said, "It's wonderful, fantastic. How about you do one more take just for the fun of it?"

He stared at her for a full 30 seconds. Finally, he turned toward me. "What do you think?"

"I think we're good."

Elton could not have been more cordial to everyone as he left. He told Sue he would see her in the morning on the set. He thanked me; he thanked Rick. And then he was gone.

We collapsed. Immediately Sue called the client, Mike Beindorff, then the account team in New Orleans. They would be able to present the video at the following morning's session.

We spent the next hour trying to recover — helped by a couple of bottles of the very good vintage wines Coca-Cola had provided. We felt we deserved them.

My luck had held once again. Disaster averted; the ever-lurking dragons chased back into the shadows — at least for the moment.

In the beginning, things weren't always so simple...

Part I

INVENTION

Chapter 1

Sweet Revenge

———

I T WAS TIME TO GET A JOB. I had finished my Fulbright year in
Rome and come home to recover from hepatitis A. I'd contracted
it by being macho-stupid and eating raw mussels off the docks in
Bari, a town located at the top of the heel of the boot that is Italy. I
convalesced all summer at my parents' house in New Jersey, sleeping
in a stuffy attic room with my sister Janet and listening to the Lovin'
Spoonful sing "Summer in the City" through a tinny portable radio.

Even though I had been encouraged to apply for a second
Fulbright year, I'd made the decision not to do it. The life of a concert
pianist — a soloist who tours without even the companionship of an accompanist — was not for me. Too isolated. Too lonely. Not enough
fun.

So when fall arrived, I set out on the bus to New York City with my
father to begin the adventure of finding a job. At that time, Pa was
working in Manhattan as a personal secretary to one of the Rockefel-
lers — a boring, demeaning, low-paying job that depressed the hell out
of him. But we needed the money.

The Manhattan of September 1966 was a very different place from
today's. There was no Internet to help you look for jobs, only the *New
York Times* want ads. I soon hooked up with an employment agency.
They sent me out to interview day after day. There being no such
things as cell phones, in order to check back with the agency after each

interview, I used one of the phone booths that stood on every corner. A lot of the encounters with prospective employers were tedious dead ends, but some were pretty funny.

I had a couple of go-arounds with an Italian cashmere company that imported high-end clothing and fabrics. They needed someone who spoke and wrote fluent Italian. That I could do, but I really wasn't interested in the import-export business. I couldn't see myself working in a formal showroom, dressed in cashmere sweater sets. In those days, I looked more like a slightly overweight ballet dancer, or possibly a classical music chick. With long hair parted in the middle and hopelessly out-of-fashion clothes, there was nothing sophisticated or hip about my sense of style.

A less boring opportunity came in the form of a rotund, jolly little old man with spectacles and a pronounced twinkle in his eyes. Yes, he did look like Santa Claus, but without the red suit. He'd made his fortune as a macaroni king in the Newark area, and had also written a book, *Laugh With Me by P. T. Magee.* Yep, for real (and filled with bad jokes). Mr. Magee was an amateur theater nut and had plans to build a professional theater somewhere across the river in Jersey. I had dabbled quite seriously in drama during my college years, including performances as Juliet in a professional summer theater program. Despite some good reviews and my earlier childhood film experience, acting didn't interest me. I wanted to work behind the scenes.

On our second or third interview, Mr. Magee took me to Aqueduct Raceway. He told me he spent at least two or three days a week there. He gave me a hundred dollars to bet with and a few tips about specific horses. I made a couple of wagers and suddenly had $800 in my pocket! Of course I was thrilled, and couldn't wait to show my parents. I refused to place any more bets, fearful of losing. Mr. McGee waited and waited. Then, at the end of the day, he placed $2,000 on one of the favorites. He won $5,000 and was ready to go home. I guess he was a pro.

A week-long trip with him to Japan? That's what he suggested for our next interview. My mother put an end to the relationship immediately. Of course I wanted to go, but didn't put up too much of a fight. I understood her apprehension, albeit grudgingly.

I continued my daily bus trips to the City, trudging around from office to office, sometimes getting to see someone, sometimes just leaving my resume. One of those places was a company named Music Makers, Inc. I dropped off a resume and forgot about it.

I was in the middle of an interview somewhere over on the East Side when a secretary rushed in with an urgent message. I was to call the employment agency immediately. They told me to drop everything and hurry across town to the Warwick Hotel. Mr. Mitch Leigh of Music Makers wanted to see me. Apparently, he had read my resume and insisted on interviewing me right then, that day, that hour.

In those days, whatever Mitch wanted, Mitch got. I soon learned that Music Makers was not only the most successful jingle company in the City, but that Mr. Leigh had also composed the music for Man of La Mancha — the most popular show on Broadway.

I rode the elevator up to the penthouse in that most elegant hotel. Mitch was waiting for me as the doors opened. He was a big man, tall, broad and imposing. He was wearing a royal blue terry cloth jumpsuit, a scarf, and sneakers. The outfit may have been a little dramatic, but after all, he was a theater person. I spent about three hours with him and loved every minute of it. He was powerful, charming, funny and very very smart. We talked and talked about everything, wandering around his gorgeous apartment. Filled with antiques and oriental carpets, the place had a wrap-around terrace with a spectacular view.

He hired me on the spot. Told me, "Susan, you are going to be my right hand person. You will be my fingers on the piano and my very personal assistant." Although he played many instruments, he didn't do very well with the piano. "I'm off to Spain for a couple of weeks to open my Broadway show there; then I'll be back in New York. You'd better go home and rest up with your family for two weeks, 'cause when I get back, I'm gonna work your ass off!"

My eyes must have opened wide at the language because he laughed at my expression as he walked me to the door. I floated out of that penthouse on cloud nine.

Two weeks came and went with no word. Into the third week, I finally screwed up my courage and called Music Makers. I was directed to Mr. Leigh's social secretary who told me, "Oh yes, Mr. Leigh has decided there is no room for you here after all."

I was devastated. Most of all, I hated the disappointment I knew my parents would feel. As usual, we needed money.

About a week later, I answered another ad in the *New York Times*. It read: "Wanted: secretary for new music production company, $90 a week."

The interview took place in their office on East 44th Street. The place was not much more than a studio apartment with a couple of desks, a second-hand sofa, and a little spinet that had seen better days.

There I met Herman Edel and his brother Buddy. Amazingly, it seemed we had a common bone to pick. It turned out that Herman was the former President of Music Makers. He had just been through a major fallout with Mitch Leigh! Now he was starting his own competing jingle business, Herman Edel Associates. I was hired.

It was the only job I would ever have in the music business. I bought him out in 1974 and continued on my wild and wonderful 40-year ride.

Sometime in the late '70s, I took a phone call from a man named Milton Herson. He introduced himself as President of Music Makers, representing Mitch Leigh. He explained, "Mr. Leigh and I have heard nothing but wonderful things about you and your company. You're supposed to be the best in the business, and Mr. Leigh has decided he would like you to represent him. He'd like you to include him as one of your writers."

I must have paused for quite a while as my mind raced with all of the things I could say. But I simply told the man, "I'm sorry but there really isn't any room here for Mr. Leigh. Please thank him, though. For his interest."

A MAJOR CLIENT of ours always demanded, "More tiffany! More tiffany!" We never corrected him.

Chapter 2

Early Years

M Y MOTHER, CAROLINA CESARINA ALESSANDRONI HAMILTON, found her eyelids getting heavy every night as she rode the bus home from Manhattan to Rutherford, New Jersey. She had finally landed a place in the chorus of a Broadway show, and opening night was approaching. It was thrilling.

The year was 1944; things were looking up. The tide of the War seemed to be turning in America's favor, and my father, Roger Hamilton, was at home. He had been designated 1-F because of a perforated eardrum. He wasn't happy about being left out of all the action, but my mother was. Lately, though, she had been feeling unusually tired much of the time and kept having to unbutton the waistband of her skirt.

She decided to see her GP about it. The family physician, Dr. William Carlos Williams was also a good friend. Yes — *that* William Carlos Williams: an amateur writer who wrote wry short stories about his hometown experiences as a GP. He also dabbled in poetry — exquisite poetry that would one day make him Poet Laureate of the United States.

Carol and Roger Hamilton had once led a carefree bohemian life in Greenwich Village. They lived in a tiny walkup at the corner of Christopher and Gay Streets — their 'place' was the Minetta Tavern, a mom-and-pop Italian restaurant that's still there today. They had left suburbia and two sets of judgmental in-laws to pursue artistic interests among like-minded contemporaries. My father was writing; my mother, singing (she also won the 1937 U.S. Women's Fencing Championship at the NYAC). But they were forced to flee back to their hometown after a nasty run-in with street thugs that ended with my mother being bonked on the head. She had unwisely interfered with a crime in progress. Determined not to succumb to a humdrum life in a small town, they held frequent soirées in their home. Williams was a frequent guest, as was Ezra Pound and e.e. cummings — along with an ever-changing mix of artists, musicians and writers.

Today, looking back on how jaw-droppingly prominent the members of their group would become, I wish I had more than a vague recollection of my parents' frequent philosophical discussions. They would always be referring back to this friend's point of view; that one's critique. Lucky me, though: I grew up in a home where intellectual discussion was a daily part of family life.

Now, in 1944, as Dr. William Carlos Williams listened to his good friend's symptoms, he looked closely at her face and told her, "Carol, you're pregnant. I'll do a test, but I'm sure that's it." And a few days later, he confirmed his diagnosis.

He sat her down for a chat.

"Anyone can have a baby, Carol, but not everyone can be a talented singer with the chance to be in a Broadway show. I'm willing to arrange things so you can stay in the show if you'd like."

She just shook her head and said, "No, Williams." (She always called him by his last name). "I can't do that. I'll have the baby and call it 'my happy accident'."

She was to have two other 'happy accidents': the three of them are me, my brother Rollin, and sister Janet.

I have nothing but happy memories of the early years. My mother gave voice lessons at home. She was our rock — the center of our family — who did everything for all of us. I don't know what my father did for work other than making Zoomerangs (more on them later) — but he too was home a lot, tinkering in the basement or tapping at the typewriter. Even then I understood that Pa was not always available. He lived most of the time in his own world. I adored him, looked up to him, hung on his every sentence — but we didn't cuddle a lot. Most of my extended family lived in our town, so I benefitted from two sets of grandparents, aunts, uncles and five cousins. Our largely Dalmatian dog was named Girlie, and we fostered a couple of cats (one had kittens right on my bed).

At age three, I demanded piano lessons, probably because of the classical music that was all around us all of the time. There were my mother's voice lessons, my father's love of recorded opera, my grandmother's live piano performances in the living room, old scratchy 78 rpm recordings of my grandfather's arias and lieder made during his operatic career, and the huge radio in the living room, forever tuned to a classical station.

My parents found a nice lady in town who gave me weekly lessons. I loved them, and improved rapidly. My father even built one of his typically crazy contraptions: this one allowed me to reach the pedals with my stubby little legs.

After about a year, the teacher sat my mother down and told her she had gone as far as she could with me.

"Susan should study with a professional. She's very talented and very ambitious — she needs more than I can teach her. I wish you the best of luck."

Her selflessness may been at least partially due to my own intense attitude, which I was later told could be somewhat startling from a four-year-old.

My mother had read about a private piano day school in Manhattan, but didn't have any money to pay for it. She was fiercely determined, though — especially when it came to her cubs. She wangled an interview with Mrs. Fairleigh Dickinson, wife of the President of the university that bears his name. They lived in our town. One day she marched up the hill to their mansion.

How my mother convinced her is a mystery, but for the next few years, Mrs. Dickinson sponsored me, paying in full for my education. In gratitude, each year I would show my progress by making a recording of pieces I had learned. I still have those discs and am mortified whenever they are dragged out and played. Not so much with the playing, which is quite good — it's the high-pitched spoken introductions that get me.

"My name is Susan Alexandra Hamilton and I am here to play for you Johann Sebastian Bach's two-part invention in A minor, the first movement of Wolfgang Amadeus Mozart's sonata in C major, and Franz Schubert's Impromptu number two."

I sound like such a stuck-up little brat...

I met Hedy Spielter and Professor Jules Epailly one afternoon that first fall. My mother drove me into Manhattan and ushered me into a very fancy elevator. Up we rose to the top floor of an old building on West 72nd Street, where we waited in a grand foyer. The only piece of furniture in the room was an immense rectangular marble table with a noticeable quarter inch crack running through it.

The two heads of the School came in and silently inspected me. They nodded to each other, then Mrs. Spielter began to speak with a pronounced German accent. She was somewhat stout and wore an old fashioned dress with buttons down the front. It hung mid-calf above thick stockings and sensible black leather shoes with laces and chunky heels. Her grey hair was fashioned into a bun on the back of her neck — but my focus was on her chin with its dark mole and three long hairs growing out of it. I thought to myself that she looked like a real witch: the kind that could put a hex on you. I kept my suspicions to myself.

On the other hand, Mr. Epailly was a disheveled, distracted-looking man who was dressed in a collarless dirty white shirt and black shiny trousers with both a wide belt and suspenders. He had long grey hair that pointed every which-way around his face. He seemed friendly enough, but eventually I came to know better. He left the room after a few minutes. During the few years I spent at their school, he had little to do with me. I became Hedy's pupil and protégé. She invested a lot of time in me.

In that first interview, she pointed at the crack in the large marble table. She said, "When you are ready to leave here, your fingers will be strong enough to create another crack in the marble." I didn't believe her, but was impressed enough to nod my head. Then she took my mother and me on a tour of the school.

Room after room revealed the same sight: four or five children, heads bent over their keyboards, intensely practicing on silent pianos. The 'pianos' were dummies that had the feel and action of playing, but no musical sound. You could only hear a sort of muffled clicking. Weird. Mrs. Spielter explained that this method allowed more students to practice in the same room. Real estate in New York City was expensive.

At first, I couldn't even imagine playing the piano this way, but after only a few days, I grew accustomed to it. It certainly fostered separate finger dexterity while sparing the involuntary wincing every time a wrong key was hit. And it became such a thrill to finally hear the music played on a real keyboard! I still can't decide — maybe the whole Dickensian setup worked.

For the next three years, every weekday, my mother would drive me from Rutherford through the Lincoln Tunnel to the School in Manhattan, then pick me up in the afternoon. What I remember most is the drive up the hill as we left New Jersey. I'd look down and across to the Island of Manhattan, at the busy harbor on the other side of the Hudson where the luxurious ocean liners were docked side by side. I fantasized about one day crossing the sea on one of them.

The regime at Spielter's Manhattan School of Music was rigorous (if not draconian). A couple of hours at the dummy keyboards would be followed by a snack. Then two hours of academics (the 3 R's) led by Miss Pirotta in her spartan classroom. Petite, dark-skinned, fashionably dressed and well put together, she looked a bit like Condoleeza Rice. Just as strict as Mrs. Spielter, she was an extremely effective teacher as well. After we moved to California, the school skipped me a grade and a half immediately.

Following Miss Pirotta's session came lunch. Then two or three more hours at the soundless pianos.

Once or twice a week Mrs. Spielter monitored my progress. These were private sessions in her marvelous room with its concert grand piano. Although she had a throne-like chair, she always stood behind a music stand with the score of what I was performing and barked out direction, criticism, and a few jealously guarded words of praise. Although I had serious questions about her methods, even at a very young age I knew I was learning and improving at breakneck speed.

My fellow students all lived in Manhattan. They were a seasoned and tough bunch. I was younger, smaller, and most of all envied because of the special attention I was getting from the headmistress.

I remember one run-in with my nemesis, Sheila Mintz. She was a big girl who often wore girly dresses (an unfortunate choice). She had frizzy blond hair, pale white skin, and a pushy personality. One day she accosted me in the hall, shoved me up against the wall, and demanded to know "*Are you Jewish?*" I had no idea what she was talking about, but came up with the best answer I could muster. "A little bit, I think." My parents laughed their heads off when I told them about it.

Months later, at Melody Island — Spielter's summer camp on Lake Winnipesaukee — my little brother got even with Sheila Mintz. One evening, as we were all sitting around in the sleeping cabins, he marched over, drew his little penis out of his pajama bottoms and whizzed all over her. He couldn't take any more of her bullying, either.

In the spring of 1953 I was eight years old. After a private audition with the Conductor and the Board, I was invited to perform Mozart's Piano Concerto in A major with the Bergen County Symphony Orchestra. Needless to say, from then on I had Mrs. Spielter's full attention. I saw her almost every day.

After years in the music business, I have never heard of anything like the extreme paces she put me through. First, I would play a movement or portion of a movement. Then I would play the same section with each hand separately: first the right, then the left. Next, I would stand in front of her at the music stand and recite the actual notes played by each hand. To cap it off, I had to recite the fingering numbers for each hand.

To this day, I credit the insane regimen with why I have such a good memory for names and dates, and why I got a perfect math score on the SAT's..

And in the end, part of the reason why I rebelled. One day, as the summer of '53 approached, I'd just had it. I was scheduled to perform with the Symphony in the fall — but I was finished. The main reason was Mr. Epailly. He was too fond of using his belt on the young boys in the bathroom. I couldn't stand hearing them cry out. More than once I complained to Mrs. Spielter, but she would simply say, "It is none of your business; your business is your music and your career." She was completely dominated by him; likely frightened of him, as well. My mother used to call him *Mrs. Spielter's Svengali.* In contrast to my parents, who had never even raised their voices to me, he was always yelling and screaming at everyone. I was out of there.

That morning I'd seen one of my favorite boys, a kid named Benjamin, come out of the bathroom, wiping away tears. I snapped.

I snuck down the stairs and out onto the noontime streets of Manhattan, where I imperiously hailed a cab and demanded to be taken home to 345 Pierpont Ave. in Rutherford, NJ. This was in the early '50s, so the cab driver just did as he was commanded.

Upon our arrival, I marched into the house and told my astonished mother that she had to pay the driver. When she returned, I explained that I was never going back to that terrible place. After I told her that Mr. Epailly was getting worse and worse (we had talked about him before), she just sighed and said, "Oh well, it's probably all for the better. We're going to take a road trip to California this summer with your father and his Zoomerangs. We'll see how you feel when we get back in the fall."

As fate would have it, we didn't return for many years.

DOUG KATSAROS AND I flew to Toronto to record the theme music he and Arthur Stead had written for *The Jim Henson Hour*. We met up with the man himself at Nelvana Studios.

It was a difficult session. The studio was sub-par and so was the engineer. The musicians were not comparable to our New York sidemen, and Mr. Hensen, although strong-minded and extremely charismatic, didn't quite know what he wanted.

We worked well into the night. The best part was each time we solved a musical problem, it was Kermit's voice that exclaimed, *"Terrific!"*

Chapter 3

The Job

FALL OF '66. MANHATTAN. AND I HAD A JOB! Granted, only $90 a week, but I was full of hope and ambition. I had spent a few months living with my parents, sister, grandmother and Sunny the Bunny in a cramped, ugly apartment on 14th Street. Then an inheritance from my grandfather enabled them to buy a house in Plainfield, NJ. I snagged a terrific apartment in Greenwich Village.

It was a 'Sister Eileen' type. Set about six feet below ground level, it had a front bedroom on the street side, a living room in the middle, and a raised breakfast/kitchen/dining area that led back to a fenced-in garden. It was mine! My name was on the lease and I loved it. I didn't even mind the occasional drunk crashing around in the sunken trash can area just outside my bedroom window. I don't even want to think what that place costs today.

Every weekday, I rode the subway up the East Side to Herman Edel's office. It was a nightmarish ride. Hotter than hell most of the year, and during both morning and evening rush hours, the riders were jammed together, body parts against body parts. I remember one chunky, sweaty asshole pressing his erection into my backside and grinding. Fairly inured to this kind of assault, I whirled around and shouted "BACK OFF, COCKROACH!!" at the top of my lungs. He slunk off at the first stop, everyone staring.

This kind of thing could happen. Earlier that year, when I was still making the interview rounds, I'd stopped at a phone booth to call the employment agency. Suddenly, the door was pulled open by some middle-aged guy in work clothes. He leaned in close and spat out, "I want to lick your cunt!" and shut the door. My mind went blank; I burst into tears. I don't cry very often.

The City was a wilder and rougher place in those days. No young woman could walk the gauntlet past a construction site at break time without enduring a barrage of whistles, catcalls and lewd remarks. No one dared enter Central Park after dark, and there were neighborhoods all over the Island where it was unwise to walk unaccompanied... ever. I was taught never to enter an elevator alone with a single man. I learned to cross the street late at night if a guy wearing tennis shoes came walking toward me.

The first couple of months working for Herman Edel were rocky. Mostly because his older brother, Buddy, hated me from the get-go. Ostensibly, I was the secretary, and he was bookkeeper and office manager. Herman was off schmoozing with clients most of the time, or in the studio overseeing actual jobs.

Buddy had me adding up columns and columns of numbers. He was absolutely furious when he learned I could do them faster by hand than he could with his adding machine. Also, I'm afraid I tended to make a few smart-ass remarks now and then. I goaded him. I knew I could get away with it because Herman really liked me. Buddy was not only jealous of me — what he really couldn't stand was my complete lack of deference. I still have visions of him standing over my desk, red-faced and screaming, pounding the heel of his hand over and over again.

"LISTEN TO ME, young lady! I've had just about enough of your sass! I am YOUR BOSS! You have to show me *RESPECT!*" I looked down, trying not to smirk as little drops of spittle rained down on my papers.

When he complained to his brother, Herman just waved it off with, "I don't have time for this crap; I'm trying to start a business. You two get along, dammit!"

The tension began to lighten somewhat as soon as Herman started taking me to the recording studios. I had been closely observing his meetings with various composers and arrangers. I saw how first Herman would lay out the specs of the job - what kind of music was needed. Then the writer would come back a few days later to sketch it out for him on the little upright piano that sat in the middle of the living room.

Herman had good advertising sense and was a terrific salesman. But I was shocked to find out that he knew almost nothing about the fundamentals of music. He had no grasp of basic music theory or composition. He didn't even have the vocabulary necessary to clearly communicate what he liked or didn't like — much less how to change it. After watching a few of these meetings, I dared to open my mouth to offer some musical advice. I was surprised when Herman listened to me instead of shutting me down. He had his faults, but he was quick to pick up on a potential asset. And I was thrilled to see the flare of re- cognition and appreciation in the composers' eyes.

From the moment I walked into the control room of my first session, I was in heaven. 100% hooked. I drank in the smell, the sounds, the heat of the dark, smoky room, full of big machines with its glorious expanse of patch bay, web of patch cords, and there at the center, the huge console. The engineer was wheeling back and forth in his rolling chair, in charge and totally cool. His assistant stood at the ready next to the machines, clipboard in hand. I looked out through the thick soundproof glass and watched the musicians chatting, joking around, unpacking their instruments, then settling into assigned places.

For a while, I just stood in the back near the assistant engineer. But after a while I started to feel sorry for the leader of the session (the composer/arranger) as he dashed back and forth from the studio to the booth, trying to direct the orchestra, the engineer, and at the same time field comments from Herman and the advertising agency clients. My fingers itched to get on that talkback button.

I remember a startled look on Herman's face when I suddenly asked if I could speak to the musicians. After a moment's hesitation, he said, "Sure. Why not?"

I was a little nervous when I pressed the button to talk over the big speakers out in the studio, but not that much. After all, hadn't I per- formed with many symphony orchestras? Hadn't I directed a couple of chamber music groups? How different could this studio session be?

The most astonished people in the room were the musicians themselves. A girl speaking to them over the talkback? I could see their stares into the dim booth. What was the world coming to? The only females in their world either played a stringed instrument or a harp. Those women knew to keep their mouths shut. But this one turned out to be spot on-the-money with her comments...

It was a man's world during the 1960's and '70s in Manhattan. I soon became a singular anomaly in my newfound profession. There were no female music producers at the time. Not in the jingle business, not in the pop record business. To be realistic, there were not many women in power positions in any industry. And with the remarkable exception of Mary Wells, very few successful female executives in the ad business.

It took me a very long while to notice or acknowledge the pervasive discrimination, probably because all of the worlds I had experienced up to this point had had no gender bias. Classical musicians — male and female — were treated equally. Many of them were gay. Show business types were equally open-minded. Maybe females were paid smaller fees, but they were well respected, nonetheless. At Canoga Park High School, at Occidental College and in the Count's grand salon in Siena, I had managed to excel: beating out the boys in many cases. There had never been any hard feelings.

So I was pretty much fearless. My parents had raised me to believe in my exceptionalism and strength. To them, being unique — being outstanding in anything — was a plus for a girl or a boy. Why would there be a difference? I had no reason to be timid. I may have been a little too cocky as I entered this new arena, but I wasn't afraid to speak my mind.

Jumping on the talkback that first session, I sped up the communication between studio and booth, and managed to get in a few suggestions of my own. Many of the musicians came right into the control room to introduce themselves after the session was over. From that day on, Herman had me join him frequently.

A few weeks later, a veteran woodwind player did teach me a valuable lesson. Phil Bodner was a masterful studio musician. He could sit expertly in the flute, oboe, clarinet or saxophone chair. That particular day I got on the talkback and, in front of the whole orchestra, announced that his oboe was flat in a certain section.

After the session was finished, he took me aside and explained how un-cool it was for me to do that over the talkback — no matter whether it were true or not. I felt ashamed. From then on, I made any personal criticism privately, either on a break or with a whisper out in the studio.

As the weeks passed, I became more and more convinced that I was now the luckiest person in the world. I'd managed to find the perfect job. I'd begun to fall under the tutelage of several invaluable mentors, and I was learning, absorbing and mastering new skills at a dizzying pace. At the same time, being able to contribute in the studio as a music producer made me feel important and worthwhile, again connected with the world of music, but in a way I would never have imagined. I had no way of knowing that this was only the beginning of an incredible climb. I had a rocket up my ass — and I was going to be able save my family (especially my mother) from the wolf at the door.

SCHLITZ BEER was the single most difficult name to record in jingles. With one group of singers, it was "Shitz Beer;" with the other, it came out "Slitz Beer."

Damned either way.

Chapter 4

The Zoomerang

THE FORTUNES OF THE HAMILTON FAMILY rose and fell with the ups and downs of the Zoomerang. It was my father's invention and bumbling enterprise, and he always credited me, in part, with its creation.

My contribution came as a toddler. I had been down in the basement, keeping Pa company in his workshop. I started playing with an old roll of film — it was one of a half-dozen he had fished out of a trashcan and brought home as presents for the kids. He couldn't afford to buy us real toys. I held it in the middle, tilted it sideways and watched the inner core extend out into a long tube. When I tilted it the other way, it first fell back into its original roll, then spilled out the other side. As he watched, the kernel of an idea formed in his mind. The Zoomerang had been born.

A classic Zoomerang consists of a coil of three-ply glassine paper. About 3 1/2" wide, it has been heated in an oven to set its curl. It is printed with a green stripe on the top and a red one at the bottom. The *Magic Zoomerang* logo is stamped to appear every few inches. A rubber band holds the coil in place and a 7" swizzle stick provides the handle. A plastic disc with a hole in the middle is fitted just under the bottom of the coil. Its diameter is just a little larger than the coil. A rubber grommet keeps the disc where it belongs.

Originally, the stick was simply a piece of red doweling that had to have a silver tack carefully hammered into place at the top end. I remember my father built a tray that held the sticks upright to make it easier to tap the tacks in place. The swizzle stick substitution came as a welcome leap forward in Zoomerang evolution.

To play with a Zoomerang, you would remove the band, turn it upside down and shake it until the long, slippery coil released. Then you could turn it back upright and start shooting it straight up or straight out with a frisbee-like flick of the wrist. Once you had mastered the basic motion, you'd be at liberty to explore the *31 magic tricks and games* described in the instructional leaflet.

Some of the most popular tricks were the "traffic light trick," "dipsy doodle," "disappearing motor boat" and "walking the dog." (I can still demonstrate all 31).

My father had a way with words. He came up with teasers like: *Curious satisfaction from very simple action; Have you been fascinated lately?; Favorite 'fiddlestick' of fly caster and fencer;* and *The intellectual's yo-yo.* Perhaps it's no surprise I ended up in the advertising business.

My fondest memory of this period came at Christmas time. Somehow, who knows how, my father talked Gimbel's into allowing him to hawk his Zoomerangs on their toy floors during the holiday rush. As anyone who has ever seen *Miracle on 34th Street* knows, Gimbel's was the other huge department store in Herald Square. Macy's was on 34th, Gimbel's on 33rd. This was a true coup for a lone pitchman from the suburbs.

You should have seen him in action! My mother and we kids would travel into the City and ride the clickety-clackety wooden escalators all the way up to his floor to watch in awe. There would be my father, Zoomerang in hand, dressed nattily in slacks (he loved Dax slacks), shirt, tie and plaid sports coat, nimbly dancing around in the middle of a big circle of onlookers. He would be demonstrating all the tricks with the whole spiel: the rapid-fire patter and banter that went along with the sell. The crowds would be mesmerized, and when the show was over, they'd buy and buy. Day after day, well into the evening for at least three or four weeks straight, my father would be there: tireless, full of energy and loving every moment. Not once when we came to watch the show did he ever acknowledge our presence — never introduced us to his audience. We were just part of the masses. To have done so would have made him too ordinary, too plebian. We never spoke of it.

In many ways, the Zoomerang was a really good toy: small, not too expensive: the perfect stocking-stuffer. And most surprising, Zoomerangs lasted a long time.

One year, the Gimbel's appearances really paid off. Tigrett Industries, a company founded by John Burton Tigrett and based in Jackson, Tennessee, took notice of the Zoomerang. Mr. Tigrett flew my mother and father down to corporate headquarters for a meeting. This would have been in 1950, because I remember that my mother was pregnant with Janet, and I was miffed that she had been able to ride in an airplane before I could. Never mind she was still inside Mom. A deal was struck and Tigrett was licensed to produce and market their version of the Zoomerang.* Although, it had some limited success, their product could never hold a candle to the original as manufactured with care in our basement. I don't know how much money my father got in the deal, but it was not enough. By the next year, we were broke again. It seemed we were always broke. Even though we were only six and seven, my brother and I knew it. Living safely in Rutherford, where there was always the extended family to help out when needed, we didn't worry too much.

But after the Tigrett deal fizzled, I think my parents needed a break from the unspoken criticism from the rest of the family: my father's inability to provide properly for his wife and children.

So, at the beginning of the summer of 1953 — the summer I stormed out of Hedy Spielter's piano school for good — we packed our woodie full to the roof with Zoomerangs and Zoomerang parts, and took off to the wild wild West. Our 'woodie,' a 1949 Chevrolet station wagon with fancy wood trim, was customized (in a way). When the wagon had been involved in some kind of accident and lacking the money to repair it, my father built a kind of free-form sculpture of odd wood pieces to cover the hole. The result was both unique and unbelievably ugly. It looked like either a cancerous tumor or massive brown-and-tan fungal growth.

I have no idea why our destination was Southern California. We knew not a soul out there. Maybe my father had renewed delusions of grandeur following his success as a showman/pitchman at Gimbel's. Maybe it was just the universal lure of that promised land of sunshine and plenty.

I have vivid memories of our first two stops. In Reading, Pennsylvania, we took a break for a picnic lunch. My mother had brought

---

*Believe it or not, chronicled in *The New Yorker*, December 23, 1950

along sandwiches. I loved road trips, but had to ask, "Are we almost there, Pa?" I was embarrassed when they laughed out loud at me; we were only 86 miles from home.

My brother and I did torture them all the way across the country with a hundred re-phrasings of the perennial question. Even Janet, the baby, caught on to the game and chimed in.

In Columbus, Ohio we stopped at the Capitol building square with its glorious fountain and pool. It was hotter than hell, so my parents actually let my brother and me jump into the fountain and splash about until some uptight citizens objected. We were ejected by the authorities. I still remember the sheer joy of the cool, cool water as the fountain rained down over us under the noontime sun.

After the interminable plains of Kansas, we headed south. During a horrendous rain/wind/dust storm, we and a few other travelers took refuge at a gas station in the Texas panhandle. It was black outside in the middle of the day, and the sound was deafening. My mother was scared; we children were thrilled, and my father sold Zoomerangs to everyone.

Later we hit the Petrified Forest, Painted Desert, and then spent three unforgettable days in a tourist cabin at the Grand Canyon. Because it was a national park, my father had to sell on the sly. In fact, at every stop my father would pull out some Zoomerangs and start pitching. Any parking lot that had restaurants and grocery stores, any town gathering, any fair, farmer's market or carnival: all were fair game. It was always *Carpe Diem* for Pa, and it paid off. By the time we hit Vegas, we had as much money as we'd started with. Granted, we didn't have as many Zoomerangs — but we still had a lot of unassembled parts.

Before the trip, my mother had sewn Zoomerang outfits for us. White skirts for her and her two girls, white shorts for my brother and father. Navy blue tee shirts with 'Zoomerang' in cursive embroidered across the chest, and white caps to match. Whenever people would ask what it meant, we would just pull out a Zoomerang and start selling. My favorite moment came when one woman asked if that was the name of our yacht! Guess mom had done a good job making the outfits look chic...

The crap hit the fan in Vegas, both good and bad. We left it in the middle of the night and limped into Los Angeles with almost no money.

Thank heaven, my father immediately charmed his way into both The Do It Yourself Show at the cavernous Pan Pacific Auditorium and the immense L.A. County Fair, an exposition that was scheduled to last for a couple of weeks in September. By now it was decision time, a turning point for the family. Gamble by staying on in California, or retreat to safety back in New Jersey? In this instance, my mother urged my father to gamble, and she prevailed. It was usually the other way around.

While my father worked the events, my mom, brother and I kept busy assembling the toys in our cheap nearby motel rooms. The best time of day came very late. My father would make his entrance and ceremoniously dump his pockets and money apron. Coins and bills would spill right onto the bedspread in a glorious pile. We kids got to separate and count it. We relished every second.

Eventually, my brother and I were allowed to learn the pitch, the patter, the *31 magic tricks and games*, and — most exciting — how to make change and handle the money. Pa rehearsed and tested us over and over until he believed we were ready to take on the public. Both of us were under eleven. Crazy as it seems, we were sent out by ourselves in different directions with sacks of Zoomerangs over our shoulders — and money aprons ready to be filled! My mother always hung back in a supporting role, and my sister was a little too young. My father would meet with us at some central spot; then we would separate to fan out across the fairgrounds or exhibition room floor.

The next summer, we drove up the coast to Santa Barbara after my father heard about a Mexican fiesta there that was said to draw a lot of people. He managed to arrange a meeting with Santa Barbara's License Inspector, a Mr. Stroud, whose first answer was a definite 'No!" The families who rented the booths that lined the perimeter of the square had all earned their spots for years. No outsider had ever been let onto the *mercado*. Undeterred, my father was on his feet demonstrating his toy to Mr. Stroud when I popped my head in the door and asked, "Are we in yet, Pa?" He later told me that I sealed the deal, and we were allowed to participate. We did have to make a significant contribution from our earnings to the local Kiwanis Club.

This was, by far, our favorite event of all. We went year after year, and it never seemed to change. The grassy square wasn't large: a lot smaller than a football field. It was usually crowded, and to us kids, always magical. At night, strings of soft paper lanterns lent a sense of excitement. They were strung all around; their dim, shifting, swaying light made it just a little difficult to see clearly. Tantalizing aromas wafted from the six Mexican food booths; the air was heavy with their exotic, delicious smells. Then there were the colorful *piñatas*, maracas,

Mexican jumping beans, pottery, *sombreros* and *serapes* displayed everywhere. Live mariachi bands played all day and night from the bandstand, and people danced: especially old people and little children.

But for me, the best show of all was performed by the glassblowers. Well, they weren't really glassblowers: they didn't make things like vases and decanters that required blowing through tubes into a globs of red-hot glass. These were artisans who could take a couple of wands and very quickly stretch and shape the molten glass into delicate little figurines of animals, flowers, doll-like girls; it seemed, almost anything. I coveted them all, but never had enough money to buy more than a single one each year. Of course, they were extremely fragile and eventually broke, but I cherished them anyway.

I also loved all of the families who ran the booths. We remained friends for years. I thought they were beautiful to look at and they were always very kind to me, sneaking me free food and drinks out of the backs of their booths. I met my first childhood boyfriend there. We were maybe nine or ten, and were best friends. We were young enough that both sets of parents smiled on the relationship. They looked on fondly while we talked and played incessantly.

During the prime Zoomerang years, my father was home whenever we were not pitching at a show. He would happily spend all day out there in his Zoomerang factory (the garage), making and baking his precious toys, radio blaring. He loved opera or talk programs of any kind. I have to confess, he wasn't the most affectionate or involved parent in the world, but he certainly was interesting. An intellectual and agnostic thinker, he had a facile way with words combined with irrepressible need to show off (especially to the opposite sex).

The next big event in the Zoomerang saga happened when my father secured a spot as a contestant on *You Bet Your Life*, the popular Groucho Marx quiz show on NBC TV. This turned out to be a classic episode — one that was rerun again and again for many years.

And he won the jackpot! He was teamed with a WAC sergeant. Uniformed and stiff as a board, she served as a perfect foil to my flamboyant father. Moving about freely in front of the other contestants, Roger Alexander Hamilton not only demonstrated a couple of his favorite Zoomerang tricks, but he and Groucho wound up in a Zoomerang duel, thrusting and parrying across the stage. It was hysterical!

When they finally got around to the contest part of the show, the category was 'spelling.' Practically a walking dictionary, my father polished off spelling all four words — calendar, porcelain, poinsettia and brethren — without hesitation. Groucho joked, "You sure are a

very smart fellow for someone out of work." To which my father replied, "Well, I have a lot of free time to read."

When the big moment — the jackpot moment — came, the wooden
WAC and my father waited as Groucho posed the question slowly and
clearly. "What is the other name for the famous painting by Leonardo
da Vinci, best known as the 'Mona Lisa?'" The music that plays while
the contestants are supposed to be discussing their answer had barely
begun when my father drowned it out by shouting, "*La Gioconda!*"

One of the funniest moments came later, when Groucho asked my
father how he was planning to spend his share of the prize money.
"Well, I have to admit that I was a bit embarrassed to run into my
children's dentist, Dr. Rex Waggoner, here on the show." (The dentist
was a fellow contestant.) "I owe him a lot of money, so I guess that's
the first bill I'll pay!"

The winnings did temporarily relieve us from our usual financial
troubles, but the true irony of the whole episode was that when the orders poured in by the thousands for Zoomerangs, we had no stock on
hand. Nor enough money to buy the supplies needed to make them. It
was a shame.

Hyman J. Sobiloff was a great philanthropist, industrialist and
billionaire. He sat on the board of half a dozen large companies. He also was a published poet, albeit a mawkishly sentimental one. Devoted
to the art, he employed some renowned poets of the day to give him
weekly lessons. How he met my father, I do not know, but he was hired
to travel with Sobiloff as his personal secretary. I think it was because
my father had mastered the Gregg shorthand system, which made him
a whiz at taking dictation.

Mr. Sobiloff needed my father to be with him at all times while traveling in his limousine, by plane or train. My father told us how he
would be seized by sudden inspiration and loudly blurt out lines of
poetry. My father would take them down on the steno pad kept at the
ready at all times. This arrangement went on for several months, but
Mr. Sobiloff eventually took my father aside and told him, "Roger, I
think it's time for you to go back to your Zoomerang. And I will
finance the operation for you."

Personally (through some comments dropped by my father), I
think Mr. Sobiloff had gradually grown uncomfortable with my father's personality. I gathered that as Roger became more and more
comfortable around Mr. Sobiloff, his own ego started to emerge.
Eventually, he chose to expose his own poetry to Sobiloff — along with
some constructive criticism of his employer's writings.

Sobiloff made good on his promise. And so it was that we were back in the Zoomerang industry. That didn't last too long, probably because many more modern toys were now flooding the market.

My father had to take a day job at the local paint store, which sent him into a serious depression. I remember he would come home from work around 4 pm and just go to bed to sleep and sleep and sleep. He always had the little portable radio next to him. I would hear the far-off, scratchy sound all night.

But the Zoomerang did reappear. I invited my parents to come to live with me in the early 70's, very soon after I bought my weekend country house. Finally, they could relax in modest luxury, and my mother would never have to worry about money again.

The new arrangement was beneficial to all. By inviting them to live with me in Vermont, I gained both house guardians and company for the weekends. My parents could spend their time pursuing any interest they chose.

My mother made friends with most everyone in town. Immediately, she became involved with helping and advising them about any and all problems. For my father, of course, it meant inventing other toys...and reviving the Zoomerang! He called his new company, "Born Again Zoomerang, Ltd.," and spent most of his time making them, playing with them, and fantasizing about future grand success.

THE BEST ZOOMERANG TRICK of all was rarely performed. My father would save it for closing time at the fairs. It was his *pièce de résistance.*

He would pull out a three-foot wooden dowel with a foot-long coil of glassine at one end. With a big swing of his whole arm, the coil would shoot more than 15 feet into the night sky.

He called the trick, *The Dinosaur's Night Out.*

One night, two men in suits confiscated the coil. He'd made it out of old Lockheed Aircraft plans he had fished out of the trash when he worked there.

Chapter 5

Susan was one of those musicians who possessed an ear far beyond those of mere mortals. She'd listen to an orchestra run through a piece and say, "In measure 35 on the second beat, the oboe should be a b natural instead of a b flat." Not even the conductor heard that nuance. In an era when music production was completely dominated by men, she ran the biggest and most successful 'jingle-house' of the era.

— Glenn Berger
A&R Recording

The Studio

———

IT SOON BECAME OBVIOUS that Herman Edel Associates needed a new secretary. Business was picking up, and I was spending more and more time in the studio. Within a year, I was producing sessions on my own while Herman concentrated on bringing in the jobs.

Sherry Lee Reaser looked as if she had been personally groomed by Emily Post or Miss Manners. Tall and slim, she arrived for her interview wearing a below-the-knees skirt and a cotton sweater set. It was an outfit straight out of a JCPenney display window from the '50s. I think she even wore little white gloves.

Buddy loved her immediately. Herman hired her at the end of the interview. Born only a week apart, Sherry and I soon became best friends. Despite our polar opposite fashion senses (my usual work outfit consisted of embroidered bell bottom jeans, tie-dyed shirt, and cork platform sandals), she and I found that we shared common attitudes toward just about everything else. After a while, she did take to wearing jeans at the office. We became inseparable.

The next addition to our quickly expanding staff sauntered in one afternoon in 1967. Bernard Drayton was a tall, handsome African-American with a super-cool attitude and Afro to match. Herman took him on as a second salesman, figuring he would give the company a hip, young image. It worked well enough that Herman, Bernie and I were sometimes called 'The Mod Squad of Madison Ave.'

The studio workload got heavier. Thank God, some of the composers I worked with had taken it upon themselves to mentor me. Let's face it: there were major gaps in my knowledge. I was familiar with all of the instruments and sections of the symphonic orchestra, but had everything to learn about rock bands, jazz groups and country anything.

It started with the normal makeup of a rhythm section: drum kit, electric bass and the choice of all kinds of guitars and keyboards. There were words like "groove," "feel," "kick," "backbeat," "push;" jazz notations such as "plus this" or "diminished that." There was the difference between using a pick or using fingers when playing bass or guitar. I was amazed to find that there were four sizes of saxophones (saxes are underused in the classical repertoire). I had to get to know all the crazy, hilarious percussion instruments: slapstick (whip sound), cabasa (originally a dried gourd with beads wrapped around it), cowbell, jawbone (from a real animal), samba and slide whistles, claves and cuicas (called "laughing gourd" for its high squeaky sound), ratchet, sleigh bells, mark tree, bell tree, and sand blocks, wood blocks, the thunder machine, and my favorite: the vibraslap (sounds like a rattlesnake). I wanted to learn it all — as soon as possible!

This was all happening right at the beginning of what was rapidly becoming a complete transformation of the recording studio universe. When I started in 1966, studios were for the most part dark, dirty, stinky places. The elevator at 112 W. 48th St. — A&R's first studio — reeked of urine. You didn't want to even brush against the gate or walls.

At that first A&R studio, I worked mostly with their senior engineer, Don Frey. But the great Phil Ramone also engineered a few of my sessions. We recorded everything on a 4-track tape machine with some subsequent bouncing and overdubbing.

In that era, engineers had to have even keener musical sense than they do now. We had only two tracks for the band and two for the singers (just one if we were dealing with a TV spot and had to lay a sync signal on the fourth track). Many instruments had to go together on those two tracks, so they had to be balanced perfectly. There would be no after-the-fact fiddling with volume or equalization on any individual player or section.

As the recording scene changed, and we found more and more tracks at our disposal, I grew to value the composers and arrangers who had either a classical symphony background or who had worked in the studios under those earlier limitations. Their compositions were so much easier to record! You could put up a single room mic, open up the faders, and hear a decent balance of instruments from beginning to end. Later on, many of the younger composers' orchestrations depended on dramatic moves by the engineer to dig out a melody here, counter line there — or that one particular guitar riff everyone loved. Definitely more work for the producer and engineer, and ultimately not as natural-sounding.

But I think it's fair to say that Don Frey didn't much like working with a smart-mouthed girl. Nevertheless, he was an effective teacher. Much later we became friends, and still are. Generally our sessions would be recorded in the daylight hours. We would just be wrapping up as groups like The Lovin' Spoonful would start to wander in to record all night. One morning I arrived to find a clean-up crew scrubbing furiously. One of the groups had decided it would be funny to defecate all over the studio. Nice.

For me, the other memorable studio from that transitional era was Olmsted. It was on the south side of West 40th Street, in the shadow of the massive New York City Public Library with its two great stone lion guardians. The studio was built into the stunning duplex apartment William Randolph Hearst bought for his Ziegfeld girl mistress, Marion Davies. The control room was perched high above the wooden floor of the magnificent two-story ballroom. This was where the musicians gathered, so there was a lot of running up and down stairs. From time to time, I would catch myself daydreaming about being a guest at some elegant cocktail party there in that ballroom, back in that much more glamorous era...long, pearlized cigarette holder in gloved hand...

Charlie Calello and Artie Schroeck introduced me to Olmstead and its extraordinary engineers, Gene and Bill Radice. Charlie and Artie were atypical jingle arrangers for the times, and Gene was maybe the best engineer in the City. They treated me like a kid sister, always joking around, jostling me, throwing an arm around my shoulders. But they also respected me as a producer — listening to what I had to say and (most of the time) agreeing.

I had been working with revered musician/composers like Dick Hyman, the fabulous pianist; Walter Raim, the hip jazz and folk guy; Bob Freedman, just starting his career as a fabled jazz arranger to the stars; and Robert Maxwell, perhaps the most renowned harpist/composer of the day. But Dick was serious: an intellectual and (to be honest) a bit stiff and stern. Bob soon moved on and up. Robert was a lovely man, but his music also leaned more toward the classical. And Walter — well, Walter became my first husband.

Charlie and Artie spoke in what was almost a new language for me. I guess you could call it New Jersey vernacular. They came out of Berry Gordy's Motown world — closely involved with the hits of Frankie Valli and the Four Seasons. Charlie arranged for them, even sang in the group from time to time. Artie did arrangements for songs like "Can't Take My Eyes Off of You." They became my basic rock 'n roll mentors: drum sounds, guitar sounds, funky electric keyboards, riffs and fills, simplicity, rhythmic authority — the concept of less is more. I learned to adjust to not reading a score, with everything spelled out for each musician. This casual, improvisatory scene in the studio with the 'cats' became my favorite way to make pop music.

Charlie was the brash-but-charming slick front guy: the guy with limitless energy. My mental picture always has him in a black suit, white shirt, and pointy black leather shoes polished to perfection. He got along well with Herman. Charlie's shy and quiet partner, Artie, wrote great melodies: his arrangements always had at least one or two totally original musical touches. His wardrobe was more casual, frequently disheveled. Also, he was the sly, funny one. The two of them went out of their way to make me feel like one of the guys — an atmosphere I would strive to replicate over the next 40 years.

Not that they didn't have their quirks. As Jehovah's Witnesses, both later moved to Idaho to await Armageddon. I'm still not sure why Idaho. When it didn't happen, they returned to the music scene. They married the same woman, though not at the same time. I once asked her (the incomparable jingle singer Linda November) why she married Charlie first, a thoracic surgeon second, and Artie third. She told me, "I finally got it right." It took me a lot longer...

Technological advances utterly transformed the recording studios during the period from late 1968 through the 70's and 80's.

We went from ½" 4-track tape to 1" 8-track; then, a little later, to 2" 16-track. That in turn advanced to 2" 24-track tape for some years — before all of them went completely out the window when analog recording was supplanted by digital. Although the tape width went back to ½", we now had 48 separate tracks at our disposal. At the height of the madness, we sometimes linked together two of those 48-track machines!

Now, of course, tape machines are mostly relics of the past. Everything is pretty much done on computers. But my personal favorite sound of them all came out of the 24-track analog machines. Although I'm now accustomed to digital, to me it still sounds just a little too clean and sterile.

Throughout all of this nonstop technological upheaval, as a music producer I needed to be able to communicate what I wanted to the recording engineers. Soon enough I learned how a bad engineer could make my beautifully composed and executed track sound like a pile of mush. So I had to keep up with their lingo.

Unfortunately, the greatest engineers were often the worst teachers. Many of them were also prima donnas. Prying the information I needed out of them was not always easy. I spaced my questions over the hours, and kept them short. If I were lucky, a two-or-three-word answer would be barked back at me. Gradually, I was able to piece all the bits together. Still, I preferred this method to the wordy explanations that could be offered by some of the less-talented, obsequious guys behind the console.

There were those engineers who were so accomplished they didn't need any direction — they were that good. Others needed a lot. The relationships I built with the great ones contributed not only to my own success, but also to my ability to direct the not-so-good. Of course, working with and being married to one of the finest (Eliot Scheiner was my second husband) didn't hurt my education, either. Eliot taught me a lot.

The vocabulary of the studio was heavy with jargon dealing with the equipment and techniques for using it: EQ (equalization), frequencies (highs, lows and mids), bouncing tracks together, punching in and out on tracks, creating fades, sync tones, compression; all the different microphones, baffles, gobos, pop screens, echo/reverb, leakage, overdubbing and doubling (stacking)... it went on and on.

I didn't know it, but I was destined to spend most of my days and nights for the next 23 years not in my office or at the advertising agencies, but in studios all over the world. They became my homes away from home. It wasn't unusual for me to live there for 16 hours a day, day after day. I ate my meals in them, brushed my teeth in them, and occasionally slept in them. In the late '90s, when I again set foot in a New York studio after a hiatus of a few years, I couldn't stop smiling. It felt so good: so completely familiar.

Another essential skill I began to pick up was the booking of the talent. There were hundreds and hundreds of gifted musicians and singers on the scene: it took me quite a while to recognize and differentiate their strengths and weaknesses.

When I first started working for Herman, the writers would choose their own musicians and singers — even book them for their sessions. As my confidence grew, that changed. I soon had favorites for every seat in the band or orchestra. I was absolutely in awe of certain singers. Most of the players and vocalists were better in one or two styles of music, not perfect for others. But there were a few I could book for almost any session. After a while, the composers/arrangers let me book everything — with the exception of drummers. Each one had to have his favorite. Most of them were so good I didn't mind at all. But eventually, I picked the drummers, too. By the time I was producing two or three sessions a day, personally doing the booking had become impossible. I got help.

Radio Registry was then the nerve center of the music business in New York City. Their sister company, Artists' Service, functioned the same way with singers. All of the eligible musicians and singers for session/studio work were on their rosters of clients. Whether the work was for jingles, records or movies, we producers would call Registry and/or Artists' Services with our wish lists of needed personnel (first choices, second choices, third choices) for each impending session. Registry or Artists would call back with confirmations or, in rare cases, the need for more names. Sometimes the final filling of a seat might come down to the wire — an hour or two before the scheduled start time — but they always came through.

It sounds simple enough, but both ends of this task were pressure-filled and nerve-wracking. A session without a key player would be ruined. I don't know how many of my dinners were interrupted by having to go to the phone to check in with Registry. Ditto, nights' sleep. Calls at three or four in the morning became regular occurrences.

One day, on a whim and having an hour to spare between sessions, I decided to visit Radio Registry. I had developed phone relationships with all of the operators, but never had met them. I don't think I knew anybody who had. As soon as I walked through the big wooden door at the address I'd been given in the West 50's, I felt like I'd been spun back in time. It was like walking onto a set from a 1930's black-and-white movie.

The room was small and dim, windowless, filled floor to low ceiling with bank after bank of switchboards — the old-fashioned kind with rows and rows of holes with hundreds of patch cords connecting them. Three or four figures, their backs turned, headsets on their heads, bustled back and forth, avoiding one another like a well-rehearsed dance team, crisscrossing, reaching out to plug and unplug, connect and disconnect. They were all muttering into their headsets, completely oblivious to the alien who stood observing them in their strange enclave. I just watched, fascinated, for a few dumbstruck minutes.

When I finally cleared my throat, they turned and looked at me quizzically. But when I told them my name their faces broke into beaming smiles, and the lot of them crowded around me, introducing themselves so I could match familiar telephone voices with faces, shaking my hand and patting me wherever they could. They all seemed about four feet tall, plump, hunched over, and dressed in black. They were very glad I had come to visit, and so was I. Apparently, few clients did.

All those days, hours, and years in the studio were probably the happiest of my life. With the help of that galaxy of talented musical colleagues, I was directing and creating good work: work I could be proud of. Sure, some of the advertising agency clients could be assholes, but others were right there with me, every bit as determined to create music that was the best it could be — and some of them became my friends and partners in the process.

These were my glory days, and the Golden Age of Madison Avenue, as well. The confluence was magical. I was an extremely lucky woman leading a charmed life.

I had landed in the right place at the right time.

NEW YORK CITY IS KNOWN for its watering holes: there are those for actors, writers, TV execs, journalists and Wall Street people. For jazz and studio musicians, there was "Jim and Andy's" — the home away from home for everyone from the most famous to the greenest rookie anxious to break into the business.

Located at street level next door to A&R's old 112 West 48th studio, the bar belonged to Jim Koulouvaris, who presided over his establishment like a friendly uncle.

His tough guy exterior hid a heart of gold. If you were a regular, he'd accept your checks. Down on your luck? You'd find you had credit. He took messages; let the guys store their instruments in the coat closet.

A&R ran a line down to a speaker above the back booth. Every so often, it would squawk out a request for a player needed on a session. (What the guys didn't know was that it was two-way speaker: up in the booth, we could quietly flip a switch and listen in on some pretty funny conversations).

Sooner or later, newbies would ask who 'Andy' was. That was worth a laugh: he was Jim's cat.

Then Andy had kittens.

Chapter 6

Las Vegas

———

IT WAS 120 DEGREES AND pitch black as we drove from the
Grand Canyon over the high bare mountains toward Las Vegas.
Our 1949 'woodie' — the Chevrolet station wagon with no air
conditioning — was only bearable when we kept the windows mostly
closed. Putting your hand outside was like sticking it into a blast
furnace. The absolute darkness of the highway coupled with the
intense heat frightened my parents. Their fear spread to my sister,
brother and me. We were uncharacteristically quiet. My mother fed us
a steady stream of ice chips from the cooler. She and my father sucked
on them, too.

We crested the last hill and suddenly there it was, a distant glowing bowl of light in the vast expanse. To us, it could have been an enormous flying saucer landed in the middle of nowhere.

We were lucky enough to find a motel right next to the brand
new "Jewel of the Desert," the Sahara Hotel. The room might be a
little expensive ($16 a night), but it had *air conditioning* and a *pool!* My
parents decided to go ahead and splurge. After all, we still had almost
as much money as we started with back in Rutherford: nearly nine
hundred dollars.

We kids were in heaven. We loved it all: the pool, the A/C, the
cheap food buffets at the hotels, the blazing lights of downtown Vegas
that transformed the middle of the night into broad daylight. We were

mesmerized by the sights and sounds in the casinos. The blinking lights, the haze of cigarette smoke, the machines chirping a C major triad over and over. Of course, we children were only allowed to walk by the gamblers slowly, but that was enough to give us a taste of the experience.

I was most amazed by the people who would sit for hours and hours in front of the slot machines, pulling the lever again and again. Their faces never seemed to change expression, even when they won. It baffled me.

On the third day, two bad things happened. I had already spent hours in the pool, but this time I ventured too far toward the deep end, stepped off a hidden two-foot ledge, and sank like a rock. It took a minute, but both fully clothed parents dove into the pool simultaneously, and together pulled me out. My mother swore that we would start swimming lessons as soon as we got to California.

The second bad thing happened later that afternoon. My father got cocky, stepped up to the gaming tables, and lost all but a hundred dollars of our money. My mother was devastated. My brother and I were stunned, scared and silent.

Money — actually the lack of money — was the real boogeyman of my childhood. It was a wolf that seemed to be forever pacing just outside the door. Money was a constant worry for my mother, and it always made me sad to see her upset or depressed. She was by nature the opposite: energetic and positive about everything. That night, we all went to sleep in a very bad place. I doubt my mother slept at all. My aversion to gambling was born. It would take me another 30 years to get over it.

The next morning my father announced that he had a scheme. My mother put my hair in pigtails and got me as dressed up as possible given my limited wardrobe. I wore a little plaid skirt, white sleeveless blouse, and white-and-brown oxford spectator shoes with white ankle socks.

Off my father and I went, next door to the Sahara Hotel.

Just outside the lobby doors, he bent down and whispered, "Now listen up, Sue...I don't want you to say anything. Just do what I say and follow my cues. Maybe we can stir up something...Okay?"

"Okay, Papa." More than anything, I always wanted to make him proud of me.

We went inside and strode up to the front desk. "Can you tell me please who the Entertainment Director is?"

"Mr. Stan Irwin, sir," the nice lady replied.

"Thank you very much ma'am."

Then to a passing bellhop, "Can you tell me where Mr. Irwin's office is, please?"

"Right over there, Sir."

"Thank you, my fine fellow." My father always had a dramatic flair.

Then straight through the big doors right into the office. "Mr. Irwin?"

"Yeah, who the hell are you? I'm busy..."

And so it was that my father pulled out a Zoomerang, confused the poor man with its action, and launched his spiel. As instructed, I just stood there and smiled shyly. Through some miraculous verbal gymnastics on my father's part, Mr. Irwin — who was pressed for time and on his way to oversee a rehearsal of the current show — agreed to take a few minutes to watch me perform.

Off we traipsed to the Grand Showroom, and as soon as the cast was on break, I trooped up the stairs onto the stage to perform. I went right into my audition routine: a piano piece of classical music, then a skit from "Hansel And Gretel" in which I sang, danced and played both parts.

The whole cast (including Gene Kelly) broke into applause. Stan Irwin flipped. He told my father that he and Larry Sloan, his partner in L.A., would turn me into a star. He said something about me being like oil coming straight out of the ground: crude, but the real stuff. That I needed some polishing and training, but they were just the people to do it. He said he would meet us in Los Angeles, and gave us information on how to contact him once we were settled in.

So it was that in the middle of the night we drove off from Vegas to face the ordeal of crossing the great and fearsome Mojave Desert. We had our chest full of ice chips; only $125 to our name — but things were looking up! Once again we had hope.

Later, as I was growing up during the first half of the 1960's, we made quite a few trips to and through Vegas. Every time we drove across the country to visit the relatives back East, we would stop there. On the way to and from my summers at the Aspen Music Festival, we stopped. And sometimes, when we grew bored in Canoga Park, we'd pile into the car and drive off to The Strip. We loved the place.

As Janet and I hit the pre-teens and beyond, we would spend most of our time hanging out by the ever more luxurious hotel swimming pools. We were girls, and we were into tanning.

I would lie on a chaise lounge as long as I could stand it and then break for the pool. Over and over again until I turned a dark caramel color and the hair on my forearms was white blond. We drank quarts of iced tea, and I developed my fetish about ice... or perhaps it goes back to those first car trips across the desert. To this day, if I want to drink something cold, it needs to be poured into a tall Tom Collins glass full to the brim with ice cubes. It doesn't matter if it's water, lemonade, Coca-Cola, a Greyhound, Tanqueray and Tonic, or a Scotch n' Soda. The ice is the indispensible ingredient.

After I left for Europe in 1965, trips to Vegas didn't resume until the latter part of the '70s. By that time, Vegas had changed drastically, in many ways for the better. It had lost the dirt, grit and character of the Wild West gambling town, but it was bigger, more enticing to more people — especially families. New, spectacular theme hotels were being thought up and built every year. But you could still get a taste of the old Vegas if you dared take the cab ride Downtown.

My favorite hotel during this era was The Mirage. The gigantic fish tank in the lobby, Siegfried and Roy's show, the tigers themselves, the elegant casino, the showy theaters and the fancy restaurants. True, the rooms weren't great, and worst of all, the walls were so thin that you could hear everything that went on in the next room. Often, too much information.

During this time, I visited the town with Eliot: played some roulette, won some money, and lost my distaste for gambling. On later visits I learned to enjoy playing cards, craps and roulette.

Many years later, after Michael and I joined forces and blended his four kids with my one, we trooped off to Las Vegas often. He knew and loved the town. He and his brother had practically grown up there, vacationing with their parents from Southern California several times a year. His father had one of the original players' cards from the Flamingo. Its number had only three digits. By the mid-90's, all kinds of wonderful themed hotels were competing for attention. The number of world-class chefs headlining famous restaurants had quadrupled. Our favorite hotel, by far, was the Venetian. Win or lose, trips to Las Vegas always provided some light-hearted relief from our daily routine.

It was not until 2007 — on our trip to the new Wynn hotel — that we could no longer say that. It represented the worst time in both of our lives.

THE OHIO PLAYERS were scheduled for an evening session in Chicago. They never showed, but finally called to say their private plane had mechanical problems.

I remember the date, May 25, 1977, because we ended up going across the street to the midnight premier of a movie called *Star Wars*.

We did get their track done the next night (and I have to say I don't remember a thing about it).

But — *Star Wars!*

Chapter 7

Madison Avenue

———

DURING MY FIRST FEW MONTHS of working in both the studio and the office, I didn't pay much attention to the people from the advertising agencies. Completely focused on helping the composer/arranger get the track right, I just tried to ignore their chatter. It would take a few years before I had the authority to suggest that they take their conversations out to the waiting room. In any case, Herman handled them well. Most of the time.

But more of the clients were beginning to take notice of the girl with "eagle ears" (as some engineers and musicians dubbed my ability to catch wrong notes or rhythmic mistakes in even the most complicated orchestral score). A few started to ask Herman to bring me along to the pre-production meetings at their agencies. These were the meetings where the advertising goals of the campaign or spot would be presented, followed by what kind of underscore or jingle the agency 'creatives' had in mind. In the new jargon I was now learning, these were the 'specs' (specifications) of the project.

A typical agency assignment was supervised by a team consisting of a writer, an art director and a producer. Often, they would be overseen by a group creative director. All of these positions were considered "creative" as opposed to the account people (client liaisons) or the money people (bean counters).

I was strictly an observer in those first meetings, but I did notice a couple of things. The hierarchy at an ad agency in those days was rigidly structured. Almost everyone lived in fear of his immediate supervisor, not to mention the immortals at the very top. Alex Kroll at Young & Rubicam pops to mind. His underlings — even if they were creative directors themselves — practically shook in their shoes at the mention of his name. I really liked him; never feared him. He was an ex-football player. I thought he was hot.

Seeing how people behaved there in the real world made me wonder. What was the matter with me? I wasn't afraid of anyone in my life; never had been. My father didn't scold or abuse me (at least not until much later in life — and even then, he made me sad, not scared); my siblings, mother and grandmother loved and championed me; and now my one and only boss needed me. Hedy Spielter had protected me from Mr. Epailly (he was full of hot air anyway). Even the creeps on the streets of Manhattan weren't much of a threat in the daytime crowds. As my children know, I am only truly terrified of scorpions and tsunamis.

Back to the meeting scene: Herman and I would be shown either a rough cut of a film for a TV commercial, a script for a radio spot, or a storyboard (a comic strip-like panel that illustrates a spot with the dialogue or narration written underneath). In the case of a new jingle where lyrics had yet to be written, we would be given "the line" or slogan (like *We Do Chicken Right*), some selling points, and often some sample lyrics. Most of the time, those were terrible. In my experience, it is unexpectedly difficult for people who are not musicians to write lyrics. It doesn't matter if you're a good prose writer or even a poet: it's still challenging. The less than obvious constraints of the discipline are not easily fathomed.

The meeting would then get around to musical genre. What style would fit the demographics of the audience? Rock, Jazz, R&B, Folk, Classical, Show? Generally, the creative team would have some idea, even throw out a few examples. Often they were right. But sometimes, they were dead wrong. To my amazement, if they were adamant about their choice, Herman would cave: go along with the plan. We would produce the track or the demo. More often than not, it would be tossed. Total waste. Later on, I tried much harder to change their minds...

Herman Edel Associates was a unique jingle company. The rest of the bunch were built around a single composer (e.g., Mitch Leigh of Music Makers). Herman, not being any kind of musician himself, came up with the idea of offering a stable of composers, arrangers, and lyricists. He would act as liaison and businessman. This talent pool was 'exclusive' to the company, but only for the jingle world. Many of them were quite famous in other sectors of the music business.

Even though I didn't realize it at the time, I was in the process of carving out a new job position for our industry. At the time, there were no jingle music producers in the studios or on staff at our competing companies. And certainly no female ones.

But for our company, the position turned out to be invaluable in a couple of ways. First, it improved the efficiency of the sessions. When I was producing while Herman was schmoozing the clients, the production stayed on schedule. We usually came in under budget, which upped our profit margin. Second, despite my refusal to kiss up to them, the ad people liked and respected me. I learned to bank on it.

As my position grew in scope, I became bold enough to start suggesting musical changes to the writers when they brought back their first sketches. Melodically, harmonically, and structurally. In essence, I became an editor of their compositions. Maybe because my ideas weren't stupid, the composers didn't resent me. The company's batting average for creating winners for the agencies went up steadily, and the paychecks for the composers/arrangers increased accordingly.

People sometimes ask me, "What were the agencies like back then? Were they like *Mad Men* — the TV series?"

Not quite, in my experience. Maybe I came onto the scene a few years too late, but I had a problem watching episodes of that show. Not because they aren't fabulous entertainment; they are. More because the show is so stylized, so different from what I remember. I agree with Jerry Della Femina's opinion, "*Mad Men* is set a decade too late."

I entered the business in the fall of 1966 — the onset of a period of upheaval throughout the country. Some could argue it was the start of a kind of soft social revolution that lasted until the end of the decade. The Vietnam War controversy fueled a great deal of it, but wider social issues led to turmoil, as well. I didn't pay much attention to any of this. After graduating from college in 1965 at 20, and then spending a Fulbright Scholarship year in Rome, I had something else on my mind — making something of myself — as I hit Madison Avenue.

Still, within a couple of years I could tell that a definite schism was developing in the advertising world — one that reflected the other transformations going on all around us. At 'Man in the Grey Flannel Suit' firms like J Walter Thompson, Grey, Bates and Y&R, most of the men (even the 'creatives') wore suits and ties and were fastidiously well-groomed. Slick, short haircuts. They all chain-smoked. They disappeared into their three-martini lunches, and although I didn't spot many shirt-waisted dresses with full skirts, the women (mostly secretaries) were never seen in jeans or trousers.

A few of the bigger agencies had music directors. They ranged from the avuncular, pipe-smoking, never-make-waves Buck Warnick at Y&R to the large, loud and obnoxious Arnold Brown at Dancer Fitzgerald. He always made trouble, but I liked him anyway. He knew his stuff and could be both cultured and crude. Well-versed in literature, art, opera, and gourmet food, he had a remarkably foul mouth and insisted on female singers with big tits: in other words, a throwback to the *Mad Men* days. I was invited to his Village brownstone a few times for dinner and cognac. Arnold taught me to sear and cook a strip steak perfectly (I still use his method). Besides, he continued to work with us even after I stole his super-smart assistant, Kathy Brega.

Thinking back, I believe one of the reasons I was treated as an equal even though I was young and a woman had to do with the "mystery of music:" a language — a code — that was uniquely difficult to crack. To most of the ad people, I was a kind of sorceress. The good kind: one who could bring them what they wanted. They felt well equipped to talk and opine about the other arts: writing, photography, drawing or graphics. Command. Control. The music was more elusive.

The other emerging face of the industry — represented by agencies like Doyle Dane Bernbach and Jack Tinker and Partners — charmed and intrigued me. At DDB, the creative guys wore jeans, sneakers, work shirts, and let their hair grow. Although most smoked Marlboros, a lot of weed was around, too. Tinker was housed in the former Dorset Hotel on West 54th Street. It reminded me of a college dormitory. People wandering around, chatting in groups in doorways and halls. I was there one day when I ended up in a conversation with the great Gene Wilder. He was there to do yet another voiceover for Alka Seltzer. He came across as funny, but weird. I was too uptight to accept when he asked me out. My loss.

The music projects assigned by these agencies were more likely to be challenging and fun. Their ideas were different — sometimes even irreverent — and I loved them.

We scored one of the most bizarre spots. It was part of the "The Blahs" campaign for Alka Seltzer. A man in an ill-fitting brown suit, carrying a heavy briefcase, wanders slowly and awkwardly across a barren, hilly landscape. He looks uneasy, keeps glancing around and back over his shoulder. The voiceover speaks of a feeling of 'dread' — the kind you can't quite put your finger on. He recommends Alka Seltzer. After the "plop, plop, fizz, fizz" beauty shot of the product, the scene cuts away to a closer look at the landscape, where — now in utter silence — a mushroom cloud blooms over the distant hills ...

I sometimes tried to inject some of that irreverence into my meetings with the more straightlaced groups. Generally, those suggestions fell on deaf ears; were scoffed at, in fact.

Those different and more creative agencies spawned some of the greatest: Wells Rich Greene, Case McGrath, and Scali McCabe Sloves were three.

Gene Case was tall, blond, blue-eyed: he would have been quite patrician in manner if it weren't for his boyish habit of constantly pushing his longish bangs out of his eyes. We did a lot of work together and became friends. Beneath his somewhat cold exterior, he was a really kind man. One night I ran into him in front of my apartment in the Village. I was upset and teary-eyed, having been stood up by some asshole art director. Gene rescued the evening — took me to a bar, joked me out of my bad mood, and spent the night. Later, I met and hung out with his weird goth girlfriend, nicknamed (at HEA only) *Dora Death*. She was a strange one, complete with all sorts of rituals. I remember her telling me that she stole some of his hair and fingernail clippings, put them in a condom, and hid the little packet under their mattress. Supposedly to bind him to her forever. She died a few years later (OD'd, I believe).

As we entered the '70s, things grew progressively wilder. Disco, drugs, sexual freedom and disregard for tradition dominated. Now female TV producers appeared more and more often as part of the creative teams. My closest friends in the ad business were experimenting with all forms of sexual encounters, sometimes with the added combination of cocaine and skin-popping heroin. I never participated, but I was scared for them. And it turned out I had every reason to be...

In the meantime, Herman was once again expanding my job description. Given my popularity at the agencies, he decided I should start selling, too. We put together ¼" tape reels of our best work. He made me start cold-calling important personnel: ones who weren't already familiar with us.

For some reason, I didn't mind. I had never seen myself as a salesperson, but this gig was different. I believed 100% in the product, sold it with conviction, and won many victories in what (once again) had always been a man's world.

As our business increased, so did the travel. I met with agency people frequently in Chicago, Detroit and Los Angeles. Less frequently in Philadelphia, Cincinnati, Dallas and Miami. I was asked to produce in London, Nashville, L.A. and Memphis. Work trumped all aspects of my life. I sacrificed a lot to answer to that master, but that's the way it was. *The Project* always came first: before love, grief, friendship, vacations — everything (except children). My whole world was consumed by my job, and I didn't mind one bit. It was more fun than anything! Even today, I feel most alive — most worthwhile — when I have an assignment to throw myself into.

I did occasionally indulge in a somewhat inexplicable fantasy. I can't say why. It started one night in the Pan Am building in Manhattan. I was set to take the helicopter to JFK. As I followed the stewardesses in their form-fitting, gold-trimmed black uniforms down the corridor, I fantasized about what would happen if, instead of going to London, I just hopped on a plane to, say, Marrakech or Rio... and disappeared. How long would it take to find me? I'd stare at the departures board and pick the most exotic destination. Why? Maybe I didn't understand that I had so much further to go in the business. Maybe it was just a sudden rebellion against having a predictable future in front of me. I never did act on the impulse...

In the early '70s, a crisis started to brew. A couple of years before, Herman had asked for my opinion about where he should take his family for a vacation. I suggested Aspen. He took me up on it, and fell in love with the town. Many visits later, he decided he would move his family there from Scarsdale, and just fly into Manhattan once a month to check up on the business. He also changed the name of the company from "Herman Edel Associates" to "HEA Productions" to reflect his lesser participation. Later, after I bought the company, I decided against changing the name — it was too well known. Whenever anyone would ask what 'HEA' stood for, I would improvise (usually, "Hamilton et al").

When his wife underwent major back surgery, Herman didn't put in an appearance at the office for six or seven months. After that hiatus, although he did make it to NYC for a few more months, the horse was already out of the barn. I had grabbed the reins; business was booming, and I didn't even have any questions for him.

The fact was, he annoyed the hell out of us by counting paper clips and accusing us of using too many stamps on our letters.

Before his move, Herman had spent months prepping me. He had explained most of his business and financial practices. My favorite new activity became figuring out bids for jobs, then discussing them over the phone with the clients. I discovered a major advantage: many clients were reluctant to nickel-and-dime a girl on budgets, and certainly not over the phone. As a result, I frequently got away with murder (especially when I was efficient in the studio and could bring the project in under bid).

Why he did it, I will never know for sure, but Herman literally handed over the keys to the kingdom. He certainly wouldn't have done it had I been a man. I think that with his alpha male orientation, there was no way he could have seen a coup coming. He simply could not imagine such a scenario being led by a woman. Still, I felt incredibly guilty about everything. He had treated me like a daughter. I was officially "Daughter #2," and had a three-tiered gold necklace with a printed pendant to prove it. He had taken Buddy off with him to Aspen (sigh of relief: there would have been blood on the walls). Between hiring a new full-time bookkeeper, Sherry Day, and his in-depth explanation of the financial workings of the business, he had left me fully equipped to run everything by myself.

In fact, I had lost a bit of faith in my mentor in an earlier episode, after letting myself into the office one night.

It had been around eleven, and I needed to pick up something I'd left behind. I unlocked the front door and surprised a favorite married client on the couch with some chippie. Oops. I wasn't embarrassed at all, though the client looked terrified. I was disgusted. I came to learn that this pimping out of the office was a special perk Herman allowed from time to time.

I never mentioned it to him. Would have been awkward.

I'd had more than six months of running the company with the bit in my teeth and no supervision. Herman was proving to be a pain in the ass: actually a hindrance whenever he came in to check up on us. I really didn't want to confront him, but I felt held down — held back.

It was probably inevitable anyway, but then came the final blow. It infuriated me. After a year of bringing in well over a million dollars worth of business, for no conceivable reason except greed and the certainty that he could get away with it because I was female, he cut my bonus from $30K to $25K. When my secretary Kathy told me what he had done, that tore it. *Not right!* I was ready for the fight. I also had the urging and backing of the most important writers, including Jake Holmes.

Fair was fair.

IN 1971, I PRODUCED the background score to one of my favorite ads of all time for writer/creative director Ed McCabe and art director John Danza at Scali, McCabe, Sloves.

The Volvo commercial shows two giant car-carrier trucks meeting at a flatland crossroad. The silhouette of a metropolis is off in the distance. The truck headed toward the city is full of bright shiny new Detroit autos; the one leaving is stacked with pancaked junkers. "Are those the new ones?" the second driver asks admiringly. Their chat is interrupted when a spiffy-looking Volvo beeps its horn. It breezes by as the announcer sums up: "Beat the System. Buy a Volvo."

Brilliant. Classic. The ad debuted before a large audience at the opening of the Volvo dealers' convention. I have always heard it was by accident, but Ed tells me the version played to conclude the convention was no mistake: the same ad, this time ending with, "Fuck Detroit. Buy a Volvo."

Needless to say, joyous rioting engulfed the auditorium...

Chapter 8

Kiddie Showbiz

IF MERVYN LeROY HAD HAD HIS WAY, my life would have been much different. The powerful director was butting heads with the executives at Warner Bros. Pictures. He wanted me, an unknown, for the title role in his upcoming movie, *The Bad Seed*. The studio people wanted Patty McCormack, a proven child actress. He wanted dark hair, green eyes and intensity. They wanted blond hair, baby blue eyes, and seeming innocence. I even did a screen test for him, but to no avail. The studio won.

My career in TV, movies, and as a concert pianist began when I was five. (I also studied classical ballet, but found out soon enough it was not to be. My legs were too short).

I made several guest soloist appearances in concerts at Fairleigh Dickinson University. Around that time, there was also a weekly television program hosted by a well-known musicologist and conductor of children's concerts, Wheeler Beckett. I performed on his show when I was six. I remember sitting around on a fuzzy white carpet with other children, waiting my turn. Two older children were standing next to the big piano, blindfolded for dramatic effect. Mr. Beckett was seated in front of the keyboard, playing simple chords and asking the two to identify the individual notes. He was giving the audience a demonstration of people with "perfect pitch." I listened to the nervous children's hesitant answers; neither was doing very well. Finally, I could contain myself no longer and just blurted out the answers.

The camera swung around to me as Mr. Beckett pointed and proclaimed, "Ladies and Gentlemen, that girl has perfect pitch!" I really didn't understand what all the fuss was about. Until that show, I had assumed that everyone had perfect pitch, much in the same way a person who is not color blind assumes that everyone else can tell one color from another.

My parents, figuring I could put some money away for the future, tried hard to get me into show business. They paid for a series of diction and elocution lessons in New York City which may account for what some people still tell me is my odd accent. Even now, perfect strangers sometimes ask me where I'm from and are surprised to hear I'm American born and bred. Anyway, Ma and Pa were miserable agents, and I got nowhere fast.

They did, however, get me some bit parts here and there. I appeared on various TV shows originating out of New York. I had small parts on *Live Like a Millionaire, The Four Star Playhouse*, and *The Ethel and Albert Show*. On that last one I also got to do a live commercial for Log Cabin Syrup. The spot featured the syrup being poured over vanilla ice cream. I hated the taste of it. It was revolting — especially having to smile as I shoveled it into my mouth, then finishing with the required, "Mmmmm, Mmmmm, Mmmmm!"

As I remember, all of these shows were done live. Rehearsed, but then shot live in huge studios (*Four Star Playhouse* was the only one shot on a stage in a theater). It was kind of like movie sets today with everybody around — cast, crew, huge cameras, sound guys, audience, make-up, friends and family — but *live*, on air!

My budding career had come to a complete halt when we left for our cross-country adventure to California, but returned to life after the incident at the Sahara Hotel in Vegas.

I was now under the wing of Stan Irwin and his partner Larry Sloan; they were going to make me a star! Stan Irwin, who was Head of Entertainment at the Sahara when I auditioned for him, was rightly considered a pioneer and innovator in multiple areas of show business. He was an actor, comedian, writer, producer of *The Johnny Carson Show*, and a major talent scout. He put together a consortium of people to sponsor my career in Hollywood. Besides him and Larry, there were Nat James from RKO Studios; Harry Crocker, an actor in

Hollywood and member of the Crocker National Bank family; and Sally Hamilton, personal assistant to director William Castle.

As soon as my family was safely moved into the house in Laurel Canyon, my mother insisted on having Stan and Larry over for dinner. This was an utter disaster.

My mother cooked her two Italian specialties, stuffed artichokes and spaghetti with meat sauce. They hardly ate a bite. Guess they were steak and potato guys. She felt terrible; I felt ashamed; my father didn't give a damn. He turned out to have the right take: it didn't matter at all.

I embarked on a regime of lessons, lessons, lessons. Classical piano, jazz piano (with the absolute master, Harry Fields), ballet, tap dancing, singing, acting and dialogue coaching. Thanks to Miss Pirotta, regular school was a breeze at the Colin McEwen School on Highland Blvd. They had already skipped me, and I was sailing through fifth grade. The rest of my weekdays and all of the weekends were filled with lessons. Eventually, I had a suitable audition piece prepared (or so I was told). At that time in my life, I didn't question the adults. Looking back now on that hodge-podge of a routine, I know it must have been dreadful. First a little classical piano with a segue into a jazzy section. Get up, do a few ballet moves, then some fancy tapping. Stop. Now a dramatic soliloquy, then back to the piano to accompany myself singing "The Boy Next Door."

Can you imagine?!!!

I didn't mind the hectic schedule so much. Most of the time it was my father who drove me to all of the appointments and auditions; we were pals. Often, as a treat, we would go to Barney's Beanery. My father would have a drink, and I, a Shirley Temple. I loved looking at all of the characters in that fabled Hollywood haunt. Seated at the long battered and scarred bar would be a bizarre mixture of sad old habituées next to glittering, bejeweled women in their full length mink coats. On the sly, I would reach out and slide my hand down the glossy fur as I passed behind their stools. Whenever my father caught me, he would admonish, "not again, Sue" (especially if I had earlier poked a finger or two into the soft butter next to the bread basket). When in L.A., I still try to stop there every so often.

A few of the auditions paid off. I snagged a speaking role in *The Americano*, a Glenn Ford film about Brahma bulls. We shot my scene at the Chatsworth railroad station. I played Glenn's niece, there to see him off on his trip to South America, and to ask a couple of dumb questions. The only cool thing about the whole experience was the bulls themselves. There were two of them in a railroad car, and I passed the time petting their noses and talking to them. They didn't seem to mind.

The scene that ended up lasting about two minutes in the movie took all day to shoot. I couldn't believe it. Glenn, who seemed to be a very nice man, couldn't remember his lines at all. Take after take, he blew them. Twenty-nine in all. I kept count. At the time I thought, *God, he's so dumb.* In retrospect, he might have been drunk.

Late in the game that day, even I forgot what I was supposed to say on one take. The director, William Castle, stopped everything, came over to me, bent down and said, "Don't worry, honey. You're doing great. Everyone makes a mistake once in a while." It didn't bother me at all — I think he was really talking to Glenn Ford.

My entry into the glamorous world of Hollywood movies did not thrill me. I was bored and frustrated with the whole experience. It involved way, way too much time just standing around, waiting, with very little acting (or action). Much later in life, when I had my music production company, I was sometimes hired to spend a few days on projects being filmed on a set or on location. Although it was always fun to work with the talent, I still didn't like the waiting around much.

The pace of the recording studio is much more to my liking. I could get two or three separate jingles done and delivered in one day. Much better. Much more satisfying. And if one of them didn't turn out so great, so be it. It wasn't as if I were losing a big chunk of my life in the process.

My second foray into the movie/child actress biz was, if anything, worse. I was cast in a bit part in the movie *Not As A Stranger.* This one was a major production starring Robert Mitchum and Olivia de Havilland. I played a little girl who had swallowed a safety pin, so practically all of my shooting time was spent lying on an operating table while the scene played out around me. This was even more boring than the Glenn Ford film. Mostly, I had to keep my mouth wide open and look scared.

Another problem was that the scene involved Gloria Grahame, an actress notorious for being difficult. She refused to come out of her dressing room for hours, pleading a headache. Held everything up. One day, when she finally did appear, she pitched a hissy fit over something and stormed off the set.

I did love looking up at Robert Mitchum with my mouth open, but that was about it for the good stuff.

My patience on the set was also tried by the union-dictated mandatory two hours of "schooling." The complete idiots they hired as teachers were generally scared of me and acted as if I knew more than they did. I believe it's possible. We usually spent the time reading out loud or coloring stupid pictures.

The only thing that could have changed my scornful attitude would have been landing that title role in *The Bad Seed*. I loved the script and the director, and really yearned to play someone so inherently evil. But it was not to be. One studio — I think it was Warner Bros — offered me one of their infamous seven-year contracts. My parents talked it over with me at length. We weighed the pros and cons, but ultimately turned them down: I wanted to concentrate on the piano.

My former agent still occasionally called with an assignment. One of the strangest involved a concert at the Greek Theater. The outdoor amphitheater is in Griffith Park and seats about 5,000 people. The stage building was modeled after a Greek temple.

I think this particular promotional event was connected with the Walt Disney Company. My part of the show involved dragging a huge clock with a giant minute hand onto the stage. The emcee would then introduce me to the audience and explain that I was going to attempt to play "The Minute Waltz" by Frederic Chopin in under a minute. It was literally a race against the clock. Needless to say, I won with just a couple of seconds to spare, making it exciting for the crowd. I had practiced diligently to be able to time it correctly without looking up at the clock. The audience loudly counted down the last ten seconds, anyway. Boy, some weird things were going down in L. A. in the '50s...

Don't ask me how or why, but when I was about 14, I had a half hour weekly radio show broadcast every Sunday from Pasadena. My father would drive me, of course. I would play a classical piece or two on the piano, and then spend the rest of the time interviewing various people. Pa would help me write some of the questions, but mostly, I winged it. He was my first guest: the inventor of the toy sensation, the Zoomerang — but after him, I interviewed our fascinating but intransigent lodger, The Colonel; a snake handler-trainer; my crazy "uncle" Lee, who was in a motorcycle gang; and my current piano teacher (that one was kind of dull). *The Susan Hamilton Show* lasted only six months. I got burned out, making the long drive every week to sit with my guest in an empty studio. The utter lack of any audience response at all did it in. That's radio. Also, by that time there were too many upcoming piano competitions and performances.

There was one other early seminal experience: another my agent arranged. It was Christmas time, and he had received a request for a pretty child who could play the accompaniments for Christmas songs and carols on the piano. The venue was a holiday party at a Beverly Hills mansion. They would pay $250 for the evening. I jumped at the chance. It was a lot of money to my family, and was sure to make our Christmas a lot merrier. I was dressed in my finest as my father drove to the fancy address in our drafty jalopy of a car. He accompanied me to the door, where a maid told us that he could come back to pick me up in two hours.

Once the maid had taken my shabby coat and introduced me to the host and hostess, I could only stare in wonder at the house and its magical interior. The rooms were decorated to the hilt: I had never seen such splendor. Every square inch was stuffed on all levels with ornate figurines depicting all the characters of Christmas; overstuffed vases of red roses and white amaryllis; garlands; life-sized stuffed animals; candy bowls; nut bowls; gossamer angels hung from the ceiling — you get the picture.

I took my place at the baby grand piano. It too was fully covered by an elaborate crèche scene. Children, maybe 15 of them, crowded around and demanded first this song, then that one. I obliged as best I could. After a while, some of the adults joined in, and pretty soon we were all really having a good time. Everyone was complimenting me and patting me on the back. I was flushed with success, so when the children of the house invited me to go to their playroom with the rest of the kids, I was pleased, and got up to follow.

The strong hand of the hostess on my shoulder stopped me dead. She smiled brightly and told me, "No dear, you can't. Go into the kitchen and wait for your father. Cook has a cup of hot chocolate for you. That is where you belong." Naturally, I did as I was told, but I was mortified.

That experience has led me to empathize with 'service' people whenever and wherever our paths cross. It's the reason I always made it a point to treat everyone in a support role first as fellow human beings. The assistants in the recording studios and editing houses; the grooms in the horse world; the secretaries of the bigwigs; the shampooers at the hair salons; salespeople, flight attendants, waiters: everybody. To recognize their existence — greet them by name if possible — has always seemed to me to be the natural way to behave. And should one of my colleagues demean one of these people in some way, I would deliberately involve that person in our conversation.

I can truthfully report that I have never in my life snapped my fingers at anyone.

That incident in a Beverly Hills home was hurtful, but I have never regretted it. Instead, it instructed me.

MY FATHER WAS LOST ONCE AGAIN in our own town (Canoga Park). As he stopped to grab a map, he was momentarily blinded by sunlight reflecting off something overhead. He looked up to see a perfectly shaped flying saucer hovering above a palm tree.

He lunged for the miniature binoculars we kept in the glove compartment, and focused them just in time to watch it dart off. Within an instant, it was a dark speck on the horizon.

When he returned home and calmly told us the story, I just grinned.

"Yeah right, Pa. Why don't you report it to the Air Force?"

He did.

Later that evening, the doorbell rang. My mother opened the door to find two unsmiling uniformed Air Force officers. They spent quite a while interrogating Pa in the living room: two of their airborne pilots had reported similar sightings that afternoon.

I didn't make fun of my father anymore. At least not for a few days.

Chapter 9

An Affair to Remember

I THOUGHT MY NEW CAREER was over as the boat tipped sideways and threatened to sink in the Hudson River. The usually taciturn 75-year-old Scottish captain of the Circle Line boat had just screamed at me, "In fifty years on this river, I've never had a man overboard! *What is the matter with you people?*"

The whole affair had started innocently enough. It was the late '60s, and I had begun to feel my oats as a music producer for Herman Edel Associates. One of my favorite ad agencies to work with was Doyle Dane Bernbach, one of the most creative. I loved producing tracks for writer-art director creative teams like Paul Margulies and Bob Wilvers. My favorite television producer was Jay Eisenstadt.

Jay was not that much older than I. He had not only given me work, but had also taken me under his wing. I adored him. So when he asked me to find an appropriate band for his brother's engagement party, I said yes immediately. Of course, I had no idea where or how to find and hire a band...but I had friends.

I went to one of my musical mentors, Bill LaVorgna, Judy Garland's former drummer (some say lover). He was the top studio drummer in NYC at the time. I asked him what I should do. "No problem, sweetie," he said, "I'll put something together and we'll have some fun." I negotiated the fee he requested for a four-piece band, even upped it a bit, and put the whole thing out of my mind. It wasn't happening until late May.

Now, Jay had told me the party was going to be held on a big boat which would depart from a pier somewhere downtown on the west side. He also informed me that the whole affair was black tie, very *chi chi*. My people and I should dress appropriately. In addition, he explained that his brother worked for the Treasury Department: I could expect a somewhat staid crowd with some Very Important People. About 140 of them, in fact. I didn't know enough to be worried about combining New York hep cats with government bureaucrats.

In my mind, I'd envisioned a huge, fancy yacht. But hey — I hadn't lived in New York that long. The 'pier downtown' was the Circle Line boarding dock. I was disappointed; the big tub looked pretty ratty to me.

Also, the weather was crap. End of May, you'd think *warm and balmy*. Instead, it was cold, damp and spritzing heavily. The boys in the band weren't too happy, either. They hated wearing monkey suits, and their instruments couldn't get wet. I had to spend a lot of time convincing them to even get aboard. All of this in an expensive, bought-for-the-occasion strapless black and white floor-length gown with very high heels that were growing more painful by the minute.

The crowd seemed happy enough. There was an inordinate amount of food and an open bar. They wore fancy garb, but in slightly frumpy fashion. Despite their average age of about 60, there were a lot of aquas and pinks, poufs and flounces: a dowdy lot, for sure.

Thank God, the weather cleared up. The moon came out and we were able to move the whole band out onto one of the decks.

The band members included Bill LaVorgna, drummer; Chet Amsterdam, upright bass; Alf Nystrom, straight man accordion player; and Gus Vali, famous Greek singer/songwriter and super-pro bandleader. Gus was the darling of the Greek community and did everyone who was anyone's wedding and/or party. He was well-known for being able to play two different saxophones at one time. He did so at this party, to the delight of the crowd.

By about 8 pm all was going well. Everyone was dancing and enjoying music under the stars. But there was one small problem.

Chet Amsterdam, the tall, blond upright bass player, motioned me over to him while the band was playing. He whispered angrily into my ear. "If that mother-fucking guy in the striped suit touches my ass one more time, I'm gonna deck him." I personally delivered a glass of champagne to the fellow in question and quietly asked him to please refrain. He fled into the crowd.

Later on, around nine, nine-thirty, the party was rockin' like crazy. People were dancing to the tunes and seemed to really enjoy the band. The ship had taken us around Manhattan Island a couple of times and was headed back to the pier. Gus was leading a long single file line of partygoers in a boisterous version of *"Hava Nagila,"* all of them weaving and bobbing through the crowd on the deck. He was playing his soprano sax. Every once in a while he would throw a leg over the railing, then pull it back and continue on with the dance. I don't know why he did it, but the last time he did, he was right next to me and slipped on the wet deck. I instinctively grabbed for him and caught the sax. But not Gus.

He dropped like a stone, a long, long way down into the dark waters of the Hudson River. I saw him surface for a moment, but the current was so strong he disappeared from sight a moment later. Bill and Chet ran to the stern. I followed, but when they frantically started to shed their dinner jackets. I grabbed them and pleaded, "Stop it you guys! There's no point! The river's moving too fast. We'll just have three people to rescue instead of one." Thank God they listened.

Of course, people were screaming, *"Man overboard! Man overboard!"* which sent everyone stampeding to the side where Gus had fallen. The boat started to list. The entire crew rushed out to shoo the folks back from the railing. A long, loud air horn sounded; the boat slowed and began to come about. The very angry captain got up in my face, "You crazy musicians! What the hell was he thinking? In 50 years on this river, I've never, I mean never, have had a man overboard!" I had nothing to say.

The two huge spotlights trained on the water finally picked up the tiny floating figure of Gus. He was in high, high spirits. Everybody could hear as he shouted, "I'm fine. Come on in, the water's beautiful, fuckin' beautiful!! It's god damn fuckin' gorgeous out here." Over and over with the "f" word. I wanted to die. Some of the ladies were tittering. Others looked shocked. Some men were amused. Others pretended to be outraged.

Needless to say, I was immensely relieved that Gus was okay. They threw him a life preserver — the classic white ring — and then hauled him in. The crowd sent up a cheer as his feet hit the deck. He was freezing and trembling despite his spirited rantings. The crew pushed him down into the boiler room and made him strip.

The next surprise was a doozy. It seemed that Gus had more than $100,000 worth of negotiable bonds in his pockets. When I was allowed to climb down the spiral ladder to visit Gus, bonds were plastered all over the boiler, drying out. To this day, I have no idea why Gus would be carrying them: but they were certainly soaking wet, now. Gus was wrapped in some grey blankets. He was cheerful as hell. I didn't have the heart to chastise him about anything. What good would it do?

Everyone was still buzzing about the episode as we neared the pier. Gus had to have the last word, though. Draped in blankets, he defiantly danced through the crowd playing *"Hava Nagila"* as we made land.

Although I feared all kinds of repercussions and punishments, they never came. Jay told me later that most people told him it was the most entertaining party they'd ever attended. He agreed with them.

BILL AND CHET stumbled through the door of my Hudson Street apartment. It was the middle of the night, and they were in rough shape.

I was alone, 22, and inexperienced about drugs. They were shaking, sweating and vomiting. Bill managed to croak out, "Bad batch of 'H'..."

I went to the phone to dial 911 but they took the phone away. "Just make coffee. Make us drink it. Keep us moving. Can't go to hospital..."

Both men were over six feet tall. I took turns trundling each one up and down the hall for hours with them leaning on my shoulders.

That night almost killed *me*.

Chapter 10

Good Witch, Bad Witch

————

MY TWO GRANDMOTHERS WERE WITCHES. Both lived in the small town of Rutherford, New Jersey, only a few miles from New York City. I didn't know the 'good' one very well; she died when I was very young. Her name was Etta Jackson Hamilton. She was married to my grandfather, Hyman Hamilton, and was mother to my father and his four siblings. A woman of extraordinary abilities, she was a Rosicrucian.

Rosicrucianism is a philosophical secret society founded in medieval times by alchemists and sages. Its doctrine was built on esoteric findings from the ancients whose teachings provided insight into the mysteries of nature and the metaphysics of the physical and spiritual realms. Based on the occult tradition, Rosicrucians believe in reincarnation, second sight, and the ability to foretell the future. Their symbol is the Rosy Cross, which is associated with the fourteenth century's semi-mystical alchemist, Christian Rosenkreuz.

Soon after my birth, my mother took me to my paternal grandparents' house. Etta held me in her arms for a long time before she looked up and said, "Why Carol, you are very lucky. Susan is an extremely old soul, and she has a completely blue aura." I heard this story many times as I grew up. I understood the 'old soul' remark because reincarnation had been explained in detail. But not the 'blue aura' part. I had no idea what that meant, and put it out of my mind.

In the early '90s, I attended the 40th birthday party in Malibu for my good friend, Richard Gitlin. Richard was a Warner Bros. executive. The party was held in front of his father's house on the beach, and it was a big deal.

Hundreds of people attended. It was catered to the nines. A great band played into the night, and a dozen circus entertainers wandered through the crowd. Off to the side, there was a small, tented booth. A sign over the door read 'aura pictures.' My friends were going in and coming out with Polaroid prints that supposedly showed them with their 'aura.' The 'auras' looked like bursts of lights all around the seated figures. Most were multi-colored, some very bright, some muted. They all had at least two colors, but no blues at all.

My friends made me do it. Late in the afternoon, I finally went into the booth. A young girl had me sit in a single chair that faced a curtain. She stepped behind it. It took a minute or two for the aura experts to take the picture with their "very special" camera. Actually, I don't remember even seeing a camera.

I could hear them talking on the other side of the curtain. *Wow, that's weird...I never saw that before...Think they're quite rare.* When they finally came out to show me the photo, the hair on my arms and the back of my neck rose straight up. The 'aura' was completely blue: turquoise blue, without a trace of any other color. Of course it sent my mind reeling back to that all-but-forgotten story.

When I asked the aura photographers what it meant, they told me, "It usually means you are a very old soul. Turquoise auras go with strong, influential personalities. They're usually associated with teachers, gurus — people like that."

I left the tent in something close to a state of shock, but I took the Polaroid. Still have it. Further research came up with this definition:

> *Turquoise indicates a dynamic quality of being and a highly energized personality capable of projection and influencing others. People with turquoise strong points in their Aura can do many things simultaneously and are good organizers. They feel bored when forced to concentrate on one thing.*

There were other stories about Etta. One day when she was having lunch with her five children, she suddenly turned pale, stood up from the table, and told them in a shaky voice, "I have to go lie down now. I just saw your father's car turn over and roll down an embankment." It was true; her vision had happened at the exact moment she announced it. My grandfather was not seriously hurt.

Another time she wrote an angry response to a letter she had received from my great grandmother. The letter informed her that everything was fine up on the Hamilton dairy farm where my father Roger was spending the summer. "Don't lie to me, please," she wrote back. "I can see the bandage over Roger's left eye and I want to know what happened." Of course, once again, she was right. They hadn't wanted to tell her, to keep her from worrying; but keeping things from Grandma Etta wasn't so easy!

I gathered from my mother, father, aunts and uncles that everyone considered Etta a saint. When Aunt Dorothy, the eldest of the Hamilton children, had to be snatched and rescued from a hasty, abusive marriage, it was Etta who cared for her. She nurtured and kept her going for many many years despite some severe psychological damage. Dorothy would crawl about on all fours, searching the floor; then stop in front of whoever was around, reach out her empty hand and say, "My eyeball fell out and I just found it. Could you put it back in, please?"

Then there was Uncle Dick, who also lived in the Rutherford house with his parents and his sister Dot. I don't know exactly why or when he fell apart, but in the 1940's, he would walk around the town and return with long, detailed reports of his conversations with the people he had met: people like FDR and General Eisenhower. Their discussions usually focused on strategies for the War.

Grandpa Hy was gruff, aloof: tough. He'd fought in the Spanish American War as a teenager, caught yellow fever, and come home with bleeding ulcers. The doctors told him he didn't have long to live. He died in his nineties, outliving them all.

But it was Etta was who held the family together; Etta who was adored and revered by all. I wish I'd had the chance to know her better.

Conversely, I knew my other grandmother — the bad witch — very well. After we moved to California, she lived with my family and stayed with us until she died, well into her eighties.

Lillian Borshnik Alessandroni was an accomplished woman. A concert pianist, she spoke five languages and was a world traveler. She was also vain, proud and highly sexual.

She met and married my other grandfather, Cesare Alessandroni, in New York City. He had been the star baritone of an opera company from Rome, Italy. The troupe was left stranded in Kansas after the manager absconded with the funds. Grandpa Cesare made his way to New York where he was hired by *Il Progresso*, the Italian newspaper. He represented the paper up and down the entire East Coast, including Canada, until his death in 1943.

This set of grandparents lived in comfort in Rutherford until the Great Crash. Cesare had invested heavily in the Market and was almost wiped out. But they survived. Lillian gave piano lessons; he still worked at the paper, and, for the most part, they enjoyed life. He was an avid gardener and extraordinary cook. I believe I inherited my passion for both from him. I've heard that he grew the most amazing dahlias and tomatoes. His secret was sheep manure. The neighbors had to suffer through the stench each spring, but the flowers and vegetables made it worthwhile.

All the neighbors hated Lillian. She considered herself a superior being what with her fancy clothes, fancy furniture, worldly knowledge and perfect figure. She looked down her prominent nose at most of them, and refused to socialize. She was overly possessive and protective of my mother Carol, her only child, and wouldn't let her play often with the neighborhood children. She also refused to provide a brother or sister. My mother hated her for it.

Cesare and Lillian bought an automobile in the '30s. They wanted to put in a driveway and garage for it, but to build it they needed an additional 12-inch strip of land. They offered to pay the couple next door a reasonable price for the land, but they turned them down. Grandma had been too much of a bitch.

Well, that was not to be tolerated. Lillian marched up their porch steps and knocked on the door. When the husband answered, she looked him in the eye and proclaimed, "Bad things happen to bad people." She stretched out her arm, pointed a finger at him and hissed, "I put a hex on you and your pregnant wife." Within a few months, the wife fell down the porch steps and miscarried, and the husband lost his job.

They gave her the land.

Lillian moved in with us at the Carlson Circle house after we moved to Canoga Park. She had divorced her second husband. Cesare had died in the 40's, and grandma hadn't wasted any time. She married again quickly; the result of a tumultuous and scandalous affair. In our new house, she was given her own room down the hall from my parents' bedroom. She was nosey, opinionated, a tattler, and a perpetual busybody.

We three kids considered her fair game. We played all kinds of tricks on her: putting creatures in her room, telling her lurid tall tales about our friends and neighbors, and lighting her very long machine-gun-like farts as she ambled down the hall to her room. Grandma had a serious flatulence problem but was also deaf, so didn't really hear her jet propulsion-type expulsions. The methane blue flares were spectacular.

In later years, even Charlie and Charlene (the woolly monkeys) got it about Grandma. They would chase her down the hall and pull on her skirts much like they did with the cats' tails. She would swat at them and scold. They would sit up, bare their teeth, and chatter and scream at her. It was wonderful chaos.

One good example of the familial interaction happened when my brother and a couple of his friends decided to dig to China. They started a hole with their shovels and kept at it for weeks. It grew very very deep. They eventually had to provide an exit ladder. It drove Grandma crazy. She couldn't understand at all why they would do such a thing.

She badgered my parents, "It's just not normal; it doesn't make any sense; it's dangerous; there's no reason for it. *Blah, blah, blah.*" My parents ignored her. She became obsessed. She took another tack. "Somebody's going to fall in and die. One of the children, the horse, a wandering hobo. It's a menace!" She got in the habit of getting up each morning, and running outside to check the hole. I believe she was hoping she would find a corpse in it.

Lillian did have a few good points. She would sit with me for hours as I practiced the piano, but wouldn't interfere unless I asked for advice. She was a total pro at telling fortunes with cards, and eerily correct about many things with people she didn't know at all. She taught her system to me, but I still have mixed feelings about using it. Too many times, things both good and bad that were foretold by the cards came true.

One summer the family planned a cross-country road trip, but then Grandma had a stroke. It was a frightening moment, but Lillian was strong. She confounded the doctors by bouncing back from no speech and almost total paralysis on her left side to complete use of all her faculties within 48 hours.

My father donned the cloak of martyrdom. He volunteered to stay at home with Lillian so that we could make the trip. I suspect he secretly preferred it. He could stay in the garage, tinkering with his inventions, listening to his radio and shutting out the world. All he had to do was to make Grandma breakfast and check on her every once in a while.

Within a day or two after we left, my father had a strange experience. Grandma was still quite weak and mostly stayed in her room. But he was out in front of the house early one morning when he saw her. She was literally floating along a few feet off the ground between the fence and the road, drifting toward town. Pa did nothing except make note of the occurrence, accept it, and report it to us when we got back. He was strange in his own way, too.

Lillian and my father didn't have the best of relationships. She sought his attention and opinion on every minuscule issue and event. Nattered at him constantly. She also tried to cause trouble by tattling on our every doing and implying that my mother was having an affair with The Colonel (the boarder who lived with us).

Pa finally developed a system for dealing with her. Whenever she would approach; he would raise one hand high over his head, and wave her off while repeating over and over, "Buxtehude! Buxtehude!" (the name of a 17th century composer). He just liked the sound of it. She would walk away, shaking her head in frustration and disgust.

One morning, just before we were scheduled to return from our big trip, he forgot to make her breakfast. He was in the garage and was startled by the sound of the huge heavy sliding door being wrenched open forcefully. The supposedly recovering Lillian stood there and demanded, "Where's my breakfast!"

Lillian lived with us until she died. Even when we moved from Scotch Plains, New Jersey into Greenwich Village. We rented a two-bedroom apartment in a big, ugly building on 14th Street. She had one bedroom, my parents the other. My sister and I slept on the convertible couch in the living room. We also had Sunny the Bunny. Sunny had been the pet mascot of my mother's nursery school class. She brought Sunny home during Christmas vacation, and we all fell in love with her. We couldn't bear to part with her. So we found a rabbit with almost identical markings and substituted it for classroom duty. No one ever suspected.

One day we had to call the phone company's repair department. Our phones had stopped working. The repairman came, looked at the wires, and said, "Okay, where's the rabbit?" Nothing new ever happens in Manhattan.

Sunny died for no apparent reason. Grandma found her and simply dumped the body down the trash chute. I never forgave her — but that was typical Lillian.

Eventually, the day came when my parents, sister and grandmother moved back to New Jersey. I rented an apartment at the corner of 4th and 10th Streets in the Village.

Grandpa Hy had died and left my parents a little money. They managed to buy an old house in Plainfield, N.J., and rented out rooms to make ends meet. Most of the renters were friends of my brother Rollin, who had just come back from a two-year stint in the Army. After boot camp, he had been selected and vetted to work in the Communications Department for President Johnson. His offices were located in the basement of the White House. He had the highest security clearance in the country, and traveled the world on Air Force One with LBJ, often letting the President's daughters win at cards. Part of his job was to keep them happy.

Grandma's health finally started to decline rapidly. A form of dementia, I think. She even lured the boys up to her room to show them her private parts. My brother and his friends tried to freak me out by describing the visuals to me in graphic detail, but I shut my eyes and stuck my fingers in my ears. To the end, though, she had her lucid moments.

One day she asked my mother, "What is going on downtown? What is all that construction by the Church and Courthouse?" My mother was startled, but not terribly surprised. There was absolutely only one way Lillian could know about the messy road project underway over in the center of town. She had to have been taking another one of her astral journeys.

AT A 4A's CONVENTION (American Association of Advertising Agencies), I was placed on the dais between author James Dickey and feminist Gloria Steinem. We were all speakers at the event. I wore Chanel and Charles Jordan.

Mr. Dickey was drunk as a skunk, and kept grabbing my knee under the table. Ms. Steinem was dressed in tan bell-bottom jeans, boots, and sported a wide leather belt with a huge oval buckle.

I still can't decide who was more obnoxious.

Chapter 11

The Folkies

I HATE TO ADMIT IT, but I never really got it about folk music. I came into the business in the fall of 1966, the apex of popular American folk music. But I didn't relate to the songs of the gods of the movement: Woody Guthrie and Pete Seeger. The harmonies were simple to an extreme — sometimes just three chords — the rhythms were polite and steady, and the melodies were linear enough to be boring, at least to my ears.

Coming from a predominately classical background, my bias is predictable. Hell — compare the harmonies of Johannes Brahms to those of Burl Ives. Come on, folks! Compare the melodies of Verdi, Mozart, Chopin and Puccini to those of Phil Ochs? You've got to be kidding!

Okay, I get it that folk music was more about the lyrics, storytelling, and political activism, and its simplicity made a good platform for the message. But for the most part I pay more attention to music than to lyrics. It's the music that tugs on my heartstrings or makes my blood pound: not the words.

In those first few years of working in the jingle business, I was being introduced to all kinds of musical genres that were foreign to me. Fresh from my Fulbright year as a classical pianist, I was somewhat familiar with Broadway show tunes, Italian pop hits of the 60's, and I had just been introduced to the Beatles. But that was about it.

So I began learning about country, bluegrass, rock, blues, soul, latin, and jazz. It was exciting. I liked them all: all, except folk. I was especially fascinated by jazz. I remember being taught what a Charleston rhythm pattern was — being thrilled when I found I could execute it easily, even though it barely existed in the classical repertoire.

One August evening, about 17 years later, I was relaxing in a chaise lounge on the slate patio of my country house in Putnam County, attending the outdoor concert of insect and frog music. As I listened to the incredibly intricate rhythms they created, I imagined them accompanying the drum beats of villagers in Africa or South America. A light bulb went on in my head. I'm no musicologist, but maybe there is a correlation between climate and music composition. It is the "hot" countries that introduced us to the complex rhythms that make us want to dance: music that slaves brought with them to New Orleans and other cities. The groove, the beat, the heat. Were they inspired to develop those rhythmic patterns from the animal and insect sounds in their environment? Could be. The cold countries of Europe and North America certainly didn't produce compositions anything like them. Their rhythms are mostly straightforward and stiff. But it is those colder countries that contributed amazing melodies and harmonies. Why?

It might have to do with the whole concept of ownership. In the wilds of Africa and South America, there was little concern about who owned what when it came to art. Simple true folk melodies with implied simple harmonies were passed from generation to generation with no concern for who wrote them: it wasn't an issue. What was valuable was the rhythmic passion of the live performance. But in developed cultures, where melodies and harmonies were more important, authorship and ownership were central. Claims were staked.

Other than classical, my favorite music is Brazilian. It combines the best elements of intricate rhythm with complex harmony and soaring melody. Ivan Lins, Gilberto Gil and Milton Nascimento are some of my favorite writers. In song, the Portuguese language is beautiful, and in dance, the samba is magical. I don't know when it was that the European melodies and harmonies collided with the rhythms of the jungles of Brazil: I'm just glad they did.

My first husband, Walter Raim, was a folkie. Well, actually, he was a jazz guy turned folkie. He was a terrific guitar and banjo player, arranger, producer and composer who worked with dozens of great artists including the love of his life, Judy Collins (they had lived together for a while), Bobby Darin, Belafonte, Odetta, Pete Seeger, Theo Bikel, Peter Paul and Mary, and others. He also scored films and did an album or two for Chad Mitchell.

Walter introduced me to many of his folkie friends. Several of them were also recruited to write and arrange for Herman Edel Associates. Two of my favorites were Stuart Scharf and Bobby Dorough. Bobby wasn't only a folkie: he was and is also a delightful, charming, fey jazz pianist and singer. He wrote all of the songs for the Schoolhouse Rock series, was the only vocalist to perform two duets with Miles Davis, and produced two albums for Spanky and Our Gang (with Stuart). He also wrote a couple of great things for me.

Stuart was a serious classical guitarist as well as a sought-after studio musician. He wrote the "Like To Get To Know You" hit for Spanky and Our Gang as well as a half a dozen other songs on their albums. He was also an intimidating intellectual and Walter's best friend. I would sit and listen to their rigorous, elegantly precise arguments about anything and everything (fact: Jews love to argue). Their use of Talmudic/Rabbinic logic taught me never to assume any assertion of mine would go unchallenged. I never dared to butt in, but it was a way of thinking that would prove invaluable.

The most influential folkie in my life, however, was Jake Holmes. From the beginning he was a star writer for Herman Edel Associates, and was instrumental in helping me detach myself from Herman to head up my own company. He wrote hits like "Be All You Can Be," "Be A Pepper," "Raise Your Hand If You're Sure," and (ironically) my favorite of all: a folk tune for the Post Office, "A Little Piece of Home In My Hand."

In the early '70s, Jake took me up to Black Rock — the CBS building on the corner of 52nd and 6th Ave. — to introduce me to Kip Cohen, head of the A&R department, and to Clive Davis, the legendary producer. Jake had been working on an album with producer Elliot Mazer in Nashville, but the project was not in good shape. In fact, it had stalled completely. From working in the jingle business with me, Jake decided I should be the one to pick it up and finish it. I met with Kip and Clive, and wound up completing Jake's project. They were thrilled with the result. Kip offered me a staff producer's job — he thought I would be great working with Tony Bennett. Clive took me by the shoulder and ran me around the offices, introducing me as his new 'girl producer.'

I gave the offer serious consideration, but in the end turned them down. I really loved my life in the advertising business, in large part because projects could be completed so quickly. The disappointments and failures could be disposed of overnight, and successes were possible almost daily. In the record business, you could work for months — even years — on a project, only to see it fail. Granted, the rewards were potentially much greater, but I wasn't into long-term gambling.

Around the same time, I got another offer. Bill Chororos, head of production at Ogilvy & Mather, interviewed me and offered the job of Music Director at the agency. It was a flattering proposition, but I turned it down as well. I was on the verge of buying Herman out: I had the gut feeling that I could make more money on my own and have the freedom of being my own boss at the same time.

Jake and I remained friends. We kept on working together frequently on advertising music assignments. When he decided to go on an exploratory trip to Europe in connection with his record career, Teddy Irwin (mutual friend and fabulous guitar player) and I decided to tag along. Walter was too busy with various projects to do any traveling. His loss.

The three of us started our European mini-tour in London. Jake's record company had rented a modest flat for him for the week, so Teddy and I crashed with him. The apartment was a few tube stops from the center of the City in an area peppered with Indian restaurants. We tried them only once: my curry was so hot it tasted like pure ammonia. While Jake went off for meeting after meeting, Teddy and I explored the sights. Out of respect for his Irish ancestry, we made sure to spend every afternoon in a different pub.

Jake reported that all the record business talk was about an up-and-coming artist named Elton John. He was considered Jake's competition.

The next leg was to Paris, where Jake immediately met fiery, beautiful, exotic-looking Marguerite Takvorian. It was a true coup de foudre: love at first sight. Teddy and I played hapless bystanders to their explosive relationship. I remember standing off to the side as the two of them sat facing each other on a park bench in the Tuilleries. She was alternately crying and yelling, while he pleaded with her to come away with him. But she was still entangled with a famous French old-guy singer, so the three of us flew off to Spain.

We landed in Barcleona, had dinner and a few double espressos, then took our rental car for the drive of its life (and mine) over the mountains and down to the Costa del Sol. I drove; Jake slept in the back seat while Teddy, a sometimes race driver, navigated and egged me on. It was a memorably treacherous cliffside drive, the narrow roadway made even more pulse-pounding by the wide, lumbering trucks roaring in both directions. I was totally wired by the time we arrived in Málaga.

We spent a week there on the beach, while Jake pined for Marguerite, and Teddy and I tried to mind our own business...all under the watchful eyes of Franco's ubiquitous, Uzi-toting soldiers. I can't say I cared much for the food.

I would have to consider David Buskin and Robin Batteau friends, folkies and fun, as well. (McDonalds pun intended - we all worked on their campaign, *Food, Folks and Fun*). David and Robin entered my life well after folk music's heyday, but in my book, they are at heart true folkies. Partially because of the sound of their music, but also because they write so many songs with satirical and political messages. They are both fantastic jingle writers, and we have enjoyed many successes together.

They also introduced me to Judy Collins. She and I ended up becoming friends, and I produced a couple of tracks on one of her albums. Judy is impressive. An icon of her times, she is tall, willowy, and has those astonishing blue eyes. Strong and intelligent, she's also had to overcome more than her share of pain.

One day, Judy and I decided to try to write a song together. With David's and Robin's participation, we wrote "Test of Time." On the surface, the story is about an Anasazi Indian woman patiently waiting for her man to return from a hunting trip (I had just explored their 1,000 year-old-caves outside of Santa Fe). In reality, it was a reflection on both of our lives and our relationships with men. "Test of Time" appeared on Judy's next album, *Fires of Eden*.

PAUL SIMON was always nice to me. In the '60s, we'd sit on the floor of Stuart Scharf's apartment and discuss politics. He was patient with me.

In the '80s, I sat right onstage in the VIP section at Simon and Garfunkel's gigantic Concert in the Park. Carol Gadd and I watched spellbound as they performed for a crowd of almost a million. It was freezing cold. We killed a whole bottle of Jägermeister.

One time, I bumped into Paul and Carrie Fisher on the Concorde. We had a good conversation: they were on their way to Vienna for the holidays.

Toward the end of the '80s, after I called him personally, Paul gave J. Walter Thompson permission to use "Bridge Over Troubled Waters" for their American Red Cross public service commercials. I've always greatly respected him as an artist — but it's gratifying to realize he's a real mensch, too.

Chapter 12

The Bedlington Massacre

———

I NEVER SAW IT COMING: the massacre. Not one of us did. Yet there we were, scrambling madly in the pouring rain and mud, right in the middle of it, the whole family, blood and bodies flying through the air. We weren't very effective. They were just too fast...

The first California chapter of my life began with that summer road trip across the country. Once in L.A., we stayed in the Highland Towers apartment hotel on Highland Ave. That's in downtown Hollywood, and it was pretty raunchy. My only memory is the narrow cement walkway that ran alongside the ground floor apartments. The dusty ivy reeked of dog shit and piss.

I started at the Colin McEwen School. Just up the street, it proved easy going for me after my New York City scholastic experience. When we later decided we were going to stay on the West Coast instead of going back East, my parents found a house to rent in Laurel Canyon (my father always called it 'Gravel Gulch').

Laurel Canyon was weird. Our neighbors were weird. Just across the street, there were frequent events involving the police. Something about drugs. The rocky wilderness that pushed right up against our backyard was weird. We lasted less than a year there.

I don't know why my parents let me hike by myself in the Canyon, especially after I told them about my encounter with a mountain lion. On one of my jaunts I came across a fawn, and was enthralled with it until I glanced up to see the crouching lioness on a ledge above me, preparing to pounce. I looked straight into her eyes — will never forget that stare — and hightailed it out of there! I didn't want to think about what might have happened to the deer.

Finally, after my mother found it in an ad in the paper, we moved to 22310 Carlson Circle, Canoga Park. It was in the San Fernando Valley, over the hills and northwest of L.A. and Hollywood. Carlson Circle was a tiny piece of a street that connected Sherman Way, the major cross-valley thoroughfare, with Shoup Ave. It bordered the house and its 14 acres — all of which belonged to Mr. Carlson, a Swedish immigrant who had come to the United States in the late 1800's with $17 in his pocket. In Boston, he made his fortune manufacturing women's shoes. Then, like so many others, he picked up and headed to California. There he bought up land to plant citrus and avocado orchards. By the time we met him, he owned a large portion of neighboring Camarillo.

We all were introduced to Mr. Carlson when we made the trip out to the Valley to see the property. He was 80 years old and somewhat feeble, but very proud of the house he had built. He insisted on giving us the tour himself, and literally fell in love with my mother that day.

He'd placed the ad because his family had insisted he move out of the big house and into one of the new tract houses a few blocks away. We rented the "mansion" for $125 a month. He was so taken with my mother that he frequently sent back the rent check with no explanation (or chose to ignore any of the months we couldn't pay at all). He knew we were very poor: so poor we sometimes had bread and milk for dinner.

The owners of the local grocery store, Larry's Market, would let my mother pick through the piles of fruit and vegetables that had been thrown out in back of the store. They, too, adored her. Once they steered a guy who was sponsoring a promotional contest over to her. To win, she had to answer the question, "Who is buried in Grant's tomb?' "Grant," she answered; he asked, "Who else?" She wrinkled her brow and guessed, "Mrs. Grant?" He paid for her full grocery cart, and we all celebrated that evening. She remarked that something had told her that day to go for broke and fill the cart instead of buying just the few things she usually did.

Mr. Carlson would often insist that my mother chauffeur him up to Camarillo to visit his orchards. He would gaze adoringly at her, kiss her hand and cheek whenever he could, and once, she told me, took her hand and placed it on his lap where she could feel his erection through his trousers. She handled the situation with aplomb and never complained. She knew we owed our being able to live in that great place to him. Even after he died, when his family tried to evict us so they could sell the place, we found out that he had put in his will that we were to be allowed to live there as long as we liked, period.

For my brother, sister and me, Carlson Circle was paradise. The house had five bedrooms and two baths. It seemed huge to us. Every one of us had our own room upstairs, although I don't think my sister ever slept in hers. As soon as my grandmother came to live with us, she was given a bedroom downstairs. My parents had a room with a wonderful invention: a Murphy bed that pulled right out of the wall! They eventually put another big bed in the room (mostly for my sister), but it also came in handy for early morning family conferences and strange events.

One of those took place one Sunday morning when a pair of Jehovah's Witnesses came a-knocking. My father set up a pair of straight-backed chairs between the two beds, and held court. We three were in the big bed; parents in the Murphy pullout. There were also a few dogs and cats in attendance. My father let the Witnesses have their say before proceeding to torture them with logic and sarcasm. He enjoyed himself immensely as the meek pair sat there, speechless and paralyzed. I felt a little sorry for them.

The majority of the property was taken up by an orchard filled with mature peach, apricot, and red Santa Rosa plum trees. We kids were in heaven, lying under the trees in the heat, listening to the bees and getting almost drunk on the super-sweet fallen fruit. My mother was a firm believer in the health benefits of air baths; and the Southern California weather often supported the practice. At least once a week, the whole family ran around buck naked (Grandma excluded) in the house as well as outside on the parts of the property hidden from the street. My mother also tried her hand at a vegetable garden, but it didn't do well. There just wasn't enough water. We children also played in and around the small barn, its corral — and the real playhouse. Built solidly to kids-only dimensions, its windows were trimmed in painted wood set into strong stucco walls. The steep thatched roof reminded me of Hansel and Gretel.

My mother used the playhouse for our black widow spider lesson. My bugaboo is scorpions. Hers was black widows. We were shown their distinctive webs: unstructured, no part circular, extremely sticky, quite strong. She even managed to find a live one and show us the red dot on the belly that marked it as female and deadly. She explained that, like praying mantises, the female murders her husband after mating. Lovely.

My mother was a true animal lover. Animals of all kinds. My father was not pleased, but never interfered.

At first it was only stray dogs and cats. They would just show up on the property. Probably, word went out throughout the local animal kingdom that there was a new homeless shelter in the neighborhood. There was Floppo, a slut puppy named after her cowflop, meadow-muffin type droppings. We spayed her after one litter (though we did find homes for the "so ugly they were cute" puppies). Then there was Bijou, a tiny Yorkie mix who managed to get pregnant by a much bigger dog (she stood on an ottoman). It was a struggle for my mother, but she did manage to deliver the babies by gently squeezing out the two huge puppies who were lying lengthwise in her tiny body. Immediate spaying ensued.

The list goes on. My mother agreed to board six Afghan hounds for a couple of months as a money-making endeavor. We built a make-shift kennel next to the corral. They pretty much stayed outside, but it was breathtaking to watch them run the property in a pack. They never tried to escape — more of my mother's magical influence, I presume. Somehow in that deal we inherited an older female who had been used for breeding, but whose usefulness for it had come to an end. We named her "Shazada." Black with cream markings, she got along with everybody. Probably grateful to be part of the family. She kept stealing two kittens from their mother cat. Carefully carrying them in her long jaws, she would take them, squealing, down to the cellar one at a time, where she would lie down next to the warm furnace and try to nurse them.

Then there was "Boy," a beautiful thick-coated Alaskan Malamute who showed up daily. We located his owners, but they gave up trying to make him stay home and just dropped off bags of dog food every month. It was like having a guard wolf. He would prowl the perimeter, and with a swift head-toss, kill anything that ventured onto the land — cats (but never ours), possums, squirrels — anything. We loved him a lot. Unfortunately, he had a tragic flaw. Every so often he would take off on a killing spree at the nearby chicken farms. He would do in 60 to 80 each trip. Animal control officers eventually came to our door demanding his capture and compensation for the farmers. We denied having the dog, and snuck him back to his rightful owners, who spirited him off to a Wyoming ranch. Close call!

Most of the cats were named "Dolly." My father thought it would easier to give them all the same name because one by one, they disappeared. They were all big friendly tiger-striped pussycats.

"Whitey," however, was an amazing cat. We found him one day lounging in the center divider of the street in front of our house. He was just chillin', watching the cars go by. A half-grown kitten with long snow white hair, he had one blue eye and one yellow. He was also deaf (as are many white animals). We confirmed our diagnosis by dropping things (like ironing boards) from across the room and watching Whitey's delayed reaction.

Whitey loved to curl up for a snooze on the gas stove over the warm pilot flame. Every so often he would light himself on fire. His hair was long enough to protect him until we could throw a towel over him, but the resulting brown singed hair did have a marked affect on his appearance. Once he was lying in his favorite spot right next to a giant pot of spaghetti sauce when he had one of his bad dreams. He flew into the air, all puffed up, whirling, spitting and knocking the pot onto the floor. It landed right side up, but the resulting Vesuvius had my mother still cleaning sauce out of nooks and crannies, cupboards, moldings and the ceiling for months.

It was then, during these preteen years, that I became fully horse crazy. I was given a few riding lessons, but that December, instead of a horse, I found "Noel" the Nubian goat under the Christmas tree. I got past my momentary disappointment and soon grew to love the crazy creature. Highly intelligent and playful, she had her mischievous fun with everybody. She would rear up on her hind legs, flare her long beautiful ears, and then come down with a thud to head butt you. Depending on her mood and her judgment of your character, it could be anything from a gentle shove to a painful knock-you-off-your-feet assault. You could never tell which was coming.

Noel also learned to open the latch on the back door. She would romp down the hall to my parents' bedroom, jump on the big bed, and pee a steady stream while wagging her little tail.

My mother decided to breed Noel, convinced as she was of the virtues of goat milk. Off to the goat farm we went. Noel stayed for a week and returned pregnant. I'll never forget the intense smell of male goat and male goat urine that filled the air at the farm. It lodged itself in my cortex, where it remains. It asserts itself instantly whenever I am offered goat cheese or goat's milk. A shame, really.

The big black king snake had no name. He had a fine, commodious cage, but since he was an escape artist, it was of little use. Once he was lost for days. We finally found him curled up inside the big black typewriter. He had another favorite hiding place in the deep round blue-and-white ceramic bowl that sat on the sideboard in the dining room. Sometimes, when we had dinner guests, he would make an appearance. Rising up out of bowl like a cobra, he caused many a scream, upended chair, tipped wineglass and hasty retreat.

He was a really nice snake who loved to be handled. My favorite activity with him was to take a stroll with Rollin and Janet down the street to the little corner store. I would wrap the snake around my waist under a loose-fitting (but tucked in) blouse, and saunter up to the cash register with our purchases. As soon as enough other customers were around, I'd gently scratch his body, which was the signal for him to uncoil and slither up my chest so he could poke his head out at my collar. The screams of horror were ample reward for all of us.

The king snake was given back to the pet store after six months: none of us ever got used to watching him have dinner. The only thing he could eat was live little white mice. The image of cute mousey faces peeking out from the coils of death was just too much to take.

Our poultry flock was a source of great pride. It grew to include chickens, roosters, a bantam rooster, two pheasants, a huge tom turkey, and 14 mallard ducks. We had raised the pair and their 12 offspring from the time their little beaks pecked through the pale green eggshells under Mama mallard. Every evening as sunset approached, the whole flock would line up single file and parade around the house, at least once, sometimes twice. They did it day after day after day, no matter what the weather was like.

One afternoon, just before parade time, the flock was outside milling about, even though it had rained heavily and the ground was muddy.

The light grey, wraith-like monsters came out of nowhere and struck without warning. They only went after the ducks, swiftly and methodically hunting down each one, dispatching it in a flurry of feathers, and moving on to the next. The poor things didn't have a chance.

The family heard the commotion and rushed outside, only to behold the carnage underway. Our screaming and chasing the killers was to no avail. They were too agile, too slippery, too totally focused:

100% dedicated to their savage mission. They were Bedlington terriers after all. Our Bedlington terriers.

It is an otherwise wholly wonderful breed of dog. Loyal, loving, energetic, big-hearted. They may look like little lambs, but they are terriers — so they are stubborn.

The only explanation for the Bedlington massacre has to be weather-related. We had been through a long dry spell, abruptly broken by the heavy downpour. Long-buried scents must have wafted up from the ground to fill the air. I suspect they triggered a primal instinct in the Bedlingtons: only the Bedlingtons. Why they went after the ducks, and only the ducks, I'll never know.

DON GROLNICK was a phenomenal studio keyboardist as well as a good friend. Although he was a bear of a man with a jet-black beard covering his face, his appearance belied a sweet and sensitive nature.

He came up to the Vermont house for a needed week of rest and relaxation.

One night he walked down the hill to the Jamaica Inn for a beer. He was dressed in baggy jeans with suspenders over a woolen red-and-black checked shirt. He fit right in with the crowd of hunters.

As was common during hunting season, at some point all hell broke loose. Fists flew, bottles were smashed, and a chair crashed through the front window.

Don whispered from the pay phone in the back; I drove down to rescue him through the back door.

Chapter 13

Niagara Falls

———

I T HAD TO BE THE WACKIEST JOB of my career, and I've had some doozies. I'd been working quite a bit with Campbell Ewald, the giant ad agency based in Detroit — mostly on their main account, Chevrolet, but also on Delco Batteries and GMAC.

In the spring of 1969 I was summoned to Michigan for a meeting about a proposed new Delco commercial. It would introduce their 12-volt Energizer Battery. The premise was intriguing: to show how a single Energizer battery could provide sufficient power for a big rock band (including horns) to drown out the thunderous roar of Niagara Falls.

I came up with the band. Walter Raim had just finished producing the first album (Construction #1) for a group named "Ten Wheel Drive." It was a rock band with jazz elements, a little like Blood Sweat and Tears. A 5-piece horn group complemented the regular rhythm section of bass, drums, two guitars and electric keyboard.

And then there was Genya, the singer: Miss Genya Ravan. She used to be Goldie of Goldie and the Gingerbreads. Genya was a diva, a she-devil, and a hell of a singer. Her big powerhouse voice matched her flamboyant personality. She dressed outrageously, behaved outrageously, but always had a twinkle in her eye and a smile on her face. We got along fabulously.

Getting the band to agree to do the commercial was easy. We decided to use "Eye of the Needle," their hit from the album. At the time, they weren't famous enough to turn up their noses at the bucks and publicity. True, we were smack in the middle of the Woodstock era with its anti-'selling out' mindset, but the prospect of starvation can change anyone's mind. Also, they were going to get a free mini-vacation to Niagara Falls in the summertime. What could be bad?

To be authentic, legal, and to fulfill the promise put forward in the commercial, we had to physically film and record the band both with and without the battery plugged in. This proved tricky. Eventually, we booked a remote truck with a 16-track machine from Location Recorders. My friend and mentor, storied Phil Ramone, supervised and engineered.

The truck had to remain parked more than 1,000 feet above the filming site. The long, heavy cables were draped over the edge and dangled down the cliff. After all, we couldn't just use a regular Uher tape machine (the normal equipment for recording sound on location). This sound track wasn't going to consist of just dialogue and an underscore, or a band playing in the background. It had to sound like a professional rock concert recording; had to be mixed like a hit single. We needed independent control of each instrument, Genya, and the vocal mikes of the players who also sang backup. A multi-track professional studio set up was necessary. There was no other choice.

The road trip began. We hired a big bus to take the band, me, and their cases and cases of equipment from New York City all the way up to the U.S. side of Niagara Falls. But we weren't going to be shooting on the U.S. side. There had been many problems trying to comply with all the rules and restrictions, unions, liability insurance, State Park officials full of themselves (and eager to rub elbows with anyone in show business), local and state bureaucrats: everyone wanted in on the action. It had become impossible, so Campbell Ewald moved everything to the Canadian side.

The Canadians could not have been more accommodating. Two problems, however: first, I had to clear a rock and roll band through customs and border control during the height of the drug culture; and second, the physical challenges on the Canadian side were tougher. Exponentially tougher. And that's not even counting the snakes...

Before we left the City, I sat the guys down and seriously warned them about the consequences of getting caught with drugs while crossing the border. They all looked me in the eye, put their hands over their hearts, and promised they would remain drug-free for the whole trip.

But late at night, as we approached the border with its spotlights, barricades, law enforcement vehicles, dogs and police personnel, I took one look around the bus, gauged facial expressions, and ordered the driver to pull over into the rest stop. We were still on the U.S. side. I'll never know who had what (or even if anyone had anything), but let me tell you, their faces as they came out of the men's room were much more relaxed. Genya, by the way, had sworn up and down that she had nothing on her, and I believed her. She wouldn't vouch for the others, though.

After about an hour's inspection by the border agents (equipment only), it was nearly 3 am when we rolled up to our funky, rustic hotel/motel. It was situated right on the Falls property. Genya and I bunked together in a little room. The heavy plaid Hudson Bay blankets matched the twin beds perfectly. I was out the instant my head hit the pillows.

During the five days of the shoot, the atmosphere in the room was easy-going. At first.

We had a lot of girl gossip to catch up on. I think she was involved at the time with the hot, sexy rock drummer, Luther Rix. Not only was he a terrific drummer, a real rocker, but he had a Steve McQueen body and wore low-slung black jeans, motorcycle boots and too-short dark tee shirts. Nice...

That first morning, we got up early to get oriented. Genya complained bitterly. She was not really a morning person. Per instructions from the film company, we dressed in rough, warm clothes. Jeans, sneakers, and sweatshirts. We met up with the rest of the band at breakfast, then followed a rep down, down, down through winding walkways and tunnels.

We emerged onto a paved and fenced semi-circular area overlooking the Falls. It was the absolute lowest of the public access points, but was still about 150 feet above the outcrop where the filming was to take place: right at the base of the Falls. The director wanted the band positioned so he could shoot them with the huge Falls in the background.

We were told that the only way to get down was to climb over the wrought-iron barrier, grab onto a thick long rope that was tied to it, then gradually, carefully, lower our bodies by holding onto the rope with both hands while stepping backwards over the rocks, foot by foot, all the way down. I don't think you can really call it "rappelling," but as rock band entrances go, it was memorable.

The boys thought it was fun; I didn't mind so much, but Genya had a meltdown. The first time we made the descent, it took me almost an hour to coax her down the incline onto flat land. She kept balking, refusing to move a muscle, sort of like a fawn frozen at river's edge. I kept her looking up at all times, never down, so that she didn't see the surprise bonus feature: the dozens (if not hundreds) of green snakes slithering everywhere over the black shiny slippery rocks that littered the hillside. When we got to the bottom, she finally saw the snakes and lost it again — but she was already down. I'd been told that they were completely harmless, and managed to convince her I wasn't lying.

The method of descent and the snakes were not the only problems. Those slippery black rocks were treacherous, and on the second day, one of the Canadian grips holding a huge reflector slipped, fell, and broke his arm. These Canadians were tough, though; he was back at work the next day, his arm in a cast.

The worst problem, however, was the ever-present heavy mist that drifted over from the Falls. It didn't matter if it were overcast or if the sun was shining, we were all completely soaked after 15 minutes. A wise decision was made by the agency to put the whole band in yellow rubber slickers and hats.

But the mist caused other problems. Water and electronics don't mix very well. Although everything was covered with waterproof tarps immediately after rehearsals or shooting, instruments did eventually rot, and a lot of equipment was ruined.

All the band members were troupers to the end. Even Genya kept her chin up, for the most part. It was only in the middle of the night before the final day's shoot that she shook me and woke me up.

"Susan, wake up, wake up."

I did.

"Listen, I've been awake all night and I've got to tell you, all I can think about is the rope. I see it in front of me; I feel it in my hands and I really don't think I can go down it one more time!"

Drama queen to the end. We talked and talked; I sympathized, praised, and soothed. Told her what a great soldier she had been, and how everybody loved her. It worked, and I got her down the rope the next morning one last time.

During all the sound checks and final preparations for the actual shoot, I was busy on the walkie talkie, communicating with Phil in the remote truck way up there. To get decent reception, I had to stand on the hillside about 50 feet above the band.

About midday, when the light was at its best for filming and everything was deemed ready for a go, I suddenly got a frantic call from the director to come down to the lakefront to deal with a crisis.

"What the fuck now?" I thought to myself as I scrambled over the black rocks and shooed the slow-witted and slow-moving green snakes out of my path. I reached the director and learned the crisis involved Genya. She had suddenly got her period. It was a very heavy flow. She refused to even think of going back up the cliff to take care of things. So I found a p.a. and told him I needed a box of large Tampax immediately. The shoot, Delco batteries, the band, me: everything depended on him.

When the package arrived, we created a makeshift cloth dressing room around Genya, and let her attend to business. Needless to say, everyone was tittering, but she handled it like a pro. Came back to her position with her head held high and ready to rock. I was proud of her.

The shoot went off without a hitch. I checked with Phil, and he had everything he needed. Ditto the director. But as we were all watching and listening to playbacks, patting ourselves on the back, I noticed something unnerving.

The band sounded great, everyone's part was crystal clear. But there was one big problem. You couldn't hear fucking Niagara Falls at all. Just a nice clean recording of a rock band. Even worse, in the setup shot without the battery, there was hardly any roar from the Falls. We had so overcompensated to record Genya and the instruments that we had overlooked the whole purpose of the commercial. The members of the band and Genya had been miked so tight that the gigantic thunderous Niagara Falls had been reduced to a mild room hiss in the background. Yes, the 12-volt Energizer battery had worked. But it had worked too damned well. I had to laugh to myself.

I didn't even bother getting into it with the agency people. I just made the sound guy take out a microphone and get lots of Uher tape of the roar of the Falls. I made sure it wasn't overloaded, but at the maximum volume the tape would take. I knew we would need it (and we did).

Back in New York, my mixing engineer was the great Don Hahn. He and I ran into another problem. A sync problem. Despite assurances from all the techies, the sync on the tape and the sync on the film weren't talking to each other, and the two elements drifted apart dramatically when played simultaneously. Donnie figured out the problem and how to fix it. Apparently we had lost power at some point, which caused a disruption in the Hertz 60 cycle sync. The result was not pretty. We were forced to cut the track into many short segments, chase, edit, patch together and do everything except turn cartwheels to get it to work. I'll never forget the visual of our hapless assistant engineer trying to manually hold the big rotary knob on the Fairchild Sync generator to keep it locked. But Donnie triumphed. We restriped the tape with new Hertz 60 cycle: it matched up with the picture, and the final version went on air.

Ten Wheel Drive went on to produce another two or three moderately successful albums. Don't know quite why they didn't break through to the top; they should have. Certainly Genya should have. But she is a survivor, that's for sure. She still has a great presence in the music world, and is just as feisty as ever.

DAVID SPINOZZA, RICK MAROTTA (famous guitarist and drummer) and I had a free Saturday in Los Angeles. We were out there working together on some elaborate project — maybe an NBC convention.

They'd been teasing me about my claim that I rode motorcycles. So when they told me they were going up to the Los Angeles County Raceway for a day of motocross, I insisted on tagging along.

We rented bikes, and I let them go ahead on the track. When I passed them down a particularly steep hill standing on my pegs, they teased no more.

Chapter 14

"What Ever Happened to the Colonel?"

————

AFTER FIFTY YEARS of being out of touch with each other, it startled me a little to think that The Colonel had made such a lasting impression. Frank Denson, a college boyfriend, asked me the question about The Colonel one afternoon when we got together for a visit. The Colonel had been in and out of my life since childhood, but Frank had met him only a few times at my family's Canoga Park homestead.

Air Force Colonel Donald H. Baxter may not have been a big man, but the rest of the military officer persona was flawless: the ramrod straight bearing, chiseled features, bright blue eyes, iron jaw and crew cut. He did look like a cross between George C. Scott and Montgomery Clift. My grandmother, who hated him, called him a 'bantam rooster' behind his back. My mother used to say, "If Armageddon ever came to the United States and you actually wanted to survive, The Colonel would be your man." By the way, nobody in the family ever called him anything but The Colonel...

He was a tough guy, a self-trained survivalist. Even though he didn't see any action in WWII, when he was forced to eject from a crippled plane over the North Atlantic, he survived more than 36 hours in the frigid waters with a broken thigh.

The Colonel arrived at Carlson Circle with the six Afghans. He was a friend of their owners, who hoped to board them with us. The Colonel came over to check us out.

He never really left. My parents started to depend on him for many things. First and foremost, he streamlined the machinery for my father's Zoomerang factory in the garage.

He devised the two 15' wooden cutting machines with motors on one end and cutting blades at the other. They stretched out the reams of colorful paper to the proper length, then cleanly cut them into long strips. My father would sit at a converted sewing machine with a foot pedal and a whirring spindle. He'd drip a spot of glue on the inner-most part of the coil, then step on the pedal. With a 10-second whoosh! and a quick wrap of a rubber band, voila! The baby Zoom-erang was born.

This was all The Colonel's doing. The coils would then be placed in trays and put into old refrigerators that The Colonel had trans-formed into ovens. They would be heated to just the right temperature to set and maintain their curl. Still in the trays, swizzle sticks would be inserted in each, the toys inverted, the plastic disks slipped down the sticks, the rubber grommet pushed down to keep the disks in place, and Finis!

The Colonel moved into two empty little rooms in the garage building right next to the Zoomerang factory. He brought along his big horse, "Red," his Weimaraner dog, "Chip," and the camper he used to travel around the continent.

The Colonel was a walking encyclopedia of the practical arts. He helped my mother with her vegetable garden, the chickens, ducks and turkeys, the goats, the dogs and cats, cleaning the house, and fixing anything and everything. He even pitched in and did a lot of the cooking. My mother and grandmother both hated to cook, which is how I ended up taking over the Thanksgiving meal when I was seven. I wanted to do it, and they let me.

My mother and The Colonel were great pals who spent endless hours together while my father was off in Zoomerang land, listening to his radio and dreaming of impending grandeur. My grandmother reg-ularly hinted they were having an affair, but nobody listened. It wasn't true...I think.

When I was 10, I did have an unfortunate run-in with The Colonel. One fine morning, he decided he wanted to make a chicken stew. He picked out one of our older hens and put her in a separate pen for slaughter the next day. When I learned of the plan I was horrified, but my wails of dismay were of no avail. So I snuck out in the middle of the night and freed her. Unfortunately, she was a chicken, therefore stupid enough to just hang by the coop. After her recapture the next morning, my parents allowed The Colonel give me a few spanks with a wooden paddle. I was furious, insulted and embarrassed. I didn't speak to any of them for days.

Many years later, my son Alex and I executed a couple of similar covert releases in Malibu. We freed a big beautiful male peacock from a dark little hole where he was being kept at a heartless friend's barn. I didn't care that he screamed loudly enough to wake the neighbors. He was gorgeous and deserved to be free. For years afterward, he roamed the neighborhood, tormenting one and all. But he never was caught.

We also released what turned out to be my favorite dog of all time. "Samson" was a stunningly gorgeous Rhodesian Ridgeback, owned by an abusive owner who kept him outside in a cage exposed to the elements. Rhodesians are originally African dogs, and don't handle the fog and dampness of the Malibu hills well. One day, his master went away for a long weekend, leaving Samson in his cage. I couldn't stand it. Alex and I snuck up to his house late one night, beat down the fence to make it look as if Samson had clawed his way out, and brought him home. We lied, saying we found him on the road.

Eventually, I paid a king's ransom to buy Samson away from the guy. It led to five wonderful years together. He would accompany me to the studios, protecting me on early morning drives back to Malibu. The children and everyone else adored him. Samson later died of a terrible cystic fibrosis-like disease. He couldn't breathe properly. I blame his death on the mistreatment by his former owner.

The Colonel. He had a dark side: one he never bothered to hide at all. He was a racist and an unbridled bigot. Years before, he had been engaged to marry a southern girl, the daughter of a five-star general. At that time, The Colonel was also up for promotion: a candidate for general. All he needed to do was to pass a standard physical. Unfortunately for him, they assigned an African American physician to perform it. The Colonel refused. He was not going to let 'some nigger' touch his body. He stuck to his guns, was never promoted again, and lost his fiancée. He seemed never to have regretted his decision at all, so committed was he to his despicable beliefs.

The Colonel would often go on and on about his opinions regarding blacks. He was a complete whack job about it.

Now one might think it was terrible of my parents to let us be exposed to this kind of thinking. They chose instead to let us hear it, dispute him ferociously on all points, and then explain to us what was so wrong about his beliefs.

But if you could get past the bigotry, there were adventures to be experienced with The Colonel. After one of his trips to Mexico in his camper, he returned with a big, hairy tarantula as a pet. I was the only one in the family who allowed her to crawl on me. She (he told me she was a female) would creep slowly up my arm, stop close to my shoulder, and stare into my eyes. She had more of them than I did. Then The Colonel would pick her up and put her back in her box. She never bit me. I will never forget the feeling of those sticky feet climbing up through the fine hairs on my skin. Years later, I did capture a wild one I found on a wall at the Via Escondido house in Malibu. I named her "Katherine." She lasted for months, until a careless housekeeper left her cage out in the sun too long.

The most exciting episode happened during the run-up to the Presidential election of 1964. My parents were staunch conservatives: Goldwater supporters all the way. The Colonel climbed a tall ladder to nail a big 'Goldwater for President' sign on a stick high up on the thick-trunked palm tree next to the driveway. But for two mornings in a row, the signs were stolen. We got mad.

With the help of The Colonel, we rigged an elaborate booby trap. We helped him fill a 5-gallon bucket with donations from every animal on the place. What a stinking mess! We mixed it all with water and strong red dye "to paint the Commies the right color," as The Colonel put it.

The Colonel attached a hidden wire from the sign to the rim of the bucket so that it would tip and spill as soon as someone tried to pull the sign down. He did make sure it wouldn't fall out of the tree and clunk them on the head.

We stayed up all night, hiding on the front porch, waiting to catch any commies in the act. But dawn came, and we had to go to bed disappointed. The Colonel was restless. He decided to take an early morning ride on Red. He happened to run into two guys driving a County garbage truck up the road. They tipped their hats; The Colonel ignored them. Later on, when we awoke from our naps, we found a huge red splattered mess all over the driveway. Someone had sprung the trap: who, we didn't know. But later The Colonel spotted the same garbage truck in downtown Canoga Park — now with one driver missing and a filthy Goldwater sign stuck proudly into the garbage for all to see.

After I went to Rome on my Fulbright, and after brother Rollin was drafted into the Army, and after my parents and sister returned to the East, The Colonel moved permanently to Florida. We did hear from him frequently — he visited both of my country places. He'd stay with us for a month or so.

Once he sent me a baby raccoon in a box, with instructions to pick it up at JFK. Since he gave me only a few hours notice, I had to drop everything and hire a limo. How else was I going to transport it?

"Hijack" lived with my brother and me for a while in my Chelsea duplex. He loved Rollin, who has a gift for handling wild animals. Eventually, we took Hijack up to the Vermont farm, where for more than a year he romped and wrestled happily with the dogs (especially Tessa the springer spaniel). They would roll, clutched together, over and over across the ancient wide-planked wooden floors. We even let him outside a few times. He stayed close for a while, but as he matured, he visited less and less. At some point he disappeared for good. We weren't too sad: it was best for him.

The Colonel's last and longest visit was to my 175-acre horse farm in upstate N.Y. This time he brought "Cecily," a full-grown female otter. She was a delightful and amazing creature. Within a day of her arrival, she had taught the dogs to respect her sharp teeth and claws. They got along just fine after that. Cecily had the run of the place and would go from pond to pond, swimming, diving, fishing and stirring up as much trouble as possible before returning to the main house, where she would scratch at the door to be let in.

We did have a problem with her when she decided to join our guests in the swimming pool. When I would swim laps, she would be all over me: under, over, alongside, doing flips and splashing with her tail. Unfortunately, sometimes she would suddenly decide she didn't like someone, or that they weren't paying her enough attention. Then she would nip. She never drew blood, but it was at best, unnerving — and at worst, scary as hell. Especially when the attack came from underwater.

When the cold weather arrived, The Colonel departed for Florida. I remember watching his old camper roll down our long driveway and disappear around a curve. Undoubtedly, Cecily was lounging in the passenger seat. I never saw him again.

My mother passed away a few years later, my father six years after that, and The Colonel somewhere in between. I like to think they are all together somewhere, laughing about the good old times.

THE COLONEL rescued three featherless baby pigeons that had fallen from their nest. We put them in a shoebox in the downstairs bathroom, across from Grandma's room.

We kids were vigilant about their feeding. Several times a day we would push little bits of bread soaked in milk into their open beaks.

After their feathers grew in and they were almost ready to fly, we encountered an unusual and frightening enemy. Small triangular, hard-shelled, dark grey parasites would leave their host pigeons to chase us screaming children down the hall. They looked and flew like miniature Empire Starfighters.

We let the pigeons go. Early.

Part II

TESTING THE EDGE

Chapter 15

Ike and Tina

———

THE AIRLOCKS WERE UNNERVING. There was a whole raft of them, and there was a camera in the corner of every one. I was impatient to get through them into Ike & Tina Turner's Bolic Sound Studios in Inglewood, and didn't like the maddening wait for one door to close before you could open the next one routine. Especially because I was traveling with a small film crew and their pile of equipment.

It didn't occur to me to wonder why there were so many airlocks.

This was in the early '70s; I was on one of many trips to work in L.A. The purpose of this one was to produce Ike and Tina Turner doing their own arrangement of the new Diet Dr Pepper jingle my company had written for Young & Rubicam. Their version was scheduled for radio use only, but the film crew was there to document an interview and testimonial to be shown at the upcoming Bottlers' Convention. We'd been doing this with many other Dr Pepper artists.

The crew went ahead of me down the long hallway. There was no reception area nor receptionist. It was fairly late in the evening — late to be starting a session. I walked past an open doorway, then stopped and backed up: there she was. Tina was sitting alone in a small room, her face turned away. I started to introduce myself, but shut my mouth as she looked up. The left side of her face was swollen, along with a good-sized bruise on her cheekbone. Uh-oh, now what? This wasn't a promising beginning for what I had hoped would be a short and sweet session.

I didn't know what to say.

She gave me a tiny, crooked smile. "Don't worry, honey. I'll be fine. You run along now and get the tracks done. I'll be in there later to sing."

I nodded and continued down the hall, feeling terribly awkward. But not really hopelessly sorry for her. She seemed resigned to her situation, yes; but also strong — even tough. Her eyes weren't dead; they had plenty of life and fire in them. Had I been older, I might have handled it differently, but I was still naïve in many ways.

I had no experience with abused women: actually, couldn't even get my head around that reality. My father and mother had always treated one another as equals. My few boyfriends (okay; maybe there'd been more than a couple) had never raised a hand to me (I would have dumped them instantly). The public Tina Turner I thought I knew was spirited, strong and charismatic. Her talent was undeniable. The encounter rattled me.

I had read *The Feminine Mystique*, but there was nothing in it I didn't already know. I disagreed with Betty Friedan's views about male and female roles in a relationship. Refusing to perform tasks normally assigned to the "little woman" just wasn't me. I would pick up my man's socks and underwear without complaint, happily make him his sandwich, willingly take care of him when he got sick and carried on like a baby. To me, these things were part of the natural role of a woman: a nurturer. But in return I demanded respect, not jealousy, nor competition when it came to my achievements and successes. I expected fair consideration of my opinions and support in my battles — whether with executives in the ad business or neighborhood harpies.

What worked for me in difficult situations time and again was to just put my head down and do my work well. No confrontations on behalf of the Sisterhood. No complaining about some perceived slight. Just let the work speak for itself. And oddly enough, I found that the misogynists in business would usually relent and acknowledge good work.

Some of it may have to do with the elusive nature of music. You know when you like it and when you don't, but it's a rare gift to be able to make concrete suggestions for how to get from there to here. Most people have neither the musical knowledge nor the language to get the job done. The most fun for me came when I would see a light dawn in the eyes of the clients or musicians. Holy shit — this chick really does know what she's doing!

So whether it was dealing with Army generals for "Be All You Can Be" or the Postmaster General for "We Deliver For You," I didn't try to play nice, kiss ass, or act like a lady. I just did my job. It worked wonders. The Post Office guy (who was the worst) actually shook my hand at the end of the session and said, "You did a great job, especially for a girl." What could I say?

Bolic Sound was top-notch. I learned later that Ike had built it himself. The control room was state-of-the-art and comfortable, too. There was a big u-shaped banquette behind the console, an easy fit for at least eight people. Unusually shaken, I kept my mouth shut and my head down as the musicians gathered to rehearse. I didn't try to sit up at the board as I usually did; instead, I perched on one end of the banquette, watched and waited.

I was uncharacteristically polite and deferential as I met Ike and a number of his musicians and colleagues. Ike was scary. Lean, mean and wound tighter than any drum I ever touched, he was dressed in black, head-to-toe. Not very friendly, either. At the beginning of the session, he and the rest of the band ignored me completely. I could have been a bug crawling on the floor. It was the first time I'd been treated so poorly, working with a celebrity. Working with anybody. It was crystal clear how they felt about women. They shared Ike's views.

I sat back and listened while they worked out the arrangement. It was damn good; but unfortunately, there were a few things I needed to correct. In a quiet voice, I spoke only to Ike, suggesting fixes on a chord here, a note there, a rhythm pattern in the middle. I saw the change in attitude in his eyes. He knew I was right. He started paying attention.

I returned to my place on the banquette and listened as they continued to work out the arrangement. The band came into the control room to listen to a take that had sounded pretty good. They were in high spirits: loose, joking around. A bunch of them squeezed in to join me on the banquette. I was a young white chick from New York City in the midst of a coterie of older black men. My film crew was off in some other room, waiting for the interview. I'd never felt so alone or so white in my life. I made myself tiny and sat on the very end.

At first I didn't notice the medium-sized silver bowl that was being passed from person to person, starting at the other end of the U across from me. I was busy concentrating on the playback, my head leaning back, my eyes half closed. A respectful pose, I thought. I only spotted the bowl as it got within a guy or two from me. I freaked. The bowl was about 2/3 full of a white powder with a tiny silver espresso spoon stuck into it. I watched as the musician next to me scooped up some powder in the spoon, held it up to his nostril, closed off the other nostril with an index finger, and inhaled.

When the bowl reached me, the whole room grew silent...I felt many pairs of eyes watching. Knowing this was some kind of test, and also suspecting it was some kind of drug, I took the bowl, looked around, shrugged and said, "I'd love to, guys, but not while I'm working."

Tina came in later and sang her ass off. Easily and quickly. She wore dark glasses; had put on enough makeup to cover the mark on her cheekbone.

She and Ike were polite and friendly during filming of the little interview. A little stiff, though; there was no spice, no fun, no passion. It was acceptable, but flat.

I can't help but contrast this relationship with the brilliant and loving one of Nick Ashford and Valerie Simpson. Best friends, loving spouses, and equal collaborators on some of the greatest songs of all time, I was honored to know them well as friends — and to work with them often.

The world learned a few years later that Tina had left Ike for keeps.

Good for her.

NICK ASHFORD AND VALERIE SIMPSON were good friends and colleagues. As a wedding present, I received a lovely boxed bottle of vintage Cristal champagne from them. I put it away for a special occasion.

A few months later I ran into Valerie at a session. I made a point to thank her for her present. I told her it was my absolute favorite champagne.

She looked at me strangely, then, "But did you look at the bottle?"

I told her that I hadn't had a chance to drink it yet. She raised an eyebrow.

That evening, I rushed home to open the box. The whole bottle was intricately engraved with art nouveau flowers, vines and elaborately lettered best wishes.

Later, Val and I had a good laugh over it.

Chapter 16

Old Aspen

I NEARLY MOVED TO ASPEN at the end of '90. My apartment was at 64th Street and Madison Ave., but New York City had turned into a dangerous place, even in that fancy upper east side neighborhood. One night, less than 50 yards from the doorway, two guys came up on either side of me and grabbed my arms. I broke free and ran to the safety of my doorman. That was the last straw. I'd had it.

I was still grieving hard over the death of my mother: my best friend, my champion, the person I talked to on the phone almost every day; the person who I loved more than anyone except my nine year old, Alex.

I was due for a change of venue.

At the time Aspen was the only other place where I felt I had put down some roots. This was before my beloved mountain town morphed into an international playground complete with its own Rodeo Drive...

It was the summer of 1960. I'd been accepted into the Aspen Music Festival and School for the nine-week session from July through August. I'd had to fudge the truth about my age by a couple of years. Okay: I lied.

I was to study with the revered teacher Rosina Lhevinne, widow of the famous Russian concert pianist, Josef Lhevinne. My mother had once again found a personal friend to help pay my way. I received a scholarship from the school for the rest.

I took the train from southern California to Glenwood Springs, and then a bus up to Aspen. I was 15 years old, and it was the first time I had been away from home on my own.

I loved everything about the train. The changing views of the countryside rushing by; walking up and down the cars, trying to imagine who the other passengers were; sitting down to meals while speeding down the tracks. All of it was new to me, and wonderful. The trip took a couple of days, and every night I fell asleep to the sound of *clickety clack, clickety clack,* snug in a tiny bunk bed. I also had the comfort of my two favorite feather pillows. (I still travel with my own pillows on road trips).

Michele Bloch, an exceptionally talented clarinetist, traveled with me to Aspen. The Festival people had suggested we ride together on the train, and I was glad for the company. She was a little older and a lot more sophisticated. We stayed close all that summer, but grew apart after she was hired by the Los Angeles Philharmonic the following year. Michele is today Michele Kuvosky, the respected principal clarinetist of the Philharmonic.

I was stunned by the beauty and charm of the unpaved and unspoiled Aspen of 1960. Everything stood out in such sharp focus, I guess because of the high altitude and the dry, thin air. Huge, craggy mountains seemed to rise straight up into the deep blue sky, turning the town below into a toy village. Fluffy white tree pollen floated lazily through the blossom-scented air. It was an authentic old western silver mining town, but it reminded me of the back lot at Paramount.

All of the streets in town were dirt, no asphalt in sight. Lumbering yellow trucks came along every few days and sprayed oil to keep the dust down. I can still bring back that smell.

New friend Michele and I made our way from the bus stop to the address we'd been given. We struggled with our luggage toward the dramatic mountain that loomed over the town. The Mountain Chalet on Durant Avenue was where we were going to room for the entire program. Ski lodge in the winter, dormitory in the summer, it was modest, but clean.

The kindly housemother assigned to look after us lived on the ground floor. Best of all, she was old, drank gin every evening, and fell asleep early. Once we heard her snoring, it was a piece of cake to climb out of the windows and shinny down to the streets of Aspen. No stinkin' curfew was going to keep us in! We never were caught.

My musical education went well. I was in awe of Madame Lhevinne, and she took quite a liking to me. I never had to take lessons from her two assistants, even though most of her other students did. I worked diligently to please her every week, and it paid off. I improved a lot that summer. If some of the other piano students were jealous because I was such a teacher's pet, they got over it.

We were all immersed in an incredible musical culture. Aaron Copland was conducting; Darius Milhaud was in residence; Adele Addison and Jennie Tourel were giving master classes. The list went on and on for every instrument. It was absolutely intoxicating for all of us young and aspiring musicians to be living in a town where we bumped into our musical idols daily.

To my amazement and delight, I was hired to be Ms. Tourel's primary accompanist for her classes. That would help me to pay back some of my scholarship money, but more important to me, it was clear that she really liked me and my playing. She was known to be outspoken, eccentric and difficult, sometimes delighting in torturing the press with fabricated tales. During our working hours, I strived to be professional and invisible; in private, we got along famously. The thought that Leonard Bernstein had accompanied her for many of her solo performances was thrilling!

I practiced every morning in one of the little cabins scattered throughout the woods, or in one of the empty classrooms at the local elementary school. In the afternoons, I would go hiking up in the mountains, rock-skipping on the rivers when the water level was low, and swimming in the pool of the famous but already declining Hotel Jerome. I made new friends; we would hang out at the corner drugstore that still had a soda fountain with spinning stools and friendly service. Most late afternoons, we would all troop down to the huge concert tent in Aspen Meadows to be inspired by phenomenal performances: sometimes from faculty members, sometimes from students.

Like clockwork, there would be a heavy downpour around four as the temperature rose. The clouds would quickly stack up into towering black banks, then burst just in time to drench us as we walked to or from the tent. It would be over in less than a half hour. We got used to it.

Sometimes, late at night, we would sneak out of the Chalet to catch a ride up to Castle Creek. We would lie on the ground and stare up at the August shooting star show. Other nights, we would go even further up the road to sit on the shore of the lake below the moonlit Maroon Bells mountain range, drinking in the night sky and dreaming young dreams of the future.

It was during the second half of the session that I developed a huge crush on Won Mo Kim, a Korean violin student whose virtuosity was wowing everyone. His father was the conductor of the Seoul Symphony. Won Mo was older: 21, I think. I was a very late bloomer and didn't have much experience in the boy/girl business, but I finally fell hard. Although he treated me like a kid sister for a while, we progressed to boyfriend/girlfriend soon enough.

I was almost 16, but still didn't understand all the fuss people made about sex. Sure, I had been kissed by a couple of boys in high school, but privately thought it was kind of gross (especially the tongue part). My development may have been retarded by an earlier traumatic incident.

When I was thirteen, my mother took in three Pierce College boys as boarders. We needed the money. All were mentors (especially re girl-boy issues). Clint looked a lot like James Dean. He was the most experienced. His two friends told me that he pleasured quite a few housewives in the neighborhood.

Even though I wasn't dating yet, the boys made a lasting impression. I worshipped them — sat at their feet as they regaled me with wild stories (certainly exaggerated) about their dates and relationships with the local girls. *What a fool that bitch was... You have to be merciless when they get all clingy and needy...* They instructed me that I was never to ask a boy out (men hated pushy females). And I was always to play hard-to-get.

One day, Clint took me with him to visit his parents in San Pedro. He introduced me as his new 'kid sister.' Before driving back home that evening, we drove up to a spot overlooking the whole harbor. Without warning, he jumped me. I was furious — but scared, too — he was pinning me up against the door when I just managed to free one hand enough to reach behind my back for the door handle. The two of us tumbled out onto the pavement. He apologized over and over. I didn't say much (and never told my parents). I liked him, but I could no longer trust him. I was too young. He must have been determined to be my first.

But now in Aspen, Won Mo's first French kiss turned my brain to mush. I couldn't think; I couldn't see; I couldn't speak. That first hot overwhelming wave of desire changed me forever. My world was no longer ruled by clear-headed logic. I now had to deal with sensations I couldn't always count on controlling.

In those last three weeks of the summer program, I spent quite a few nights on Won Mo's miserable little cot. I didn't care. Who needed sleep? He introduced me to many new experiences (but never actual intercourse: I was too scared of getting pregnant). The memory that lingers is the smoothness of his hairless caramel-colored skin against my bare breasts.

In the final concert of the season, Won Mo played the Sibelius Violin Concerto with the Festival Orchestra, and I played the first movement of the Chopin Concerto #1 in E minor. We received back-to-back standing ovations from the thousand-member audience: a priceless, until then unmatched moment in my life. I was thrilled to be acknowledged as an artist; at the same time, secretly proud to have become a sexually awakened woman.

But then summer was over. When my mother arrived in Aspen to pick me up in the family station wagon, I informed her that Won Mo and I were going to be married as soon as I turned 21; that he was going to go back to Korea, but would wait for me. I also told her he was coming back to Canoga Park to spend a week or so with us before flying back to Seoul. She didn't blow up; she didn't yell at me; she simply raised an eyebrow and said, "That's nice dear; I'm sure it will all work out for the best."

And of course, it did: the unforgettable summer romance was over — we quickly lost touch. As Carl Sandburg wrote,

> *For he went west, she went east,*
> *And they both lived.*

THE COLONEL called me out onto the front lawn of our house in Canoga Park at dusk. He showed me the body of an opossum our two Bedlington terriers had killed.

When I picked it up to examine it more closely, *BAM!* the tail wrapped around my forearm with a snap! It was a postmortem muscle reflex, but I didn't know that.

I hopped, screamed, and tried to shake the damn thing off my arm. The Colonel bent over double, laughing his ass off. He knew the creature was really dead, not just playing possum. He'd also known what would happen when I picked it up.

Chapter 17

Nature Baby Trauma Maiden

———

I skipped the next session in Aspen. It was 1961 — the summer after high school graduation — and I was occupied with my first serious boyfriend.

No, it wasn't Won Mo Kim. He was the Captain of the football team, star butterfly swimmer, and Student Body President: Robert W. Bishop, Jr. I called him Jay. Months before, as I entered my senior year at Canoga Park High School, I was a changed girl. My friends noticed, but couldn't figure out how or why. I knew, but never told anybody (except my mother) about Won Mo.

When Jay asked me to the Autumn Dance, it surprised many of my classmates. Just before leaving for Aspen that previous summer, I had worked behind the punchbowl at the senior prom. Jay had shown up as the date of Gilda Lee, a blonde bombshell senior who had just won a major local beauty contest. I soaked my pillow with tears that night: I'd had a secret crush on him.

That fall, after returning from Aspen, I was determined to make it happen between us. My plan worked. I befriended his delightful little sister, nicknamed Dandi (I really did like her immensely). We spent many afternoons at their house kidding around with big brother Jay. One day, she told me he was going to ask me to the Autumn Dance. I conveniently ran into him on a semi-deserted staircase, and he popped the question. As word got out around campus, I'll never forget overhearing one of the popular girls asking a huddle of her clique, "Why would he ask her? She doesn't even have any curves!"

We went steady for the rest of the school year and through the summer. But in the end he went to Claremont, I went to Occidental, and especially after the following summer in Aspen, we drifted apart.

That summer of '61 was also when my mother, brother, sister and I made one of our trips across the country to visit the East Coast relatives. I had been driving one night when we pulled into a motel parking lot. An old junk heap of a car followed us in, and a couple of creepy guys jumped out and asked about prices for our services. I didn't know what they were talking about, but they explained they'd seen my mother's bare legs sticking up from the luggage area of the station wagon where she had been snoozing, and took it as an advertisement. My mother was horrified, told them off, and rushed us all into the motel manager's office. My brother and I thought it was hilarious.

My summer of '62 in Aspen was a very different experience. I knew the ropes (or so I thought). I had won a couple of important Young Artists' competitions in Los Angeles, and had performed as a soloist with the Pasadena Symphony, the Long Beach Symphony and the L.A. Philharmonic. I was more confident. Maybe too much so.

Joining me that summer were three members of my piano quartet: a chamber music ensemble we had formed back in L.A. We performed as a group at the Festival: Ronnie Patterson, violin; Marvin Chantry, viola; and my dearest friend from college, Beverly Lauridsen, cello. One day we had to go somewhere to play a concert: a day that also provided me with a horrifying and indelible memory.

As we got into the car, Ronnie handed me his $5,000 violin bow. I got into the seat carefully, holding the bow upright in my left hand and closing the car door with my right. *Snap!* It was over in a millisecond. I had broken off the top few inches. I don't know if I have ever felt so wretched. Such a stupid, klutzy thing to do. It may have been insured, but still...

Each of the other members was a rising star in his or her own right, and each of them went on to successful careers as classical musicians. Not I. My career took a left turn after my Fulbright year in Italy.

I was closest with Beverly, who'd been my college roommate for a semester. Then she left Occidental to join the Los Angeles Philharmonic under Zubin Mehta. She became one of the youngest members ever. Her boyfriend in Aspen (also a fellow Oxy student), was David Shostac, the now well-known and acclaimed flutist. She eventually moved to New York City, where she played on every session I produced that called for a string section.

In that second Aspen summer, I became involved with an intense young man. Five years older and Polish by birth, he was a pianist who specialized in Chopin (of course). He had by then already won some prestigious international awards. His name was Marek Jablonski. He was handsome and had the requisite dark and brooding personality. Heathcliff-like. I had been to Planned Parenthood, now used a diaphragm, and we had plenty of sex. Marek did happen to be my one and only foot fetishist (he spent a lot of time on my toes). It wasn't my thing, but I didn't mind much.

Being around him made me aware of something I had noticed before but never really thought about. Most concert soloists, especially pianists, (maybe even great artists of all kinds) have a kind of a chip on their shoulders. A conviction that they have to prove something to the world. A sense of being an outcast, not belonging — with buried resentment as a result. It could be why they are able to remove themselves from social contact so easily to be alone for weeks, months, even years to create masterpieces or to prepare a year's repertoire. It could also be why I could never be one of them. I was too social, too much of a people person. I loved life and fun too much. But I didn't know that yet.

Madame Lhevinne disapproved mightily of my romantic involvement, and told me so. She wanted me to break it off immediately. I wouldn't. But after a bad lesson with her led to one session with one of her snotty assistants, I settled down. Many necessary hours of practicing regained her esteem. She even coached me later when she came to California. She spent every September and October in Santa Monica before returning to Juilliard in New York City. She graciously allowed me to take advantage of her vacation time. I still regret that I probably disappointed her greatly with my decision not to become a professional concert pianist. But that came later.

That summer, I lived on the second floor of the Roaring Fork Hotel, facing the center of Aspen's Main Street. The building was old and crumbling. Our rooms were set up like a dormitory: they sat directly above the ground floor public area that held post office boxes and a cafeteria. The carryings-on from the street kept us up into the wee hours. I remember leaning far out from my second story window many times to chat with people during the daytime or yell at them to shut up at night. It was a scene. Sometimes there would be scratching, biting, hair-pulling cat fights in the dorm. I remember one in which two girls tumbled down the little interior staircase into the public room below while scrabbling and wrestling in their underwear.

Early one morning, in panties only, I was brushing my teeth in the big communal bathroom when another girl came up behind me, put her arms around me, and started kissing my neck and back. I was blasé enough by then to simply say, "Not now, you idiot, it's too early in the morning!"

I learned a lot about homosexuality that summer. Without bias, my parents had educated us about different sexual preferences. We knew a couple of their friends who were gay, but I had never hung out with them. My mother and father referred to them as "queers" but there was no negativity in their use of the term. It was just the old-fashioned word they'd learned.

In Aspen that second term, I soon realized that a great number of classical musicians are homosexual, both men and women. I was intrigued, and wormed my way into a clique of the most flamboyant males. I soon became kind of a mascot to them. I was the only 'outsider' allowed to attend the fabulous drag parties they held in a wing of the Mountain Chalet (where most of them roomed that summer). The scene was wild enough that someone always had to act as lookout.

Among the most prominent members was the queen mother Ronnie Rogers, who was also a student of Rosina Lhevinne, as well as a famous drag queen opera singer. There was Stanley, the cynical Jewish pianist from New York City, who actually was straight; and David, a teenager who couldn't make up his mind. David's drag name was *Flying Fish*. Our group gave drag names to everyone we talked about at the Festival. It didn't matter if they were male or female, straight or gay. I can only remember a few. Ronnie was *Rinalda*; Stanley was *Stella*. Mine was *Nature Baby Trauma Maiden*, and Van Cliburn's was *Pussy Nell*. A visiting outrageous queen from New York rounded out the group as *Priska*.

We referred to everyone in conversation as 'she.' High drama, sturm und drang, and public scenes were everyday occurrences. In the middle of one night, for instance, a completely shaved and naked Ronnie threw 'herself' onto the lawn in front of the place 'her' current boyfriend was staying. 'She' wailed and flailed while beating the ground with 'her' fists. 'She' woke up the whole town.

What I didn't like at all was the campaign they waged on poor David. The constant pressure to make him declare himself homosexual bothered me a lot. He confessed to me once that he was contemplating suicide. I didn't think he would actually follow through, and he never did. When he finally did 'come out,' there was much rejoicing and celebration, but the whole thing left a bad taste in my mouth. He didn't seem that happy. It never did stop me, however, from having many gay guys as very close friends from then on.

A side note. A favorite fixture in Aspen was a giant black royal standard poodle named "Chutzpah." He belonged to the unabashedly homosexual festival director, Norman Singer, and had the run of the whole town. His elegant stature, prancing gait and perfect grooming made him an ideal symbol for gay pride. He roamed Aspen every day, going from place to place to receive his proper adulation. Dignified and aloof, he would graciously allow only certain people to actually touch him. I was one of them, and felt duly honored. In later years I yearned to own one of his breed, but never could find one that approached his elegance.

The best thing that happened to me that summer was my friendship with Jimmy Levine — now the great James Levine of the Metropolitan Opera. I adored him as a friend and considered him a mentor even though he had barely turned 19, only a year older than I. He knew so much more than I about both music and musicality. He helped me greatly with my playing and interpretation. He encouraged me with words like, "You've got it. You can make it." I may have been good, but I was nowhere near his level; I remember being awed by his flawless and fiery performance of Beethoven's Third Piano Concerto with the Aspen Symphony.

But his heart really belonged to opera and to conducting. I was privileged to sit and listen for hours as he coached the singers for a production of Mozart's *The Magic Flute* that he was to conduct later in the summer in historic Wheeler Opera House.

Like everyone else, I loved that hall. It had been built in 1889 and fully restored in the 1950's. Its grand proscenium stage was flanked by draped box seat alcoves. The famous "Queen of the Night" arias in the opera were both performed from the one on the left. The graceful arched balcony section was cantilevered over the back half of the orchestra floor: it held the best seats in the house. There were heavy gold stage curtains and the dark red walls of the hall were decorated with gold fleur-de-lis. The coffered ceiling had stars painted in the recess areas, and the red mohair movie theater-style seats were superbly comfortable except when the bats that lived in the upper reaches of the building would decide to dive-bomb the heads of the people seated in them. Great fun!

Anyway, seated in a folding chair beside the 19-year-old Maestro on his piano bench in the small rehearsal room, I watched how he worked with his singers. The way he would coax emotional punch and believability out of the performers was positively transformative. He would play a phrase on the piano or even sing it himself to demonstrate the powerful effect created by a slight emphasis on this note, lingering a bit longer on another, or reducing the volume to almost a whisper at the end of a line. His big body and a conducting hand would lean expressively into the music as the singers tried to follow his direction. He was intense and passionate, yet I never heard him yell or lose his temper. He was simply and absolutely determined to get what he wanted. Observing these sessions taught me techniques I continued to use throughout my career.

As a reward, he let me play a tiger-like creature in the group of animals summoned from the forest by Tamino's flute. The full costume, complete with tiger's head, was stifflingly hot... but what a memory!

Those two formative summers in that small Western town greatly contributed to my skills as a musician. They equally prepared me to handle the onslaught of wacky situations that would characterize a large part of my future career.

And *Nature Baby Trauma Maiden* turned out to be a more apt alias than anyone imagined...

MY BEST FRIEND in Hudson, NY, is Dini Lamot, aka "Musty Chiffon" — fabulous singer and performing drag queen. Dini and I share a love of gardening.

One day we toured the "white garden" I'd planted in front of my federal farmhouse. I was very proud of its design.

A week or so I later, I was horrified to see that two blood-red gladioli had emerged in the middle of all that purity. I jokingly pointed out to everyone that this was *absolute proof* of the Devil's existence.

It was only when I went to pull them out that I realized they were made of plastic. My son Alex knew at once: "Has to be Dini."

Of course he was right.

Chapter 18

Adventure in Austria

———

WE ESCAPED INTO THE BAR at the Hotel Tannbergerhof, taking cover from the howling blizzard raging just outside the door. It was 1970 or '71, and we were there in the quaint, charming Austrian village of Lech am Arlberg because there was no skiing in Val Gardena, Italy (our original destination). We had been traveling through Europe searching for snow. We tried St. Moritz in Switzerland, and both Val Gardena and Cortina d'Ampezzo in Italy, but no luck. In Lech, there was more than enough. To get anywhere in town, we had to make our way down shoulder-width paths cut through nine or ten feet of packed snow. Being somewhat claustrophobic, it made me nervous.

I was with my first husband, Walter Raim, and our friend Bela Sigetvari, a Hungarian refugee, ski instructor, and guide.

We had survived a harrowing day on the mountain. That afternoon, we'd ridden up the lift on the wrong side of the valley. It landed us in a complete whiteout. The second my skis hit the snow, I felt sick to my stomach. Total vertigo. I couldn't see my feet, couldn't see the terrain, didn't know which way was up. I had only been skiing for about a year. But we did have to get down somehow.

Bela is an interesting fellow. At 14, he was hurling Molotov cocktails at Soviet tanks in the center of Budapest. He lost pieces of a couple of fingers, but managed to escape by walking to freedom over the mountains into Austria. He made his way to New York City, where he survived by doing odd jobs and eating canned dog food. Eventually, he became a banker during the week and a ski instructor at Stratton Mountain on the weekends. His violent past, however, did have lasting effects. On our ski trip, we could often hear his recurring nightmares through the walls as he screamed and threw himself out of bed.

On one of our weekly drives up to Walter's house in Vermont, Bela elaborated on his earlier choice of pet food. "It was cheap. It was good. And I didn't read English."

Bela sometimes entertained me with tales of his stint in the U.S. Army. Overseas, when he was refused assignment to his preferred mountain division in Garmisch, Germany, he took a tank on a joyride through the local town, knocking over as many mailboxes as possible. He was reassigned to Garmisch.

One of Bela's favorite topics of discussion was avalanche survival, rescue and recovery. Tips for survival included doing the breaststroke as the avalanche hurtled you down the mountain, and making sure your hands were close to your feet when you came to a stop (so you could get your boots off). Then you were to spit into an air pocket around your mouth to determine which way was up. Gravity would provide the answer. You needed this information in order to avoid mistakenly clawing your way out in the wrong direction. More grisly details for rescue and recovery involved learning the proper technique for poking for bodies with long pointed poles, and useful tips on the proper training of cadaver dogs. It became clear that Bela was both obsessed with (and terrified by) avalanches.

So I was prepared, but none too happy, when Bela started yelling, "Avalanche! Avalanche! There's going to be an *avalanche!*"

We were at the top of the mountain, and, as I said, in the middle of a whiteout. I followed Bela as he disappeared into the white fog. I felt my skis starting downhill. There was no evidence of a trail, but the going was slow enough for me to keep my balance in the thick, sticky snow. When we got down a bit, the fog lifted and I found myself on an expanse of what looked like white cement rubble. It was miserable to move in, much less ski on. Bela was still screaming up at me but the message had changed to, "*There was just an avalanche here!* We have to get down *before it slides again!*"

Walter had disappeared long before, but now Bela followed. I didn't panic; I just began doing kick turns on both sides of where I imagined the trail should have been. All the way down to a road where they were waiting. Nice guys. Later, we met a group who did confirm that Bela's fears had been justified. They had seen the avalanche we'd just passed over.

By the time we hit the bar that evening, all of us were ready for a drink. We settled into one of the ancient, heavy wooden tables and ordered. The Tannbergerhof opened in 1928 and was built in traditional Austrian chalet style. Although frequented by the rich and famous, it felt homey, relaxed, comfortable. It was the perfect place for a celebrity to bring the whole family, and many of them still do.

Suddenly, Walter said, "Oh my God! That's Harris Yulin at the bar!" We were freshly familiar with the well-known actor having just seen him in a screening of *End of the Road*. Based on a novel by John Barth, it was one of the most depressing and disturbing movies I had ever seen. It gave me headaches and nightmares for a week. The movie starred Mr. Yulin, but also featured our good friend Ray Brock as a sadistic transvestite nurse. Ray was Walter's architect and a frequent guest at the Vermont house: a wild man, always hilarious to have around. (If the name is familiar, it may be because he is the 'Ray' in Arlo Guthrie's "Alice's Restaurant").

Emboldened by the coincidence of the situation, Walter, normally too hip to interact with strangers, walked right up to the bar, introduced himself to Harris, and somehow persuaded him to join us at our table. Before long, the four of us were deep into the kind of intimate conversation that can happen when you're thrown together during a blizzard in a foreign country.

We were talking about the meaning of the movie, ourselves, and the purpose of life when Harris happened to glance at his watch. He sprang to his feet and said these exact words, "I must go and meet my beloved!" He dashed out into the snowstorm in such desperation that we were compelled to rush for the windows to see what was going on.

Like a scene out of *Doctor Zhivago*, she appeared out of the blowing snow. Lit by the dim street lamps, clad in fur-trimmed wraps and fuzzy boots, she broke into a run when she saw him and leapt into his arms, throwing her legs around his waist. It's hard to imagine a more romantic scene. They embraced and kissed for a long time, but at last came inside, laughing and shaking, stomping their boots and brushing the snow off their clothes. He introduced her, but there was really no need: it was the early '70's, and she was Faye Dunaway.

We all hung out together for the next few days. Bela gave Faye skiing lessons while Walter and I skied the upper slopes. She was a beginner, but plucky. She was forced to wear all kinds of strange headgear because she was forbidden to let the sun touch her face. This edict came from the director she was working with in Paris. In retrospect, I believe the movie must have been the first of Richard Lester's *The Three Musketeers* films.

Faye and I had a couple of conversations about men up in her room while she was primping for the evenings. She didn't like Walter at all — particularly not for me. She thought he was too old, too jaded, too cynical, too short, and not handsome enough. In truth, Walter broadcast a kind of 'know it all' superior attitude. It was most likely defensiveness on his part, especially around a woman who was such a superstar. I defended him with stories about what an intellectual he was and how much he was teaching me about music, skiing, and the good things in life. She simply said, "Susan, you can do better; and trust me, you will." It did cross my mind that Harris Yulin didn't seem to be such a perfect match for her, either. I knew he was absolutely besotted with her, but to me, she often seemed to be acting out a role in a romance movie. I said nothing.

Often, I found myself staring at her face. She was astonishing to look at: all bone structure, angles and planes. What was remarkable to me was that she wasn't pretty at all. On film and in photos she was absolutely stunning, but in person, not really. A professional photographer once told me that the camera only sees with one eye, which is why some people look so different in real life. Had I known it at the time, I would have tried looking at her with one eye covered.

The two of us really hit it off, and later spent a couple of afternoons together back in Manhattan. I recall one time when we went shopping and spent a couple of hours at the Charles Jourdan shoe salon on Fifth Avenue. She tried on maybe a hundred pairs, charming the salesman and ignoring the clot of onlookers. She bought; I watched.

But we moved in very different circles, so eventually, we drifted apart. There was one weekend when she was supposed to come up and visit us in Vermont. I think she was with Stacy Keach by this time, but the car never pulled into the driveway. I watched the empty road from the window for a long time.

And she was right about Walter and me.

ON THE CONCORDE, I was seated across from two Saudi Arabians in full Arab dress. One was a prince, the other, his toadie. After a while, the Prince deigned to speak with me directly. We discussed horses — he had about a hundred prize Arabians.

I told him what I did for a living. He offered me $25,000 to write a birthday song for his youngest wife. I declined; but the conversation continued.

After giving me his five different addresses all over the world, he finally said, "And if all else fails, you can always reach me through The American Bank in Beverly Hills."

"Oh, that's my bank!" I said brightly.

"No my dear," he replied. "That's *MY* bank."

Chapter 19

The Simian Society

TWO MALIBU CANYON LESBIANS created it in the early 60's. They lived in a spectacular avant-garde wood, stone and glass home. The property covered more than 10 acres high up in the largely arid Southern California hills.

Most amazing of all was their monkey wing, with separate quarters for each simian. There was also a communal playroom, open to the outdoors, with trees growing up through the wire walls and ceiling.

We got involved with the Society through my mother, of course. As usual, she was the one who found them.

My introduction to monkeys came early — in the Carlson Circle days (the king snake days). I may have been 11 or 12. One day, a little squirrel monkey scampered onto the property. I was surprised that the dogs didn't grab her, but then again, monkeys are smart. They move quickly to different levels when they need to escape. She attached herself to me, and I fell in love.

We later found out that she belonged to a very strange man who lived across the street. He was a professed sculptor. Probably about 50, he wasn't tall, but was in very good shape. One thing I remember, he was shaved from head to toe, completely hairless. He would come and go to check on his pet and visit with my parents. The monkey's stays lasted longer and longer, but she would occasionally drift back to her home.

At one point, her owner told my parents that he found my proportions to be the mathematical ideal of the human form. He asked permission to make plaster casts of my arms, legs, and body for a statue. I didn't mind too much and made it through the ordeal. In retrospect, I can't for the life of me figure out why they let him do it, especially since they didn't attend the castings. I suppose times were simpler then: Evil did not seem as omnipresent as it does today. Besides, the sculptor would have realized that I was the kind of child who would have ratted him out instantly. As it happened, he never made any overt move, but something made me uncomfortable enough to have them sever the relationship. No more monkey business. I later wondered if he'd sent the little creature over as a lure.

It was six or seven years later, during my junior year at Occidental College, that my roommate, Mari Ryan, received a special gift from her boyfriend. His name was "Charlie" — a six-month-old woolly monkey — a cuddly and lovable baby in diapers. We were enthralled. It turned out to be disconcertingly similar to taking care of a human infant (though one with a great disposition). Charlie slept through the night, didn't cry much, and was really good about having his diapers changed. We managed to keep him secretly in our dorm room for two weeks before somebody snitched. So off he went to the Carlson Circle homestead.

My family was fascinated. The current pack of dogs had no idea what to make of him; he blurred the line between human and animal, and they didn't dare risk harming one of ours. My mother grew to love him like her own baby. The cats were terrified — and Charlie made the most of it, chasing them down the hall and grabbing them by their tails. They couldn't even escape by jumping up on anything. Like the dogs, they wouldn't use teeth or claws, even to defend themselves. The cats regarded him as an unfortunate family secret, a hideous monster child that should have been put down.

Mom wanted to raise her newest baby properly, but had to admit she didn't know much about monkeys.

I accompanied my mother and Charlie the first time they drove up the Canyon to meet Libby, Director of the Simian Society. She and her partner Sarah loved Charlie, and of course (like everyone else) adored my mother. They gave us lots of good advice and invited us to join their Simian Society. They convened on Sunday afternoons. We attended our first a couple of weekends later.

We met outdoors in kind of a natural amphitheater. What a scene it was, spread out across the barren landscape. Everywhere were dozens of big, smooth, sand-colored rocks to sit and climb upon. Except for a bit of scrubby undergrowth, the ground consisted of dry dirt and sand. It was much like a PTA meeting or school picnic, save that each family had a monkey or two (or three) in tow instead of children. About 30 or 40 beings in all. The parents brought colorful towels and blankets, coolers full of food and drink for humans and simians to share, umbrellas and folding chairs, and a variety of toys for the monkeys and the few human children to share. There were no dogs.

There was much diversity of species. The big macaques scared me the most. They would scream, bare huge fangs, and beat their chests. The squirrel monkeys were cute little fuzzy things, scampering about and playing only with one and another. The gibbons (actually, a type of ape rather than monkey) were the clowns. With their extremely long skinny arms stretched wide, big grins across their faces, they would toddle side to side, back and forth when they came to greet you: gentle giants, like orangutans. Spider monkeys were always the fastest and most athletic, able to make full use of their thin bodies and long, effective prehensile tails. Even lacking any trees to exhibit their full prowess, they still could put on a spectacular show.

To me, the woollies were the stars. Stockier than spiders, they were nearly as agile, and had tails to match. Covered head to toe with dark, dense, short, soft fur, their hairless faces were the most expressive. Charlie was tiny compared to most of them, but they treated him kindly (especially the other young ones and the females). The big males were aloof. Charlie would have nothing to do with the other species.

A particularly striking feature of the gathering was the attire of some of the simians. Some wore costumes, yes, but for the most part, stylish human dress was the norm. Communion dresses for some females, custom-tailored suits for some males. Every type of baby, toddler and children's clothing imaginable for the others. Sensibly, those in fancy duds were not allowed to roughhouse and scramble over the rocks. They had to be content to sit with their parents, sometimes drinking politely out of teacups.

These people clearly had come to believe their monkeys really could be turned into children. Too weird for me; I never dressed any of my monkeys in anything but Charlie's utilitarian diaper. (For long car rides, some of the others needed pull-ups.)

The school year ended and I went off to Italy with my cellist friend, Beverly Lauridsen. We were on our way to master classes at a Count's palace in Siena.

Early on I started to receive letters from home with sad news. Charlie was sick — very sick — and getting worse, quickly. My mother went from vet to vet with no good result. Finally, in desperation, she went to an animal medium, who promised she could diagnose him. My mother described how the woman repeatedly swung a crystal pendulum over Charlie's little body, every which way for a long time. Finally, she told my mother, "It's his liver." And she was correct.

Reading her letter, I remembered a couple of things. Charlie reportedly had belonged to a French actress who had carried him around as an accessory à la Paris Hilton. She also fed him champagne constantly, which he loved, for the amusement of her fans. And I remembered something else. The family had once gone camping in the desert during the late winter. Charlie had come with us. I flashed on how he had jumped around the campfire at night, stealing and emptying our tin cups of hot spiced wine. Charlie was an alcoholic.

When I heard the news that Charlie had died of cirrhosis of the liver, I wept off and on for days. The tough divorcée who was my landlady didn't understand. She said over and over (in Italian), "But Susanna, it's an animal, an animal, not a child. If you want to cry about something, cry for the poor children of Italy. That's worth crying about!" She just didn't get it.

Back in California, all of our friends from the Simian Society were truly saddened by Charlie's demise, and especially sorry for my mother. Libby promised she would find a way to comfort her.

Two things happened that fall after I returned to college at the start of my senior year. First, my mother was persuaded to board a group of five monkeys on our property. The troop consisted of three woollies, a Brazilian spider monkey, and a capuchin. Once again, a big wire cage was constructed around a few trees, with a makeshift wooden shelter added for rainy days. It was quite close to the house for easy observation and to enable speedy intervention when squabbles broke out.

My personal favorite was "Sapphire," the Brazilian spider monkey. She had sparse, long black hair, over-length arms, legs and tail, and walked upright a great deal of the time. She loved people, but had an unusual way of greeting them. If she hadn't seen you for a while, she would start chirping and woofing, shaking her head back and forth and pulling hard on the little bit of hair she had on her chest. She would then jump into your arms, wrap her limbs around your body (including her tail) and more often than not, pee all over you. It was difficult to get really mad at her; it was just her way of showing unconditional love.

She did bite me hard one day — but it wasn't her fault. We were riding back home over Malibu Canyon after taking her to a Society meeting. We were in the tunnel and some asshole leaned on his horn. She freaked out, and when I tried to hold her, she bit me. Blood streamed all over the back seat. It actually wasn't dangerous, but I still have a v-shaped scar on the inside of my left arm.

I also have a vivid memory of the expression on the faces of two phone company repairmen as they watched her, high overhead, scamper out along the telephone lines that led to the street.

"Guapo" was the leader of the pack, the biggest of the troop, a large stocky male wooly. He was grayer than most woollies I had seen, and determinedly dominant. For months we had no problems, but one day he jumped my sister Janet in a pronouncedly sexual way, biting her hard on the head. Part of the mating ritual, I believe. She was screaming blue murder with the blood running down the side of her face. Head wounds do bleed a lot. My parents pulled him off, but the incident was a catalyst for the whole group's ultimate departure.

And then came "Charlene." A gift from the Simian Society, she was a two-year-old woolly. A superbly healthy, strong-minded devil of a girl. You could see it in her eyes. She had the run of the place inside and out, although we learned not to let her in when she had been punished and was bent on revenge. On one such occasion, screaming, she opened the latch on the back door, ran down the hall into my parents' bedroom, raced up the drapes next to the big bed, spraying diarrhea as she went. It was awful.

I also recall sitting at the dining room table, trying to write term papers using my father's big black Royal typewriter. In those pre-copier days, we made 'carbon copies' using alternate layers of onion-skin and carbon paper. Working with them was maddening. As usual, my pack of Marlboros would be lying on the table next to me. Charlene would casually saunter by with studied innocence. Then, if I were sufficiently absorbed, she would make a sudden quick leap, grab the pack of cigarettes, and run off with it. Once, in her haste, she dropped the pack — without missing a beat, she retrieved it with her tail and scampered away. It was her custom to then scramble up to the one place on the roof we couldn't reach, open the pack, neatly break each cigarette into pieces, and drop them on me as I stood on the ground screaming up at her.

Charlie and Charlene were my first children — well, at least my introduction to child rearing. The feeling of them wrapping arms, legs (and tails) around my neck and waist in unabashed love was only duplicated when I did, in fact, have children.

I FOLLOWED MAGGIE the Airedale puppy into my Malibu kitchen. The door was wide open to the outside patio.

Suddenly, the air was filled with a terrifying noise. Insects? No. Rattlesnake? YES! It was coiled on the mat just outside the door.

I screamed *"NO!"* at Maggie as she curiously moved in to investigate. I grabbed her by the hips and *pulled* as I kicked the door shut. The striking snake's fangs banged against the glass.

Michael came home, grabbed a shovel, and cut its head off with a *whack!* — but the snapping severed head, full of venom, almost got him as it shot past his elbow.

I gutted it, skinned it, marinated and barbecued it. Delicious!

Chapter 20

Steppin' Out

THE LATE 60'S AND EARLY 70'S were wild and unpredictable times in Manhattan. People were experimenting with multiple relationships, exotic sexual activities, and a whole pharmacopeia of drugs. Yet the times were not completely without occasional vestiges of more genteel days. One of those might be being invited over to a friend's apartment for a home cooked meal, or cocktails and appetizers.

When the head of production at Grey Advertising invited Walter and me over for dinner at his Greenwich Village apartment, I accepted with alacrity. I was a bit surprised, though, at Bob Gross's invitation. He did not seem to be the domestic type. A fascinating but twisted character, he was little and wiry, with an oversized head and piercing eyes. He dressed in low-slung jeans and checkered shirts, always with boots (sometimes even cowboy boots). At the time, an unusual look for Madison Ave.

Bob was one of the first ad biz bigwigs I pitched with a demo reel of our jingles and underscores. For whatever reason, he took a liking to me and gave us many jobs. He was an exacting client, one who knew what he wanted, and we came through for him. It was a definite feather in my cap to bring in so much business. All the more so because the boss, Herman Edel, was himself a consummate salesman.

Walter and I walked over to Bob's place from our apartment on Hudson Street. He lived on the ground floor of a well-kept brownstone. We rang the doorbell and waited. The door opened wide, and there stood my client with a twinkle in his eyes and a smirk on his face.

Bob was completely naked except for a tiny, frilly, colorful apron tied around his waist. It barely covered his privates. Walter and I tried our best to be nonchalant. Walter was inherently cool anyway, with his tiny rectangular wire-framed sunglasses and his red beard goatee. He was ever the quintessential guitar-playing, left wing beatnik.

I was fairly speechless. I thought Bob was married (knew he had two children) — but next, we met the girlfriend. She couldn't have been older than 18, was naked as a jaybird, and very pretty. She lacked the apron. She was fair — a natural ash blond with pale blue eyes. Although she hardly said a word throughout the evening, she seemed happy. And relaxed.

Bob told us to feel free to join them by taking off all our clothes. We declined. He didn't put any additional pressure on us, but I could read his delight at our discomfort. We chatted during cocktails while he popped in and out of the kitchen. He was doing the cooking, and served a fantastic meal. We sat down to a perfectly set table for four with linens, china, crystal, candles, and naked people. I still remember the menu: sausage-stuffed cornish hens, wild rice and mushrooms, petit pois, and an endive salad. Conversation was lively and interesting, and continued on into the night. I was happy that the tablecloth was ample enough to hide everyone's laps. The only disconcerting sights above the table were Bob's totally shaved chest and arms and his girlfriend's small childlike breasts. We ended the evening cordially.

My strange and intense relationship with Bob lasted a few years. Besides working together, we hung out socially and talked about a wide range of subjects. One of his goals in life was to screw every single person who wore a skirt. He tried to seduce all of my female co-workers (and succeeded with a few).

One night, Bob talked me into going to a party at a club. It turned out to be a full-fledged orgy. Over a hundred participants. As Bob and I walked in the door, we were greeted by bodies, entwined limbs, drugs, liquor, and the smell of sex everywhere. My best efforts to be hip dissolved; I couldn't handle it. I insisted on getting out of there immediately. Bob laughed at me.

Some years later, a terrible thing happened. I had known that Bob was heavily into cross-dressing and trolling the streets as a woman. It was another facet of his craziness, his love of living on the edge. Late one night, as he was hanging out in drag at a fountain in Central Park, he was accosted by a group of Hell's Angels. When they discovered he was really a man, they beat him to within an inch of his life. He survived... but gradually, over the course of time, we lost touch.

Mr. Robert Maxwell is a delightful man and one of my favorites in the group of composers who worked freelance for Herman Edel Associates. I always called him Bobby. Bobby is quite famous as a professional harpist. He has some major hit songs and instrumental compositions to his credit: he not only wrote the music for "Ebb Tide" and "Shangri-La," but also penned a composition titled "Solfeggio" which became famous as the theme song of the "Nairobi Trio": Ernie Kovacs' immortal comedy invention.

A lovely and gentle person, you'd have to describe Bobby as elfin. Small features and a halo of frizzy salt-and-pepper hair. I knew him better as a session harpist than as a composer. His style of music was somewhat difficult to sell in the 'determined-to-be-hip' Zeitgeist of the early 70's. Nevertheless, we did have a few notable successes.

He and I were kindred spirits, perhaps due to our mutual love of classical music. So I wasn't too surprised when he invited Walter and me over to his apartment for cocktails and appetizers. He wanted us to meet his lady. She was a well-respected independent film producer; they had been a couple for some years.

Their apartment was in a modern building on Central Park South: the one with the big curved façade. After greeting us at the door, Bobby showed us into the expansive living room where we met his lovely lady. The only peculiarity, one that was hard to miss, was that the big room had absolutely no furniture. It was carpeted wall to wall, but that was it. I was confused. I glanced down and saw six little plates laid out in a semi circle on the carpet. I became slightly more confused.

We were invited to sit cross-legged on the floor beside the plates. Thank God, I had worn jeans. I noticed that some of the plates had some carrot and celery sticks on them, along with a few lettuce leaves.

We settled down and Bobby hovered. His better half offered us drinks, then passed around a platter of cheese and crackers.

After a pleasant interlude he said, "I guess it's time to meet the children!" Our hosts glided out into the hall off the living room and opened a door into what I assumed was a bedroom. They returned a moment later and sat down on the floor. I didn't notice at first, but following them, slowly humping up to one of the vegetable plates, was a beautiful seal point rabbit.

Okay, I have found myself thrust into some (actually, many) weird situations, but this one took the cake. Really. Cocktails and appetizers with a rabbit?! Walter and I oohed and ahed over the lovely animal, then resumed our conversation about the music business. After about 15 minutes, Bobby's lady stood up and ushered the bunny back to his room. A different door opened and a very feminine, light-colored doe rabbit joined us, delicately nibbling at her treats while we talked on.

The third rabbit was a rougher character. He looked as though he'd been in a few fights, and my guess, he could hold his own. But he was just as polite as the other two, and polished off his plate of goodies without incident.

The conversation eventually turned to bunnies. We were led by the proud parents to admire their quarters. Theirs was a big three-bedroom/two bath apartment. Those familiar with Manhattan real estate will appreciate the fact that the rabbits occupied two of the bedrooms. The two males had one; the little girl had the other to herself. Her room was decorated to the hilt. She had an appropriately sized four-poster bed complete with silk curtains and tassels, down bedding, and some stuffed animals for company. She even had a sort of grass-like play area.

But it was the sleeping arrangements that caught my attention.

The boys had to live in cages: beautifully large, painted cages, but cages nonetheless. Bobby explained to me that all male rabbits were mortal enemies. When fighting, they would each try to rip out the other's genitals with teeth and claws to prevent any future matings.

Lovely. Thanks for the visual. Of course that's why they weren't allowed to join us as a group during the cocktail hour.

After that evening, although we kept on working together, I just couldn't look at Bobby in the same way. But I have to admit: that girl bunny certainly had it made.

JOHN BARRY came to New York in March of '68. He had agreed to score the Eastern Air Lines "Second Summer" commercial for us. He was also working on the score for *Lion in Winter*. Herman put me in charge, and told me I was to attend to his every need.

I took the film timings for him; finessed the agency people during the piano meeting; booked the studio and players, and personally delivered the neatly hand-written score to the copyist. I was also privileged to assist him with a couple of choral rehearsals for the movie score. What a thrill *that* was!

The night before our session, he instructed me to pick up the score and parts from the copyist and deliver them to him in his room at the Hampshire House hotel. I couldn't figure out why. Usually, they'd be passed out in the studio... It did turn out to be a touchy situation. I was flattered, but couldn't go along with the plan.

The next morning, his music was breathtaking, and the session went smoothly. John was polite, but cold. I held my head high. Only later did I get wind of his reputation as quite the rake!

Chapter 21

Summer in Siena

————

MASTER CLASSES IN A MEDIEVAL ITALIAN PALACE? Of course I wanted to go! It was the summer of '64, just before senior year at Occidental College. And my friend, Beverly Lauridsen, ex-roommate and then cellist with the Los Angeles Philharmonic, was going with me. Once again my mother had dug up the financing: this time from her generous cousin, Lelo Alessandroni, a prominent estate lawyer in New York City.

We flew to New York and boarded the aging *Queen Elizabeth I* for the voyage across the pond. It was a pretty heady experience to be in the New York Harbor, shipside. For so many years I had gazed longingly across the river at those gigantic ocean liners docked along the West Side Highway.

The jostling of the crowd, the tiny figures waving at us from the faraway upper decks, then up the gangplank, to be greeted by the captain...

Beverly and I were booked into a twin cabin in steerage. We became buddies with a bunch of male crew members. As a result, in secret, we had the run of the whole ship. We snuck through narrow oval hatches into their quarters for drinking parties. They took us on after-midnight tours of forbidden first class areas. We never were caught. And we never had sex with them, either. They told us they didn't fool around with American girls because everyone knew they had loose morals and would infect partners with some venereal disease. It was a relief to hear this information; made our lives easier, for sure!

We took the train from Le Havre into Paris to find our cheap pension. We settled in for a few glorious days in the City of Lights.

One afternoon, as Beverly and I dodged our way through the circular stream of traffic around one of the famous monuments, a couple of guys leaned way out of their car window, yelling and whistling at the two of us. They instantly smashed straight into another Peugeot. We scurried away from the scene of the crime before the police arrived. Our last vision was of all the men standing outside the two cars, waving their fists and screaming at each other...

Two days later, Beverly and I were maneuvering our way through *Gare de Lyon*, overladen with luggage and Beverly's cello. We were there to catch a train to Rome: I wanted to visit some of my mother's relatives before motoring up to Siena. I had taken a few years of French in school, and was proud of myself as I led Beverly through the crowds, speaking a *foreign language*! We hefted the mountain of baggage up onto the train, and, with relief, settled down in our compartment. I started conversing in French with a very nice young woman.

When I told her where we were going, she asked, "But where are you stopping along the way?"

I answered, "Nowhere."

She looked startled. "This is the local train. It stops everywhere along the line. It takes days to get to Rome."

We panicked, threw all of our stuff back down onto the platform, and barely made it off the train before it chugged away.

At that point my limited command of the French language deserted me completely, and I ran around the platform like a madwoman yelling in English for someone — anyone! — to please help us.

A distinguished-looking gentleman from Malta with a well-groomed goatee and perfect cream-colored three-piece suit heard my pleas. Calmly, he pointed his silver-tipped cane toward the numbered entryway to the proper track...and we heaved the last piece of luggage onto the open area between cars as the express pulled out.

Beverly and I calmed down, and sat back to enjoy the ride. And we would have, if it hadn't been for one embarrassing problem. No matter how many times I tried to go to the "W.C." to pee, I couldn't. I would perch above the toilet seat and make the mistake of looking down into the gaping hole and the rushing railroad tracks below. The cold air that roared up between my legs instantly killed all resolve to go. I arrived at the *Termini Roma* with a painful, near-bursting bladder. There, on terra firma, all was quickly set right.

Beverly left right away for Siena, and after a few days of getting acquainted with my Roman relatives, I joined her there.

Siena was and is magical for me. The best example of an Italian walled city from the Middle Ages, unsullied by modern structures. The narrow winding streets all lead eventually into the *Piazza del Campo* where the heart-stopping *Palio di Siena* is held twice each summer.

I rented a room from a woman of disrepute on *Via del Città*, just a block or so off the *Piazza*. She was a brash, chain-smoking divorcee with thick, spiky, dyed-jet-black hair. We got along just fine (except when she was trying to wheedle more money out of me). She taught me to make *spaghetti alla carbonara* — a recipe I follow to this day. Her creepy but manageable son lived with us, as well. In Italy, most unmarried sons live with their mothers, even into their thirties. I did catch him in my room once, fondling some of my panties. Yuck! His mother screamed a blue streak at him. He left me alone after that.

An early adventure in Siena involved trying to get my practice piano — one of those heavy uprights — up three flights of the narrow circular staircase. This caused a neighborhood sensation. Entertainment for all. Men, women and children took turns sticking their heads through the street level entrance to watch as three burly piano movers sweated and struggled to lift, push and jam the behemoth up the stairs. They yelled; they swore; we all screamed encouragement. Gouges flew out from the plaster walls, little shards of wood were ripped off the piano, but it got done. On the street, I tipped them as well as I could, and they begged me not to call them when it came time to get the monster out of there.

The list of teachers (*maestri*) for the *Accademia Musicale Chigiana* was impressive. I was to study with Guido Agosti; Beverly was looking forward to lessons with the famous French cellist, Andre Navarra; Andres Segovia was on the roster for guitar.

We did get an early scare when we found out that we were required to audition in order to qualify as a 'performing' class member. We hadn't been told in advance that only a small number of the students would actually perform and take instruction from the *Maestro*. All the others would learn what they could as spectators. Come all the way to Italy just to sit and listen? We thought *not!*

But the problem didn't materialize: we both passed our auditions.

The Master Classes were held in an assortment of elegant rooms in the impressive Palace that towers over the center of town. It still belongs to the family of Conte Guido Chigi Saracini.

The salon for the pianoforte class was incredible. It was immense, perhaps 80 feet in length, and easily 30 feet wide. High overhead, a coffered ceiling rose nearly 40 feet above us. Two concert grands were set side-by-side: the maestro's instrument next to one of the long walls, the student's closer to the spectators. A grouping of elegantly upholstered little chairs was arranged in a semi-circle four or five deep, positioned to provide their occupants unobstructed views of both keyboards. Signore Agosti had only to turn slightly to address the class.

There was no other furniture: just vast expanses of gleaming parquet floor. At the back of the room, tall, long-paned windows were bordered with heavy velvet drapes, pulled back to admit the brilliant Tuscan sunlight. Hundreds of oil paintings in heavy ornate gold leaf frames filled the long walls. The works of art were jammed together, almost touching. I had never seen anything like it in any museum or anywhere else. I was later told that the Palace housed 12,000 individual pieces collected over the course of more than six centuries.

Guido Agosti was tall and slender, of northern Italian heritage, with refined features, blue eyes, and slicked-back, salt-and-pepper hair. He dressed impeccably and spoke six languages fluently, including Russian. He started out in English with me, but I was very proud that, by the end of the summer, he addressed me only in Italian. Above all, he was a brilliant teacher.

We began with Beethoven's *Appassionata* Sonata, since I had used the third movement as my audition piece. Signore Agosti loved the way I performed the third movement, but I could never master the first movement. He finally told me I was just not mature enough to understand it. We moved on.

I remember working like a fiend on Chopin's Ballade in G minor, but at the formal final concert for the rest of the students, the Count, and some selected public figures, the maestro chose two pieces for me to perform: a Scarlatti sonata and Franz Liszt's *Mephisto Waltz*. He knew the audience would appreciate the dramatic contrast between the stately, restrained sonata and the fiery, technically demanding waltz.

That summer also provided plenty of free time. I roamed every street in the ancient town. Many days I would hike up the hill to *Il Duomo* to eat lunch with the monks. The entire magnificent medieval cathedral is faced with horizontal stripes of dark green and white marble. In their great dining hall, we all ate family-style at long, bare tables. The food was simple and good. I remember the gigantic country bread loaves that would be sliced into thick slabs. Light brown-grey in color, the texture was coarse and heavy: perfect for dipping into the stew-thick minestrone. And you couldn't beat the price — a dollar or so. For dinner, I often ate the hot, crispy pizza sold from the street vendors' carts. It was topped with anchovy filets, and I grew to love them: my palate was changing.

Despite a somewhat similar climate, the less-arid surrounding Tuscan countryside was nothing like the Southern California landscape I was used to. Here, soft green hills were dotted with simple but large sienna-colored houses and outbuildings, olive groves, vine-yards and rows of perfectly spaced cypress trees. Many afternoons, groups of students would hike together through the fields. But our favorite pastime was to creep up to the centuries-old castle ruins late at night. We would do our best to scare each other with ghost stories as we huddled together, looking out over the mysterious forms of trees and buildings silhouetted in the bright moonlight.

Beverly and I both found boyfriends that summer. Well actually, I had two. I met Gianni in my first few days at the palace. He worked there in a lowly position, but he was young, cheeky, handsome — and had the run of the place. He flirted with me one day as he swept a stone pathway with one of those cool-looking twig brooms; I flirted back, and we were fast friends for the rest of the summer. Pals only; I don't think we ever even kissed. As with the crew on the *QE*, I would follow him in his uniform of dirt brown sackcloth through secret passageways up and down, from wine cellars to belfry, through the kitchens, private quarters of the family, dining and sitting rooms, to the outside private walled gardens with their population of ancient statuary.

Once, one of the maids nearly caught us in the kitchen. We scur-ried into a broom closet and hid for about 15 minutes — trying not to giggle, praying she wasn't in a cleaning mood. Then we heard her make herself an espresso and sit down to rest and enjoy it. Of course she was breaking the rules, too!

Nobody ever knew about our relationship. I would sometimes pass him in a corridor with fellow students. He would tip his cap and wink at me; I would stick my tongue out at him as soon as my friends' backs were turned. He would have been fired instantly for consorting.

When I speak Italian, I still have a hint of the Tuscan accent: a gift from Gianni. Mostly, it is the hard 'c's that are pronounced differently. In Tuscany, people soften and almost aspirate the consonant. The word 'casa' can sound a bit like 'hasa' with a throaty sound at the beginning. Coca-Cola becomes a raspy "Hoha-Hola."

My other boyfriend was Antonio. He was a serious and sensitive fellow pianist, but unfortunately had been relegated to the bleachers — the spectator seats. At least he was only 50 miles from home. We shared many long walks and deep conversations. I credit him with teaching me proper Italian. We did some making out and light petting, but that was all. He was engaged to be married, and felt terribly guilty about our relationship. I didn't.

I met his *fidanzata* (fiancée) one day on a trip to the shore near Livorno. I was horrified for him, but never said anything. It was to be some sort of arranged marriage. I have never seen such a hirsute, unattractive female. Although still in her teens, she was pudgy, had long black hair on her legs and arms (plus a thick mustache on her upper lip). She was escorted by older female relatives — crones swathed in black — who glared at me with remarkably undisguised hatred. Not because of my relationship with Antonio (we kept that well hidden), and not for my treatment of whats-her-name, to whom I was very nice; but just because of where I came from and how I looked and dressed. Her skirted swimming costume v. my bikini was reason enough.

For Beverly, it was Massimo and his motorcycle: a sexy bad boy, quite a bit older. They had one very bad experience. They didn't realize as they rolled around naked in a grassy field that it was covered with poison ivy. To her horror, the rash showed up everywhere...

Two events indelibly defined that summer. Siena is most famous for its *Palios:* a tradition that dates back to early medieval times. The *Palios* celebrate the seventeen *contrade* of Siena. A *contrada* is like a precinct or ward, but with almost mythological origins. Each is named for an animal or symbol: goose, she-wolf, wave, porcupine, etc. In the Middle Ages, they were organized to provide equal numbers of troops for Siena's many battles with rival towns. Today they remain centers of ferocious competition and loyalty. If Scorsese's *Gangs of New York* had lasted, they might have turned into American *contrade*.

The *Palio* is held in Siena's huge town square, the *Piazza del Campo*. The 15-foot-wide perimeter of the D-shaped *Piazza* is packed with 4 inches of sand to transform it into the world's most dangerous racetrack. Large trucks rumble in daily for more than a week to dump their loads; gangs of men from the different *contrade* swarm over the piles to rake them out. The center is left open for the seventy thousand or so fans and spectators who will pack into it. Ornate buildings with balconies overlook the festivities in the square: those are the places to be. I managed to wangle a seat up there for both *Palios*.

I can't stand crowds; I would have died out there in the heat of the square. As a matter of fact, people were always having to lift unconscious fans up and across the crowd into the arms of the waiting medics.

At the beginning, the spectacle was not much more than a colorful but slow-moving parade. Each *contrada* was represented by flag-carriers, jugglers, drummers and groups of street entertainers, each dressed in the colors, symbols and costumes of his *contrada*. Interesting, but after an hour, it had begun to grow tedious. But then the muffled sounds of the drums and roars from the crowd in the center began to build. Slowly, all but imperceptibly, you could sense the tension building, hear the change as nerves frayed and tempers flared in short outbursts. My heart started pounding — and wouldn't stop. I felt faint, nauseous and breathless, even in my safe perch above the melee. By the end, it was almost more than I could stand.

It all culminated in about 90 seconds of utterly uncontrolled release and brutality. Ten of the seventeen *contrade* had been chosen to enter a horse and rider in the wild, no-holds-barred race. Thrice around the track the riders rode bareback. They carried crops and were allowed to beat their own horses (and also those of their competitors). They could also beat the other riders. It was straight-out barbarism.

Additionally, the course was nothing like a racetrack oval: it included two ninety-degree corners where all the horses would bunch together, sometimes crashing into a tangled mass. It was three times around that gauntlet. In the first race, I saw one rider and one horse die.

The second Palio in August was less traumatic. Although there was the usual pileup at the first corner, no one was hurt. One rider, however, slid off his horse in the tangle and had to crawl off the track and be dragged to safety by the crowd. His riderless horse kept on running: it won by a couple of lengths. This, it turned out, was a legitimate outcome, specifically covered in the ancient rules.

Yet that night in center Siena all hell broke loose. The drunken fistfights went on and on all night. My American friends and I were interested onlookers, but could never really comprehend the depth of the passions involved. But, then, our history as a country only spans hundreds of years, not thousands.

As I look back on that carefree summer at the Count's palace, I realize it marks a kind of turning point. Nothing really bad had ever happened to me. My heart had never been broken; nobody close to me had died; I had never faced an insurmountable challenge. Life had gone easy on me. That summer in Siena ended what I think of as my personal Age of Innocence.

MY SWISS FRIEND FIFI would often take me to
swim in the pool of the *Parco dei Principe* Hotel in the
Parioli district of Rome, right next to the *Villa
Borghese*. She knew the Manager.

One afternoon we had a spirited water fight with
a group of young English musicians. Rod Steiger and
Claire Bloom — also guests of the Hotel — looked on
as we splashed about.

Fifi and I had no idea at the time that we were
frolicking with The Rolling Stones.

Chapter 22

David E.

———

I ALWAYS CALLED HIM 'DAVID E.' So did everyone else I knew. Never 'David', never 'Davis' or 'Mr. Davis' — just 'David E.' Although he was the first of my three most influential mentors in the business, I remember far less about the advertising work we did together than about our shared adventures and multi-layered relationship.

David Evan Davis, Jr. was a pioneer and a giant in the world of automotive journalism. He mentored some of the finest journalists, illustrators, designers and photographers in the country. He went from writer to both Editor and Publisher of *Car and Driver* magazine; was the founder and Editor of *Automobile* magazine and, for his entire career, car junkies from all strata of society (and from all over the world) hung on every word he wrote.

I met him after he'd pissed off so many bosses that he had to take a break from what he really loved doing to become Creative Director of Campbell Ewald: the Detroit-based advertising agency for all of General Motors. He made sure he overturned as many apple carts as possible there, too.

A few examples: while at *Car and Driver* reviewing various products, he parked a Ford Pinto in front of a junkyard and ran the picture in his article. He also trashed Blaupunkt radios, writing that they "could not pick up a Manhattan station from the other side of the

George Washington Bridge." Speaking at a Press Association meeting, he likened GM managers to the piano players in a whorehouse who were "aware of what was going on upstairs, but unable to do much about it, even if they were so inclined."

His ruined face: it was the first thing you saw when you met him, but then you forgot it almost immediately. When he was 25 and racing professionally, his car overturned and he skidded many yards face down with the car on top of him. He lost quite a few parts of his face. Plastic surgery wasn't what it is today, so from then on he always sported a magnificent mustache to cover as much damage as he could. It didn't matter at all. He stood 6'3" tall with girth to match. Forever dressed in sartorial splendor, David E. chose three-piece business suits for the office (though English tweeds were actually his favorite). I always imagined him with a monocle and walking stick.

David E. could tell a story like no one else. Maybe it was the southern influence, the Kentucky in him. He also made me think of macho man Hemingway. I have many memories of sitting around great dining tables crowded with famous people, everyone absolutely rapt as he spun his yarns.

He delighted in causing trouble, creating mayhem, stirring the pot with all of us who worked for him and always getting his way creatively (even if it meant losing a client or two). The *New York Times* labeled him a "combative swashbuckler," but his great rival, writer Brock Yates, more precisely nailed his "short fuse and penchant for unpredictable snorting charges at friendly targets."

I like to think it was David E's fearlessness and unwillingness to yield to mediocrity that helped shape me. Years later, somebody would call me "the uncompromising terror of Madison Ave." It made me proud.

My company did a lot of work for Campbell Ewald. Chevy cars and trucks, Delco, GMAC, etc. It's all a blur. I do remember meeting Mr. Slick-and-full-of-himself, John DeLorean, with his latest wife, Kelly. She was enamored of the Manfred Mann singers. As a result, I got to take another trip to London to record them — just for a vocal tag. Speaking of tags, six background singers in the U.S. once spent about an hour in the studio with me perfecting a five second tag, "Chevrolet, Building a Better Way." It was stuck onto the end of dozens of Chevy ads; that year, each singer made about $66,000 from the residuals. I sure made mental note of that. Lesson learned.

I spent a lot of time with David E. in both Detroit and Los Angeles. In Detroit, I got to know his first wife, Norma Jean, and his three children: stayed at their home a few times. He taught me how to really drive, and when it came time for me to buy a serious car, he insisted on a Mercedes. His wife and kids had just walked away unscathed from a horrendous accident on an icy New York Thruway that utterly totaled their Benz.

He picked out a grey market 450 SE for me in Germany. I had all the chrome painted slate grey. I called it my Stealthmobile. It was four inches shorter than the American market 450 SEL and could handle the corners like a sports car. It would also drop five inches closer to the road when you pushed it past 90. The thrill of that feeling of power was yet another gift from David E.

He once took me skeet shooting at some fancy gun club in northern Michigan. He fitted me with an elegant little ladies' shotgun and guided me around the course. He told me I did great, but I had serious doubts. Every time I took a shot, he would shoot too, so I never knew which one of us hit the clay pigeon. I appreciated the experience, sort of (but ended up with a sore shoulder).

Then there was a whole week together at the Beverly Hills Hotel. I think we were actually working on different projects. But we had dinner together every night and three or four times, very late at night, he would take me up to Mulholland Drive and try to scare the shit out of me, showing off his driving skills at ungodly speeds. Subsequently, when I became friends with some of his racing buddies, they did the same. I refused to bite. I would just sit there in the passenger seat, silent and totally relaxed. There was really no point in freaking out. After all, the situation was out of my hands, and I was the one who'd put myself in the passenger seat.

Ours was a complicated relationship. A daughter, trusted friend, an acolyte, worthy combatant, a comrade in arms, an equal, a thorn in his side, a potential lover. I was all of those things at times. One night on the red carpet that led into the entrance of the BHH, he shyly asked me to come up to his room and spend the night with him. He promised, "I just want to cuddle." I had to refuse: it would have ruined everything.

I last saw him at his second wedding. I liked Jeannie immensely: she matched him in style and temperament. She dressed with sophistication (often in Halston — I still remember one scarlet silk outfit in particular). Jeannie could definitely hold her own on any stage: a suitably fiery, funny, outlandish, adoring partner for him. They had many wonderful years together.

I loved David E. in so many ways...and was a complete idiot to let him fade from my life after he left the agency. I was too wrapped up in my own work, too flush with the successes of the moment. That kind of success dissipates with time, but if tended and cared for, friendships shouldn't be allowed to languish and die.

David E., I hope you can hear me: I was foolish, and I miss you!

ONE MORNING in the middle of a big orchestral
session, a well-dressed account woman with a frown
on her face said, "It sounds kind of slow to me.
Can't you take it up an octave or something?"

Chapter 23

Fountain of the World

———

M Y MOTHER FIRST MET two of the cult members behind Larry's Market in downtown Canoga Park. All three of them were there to cull through the slightly marred fruits and vegetables that had been discarded by the produce manager. They would pick out the edible pieces for their respective families.

Carol Alessandroni Hamilton was sometimes too fearless and too naive. She had a habit of picking up strangers and bringing them home. Stray animals, stray people; it didn't matter. Once, she brought home a 14-year-old girl named Grace who came from one of the worst areas of Central L.A. My mother had been giving her singing lessons at a community center, and decided she could benefit from a few days in the country. Unfortunately, Grace wasn't unaccompanied. She gave all of us head lice.

I seem to have inherited the trait of taking in strays: I've had to go through a couple of unpleasant experiences before breaking myself of it. She never did.

Years later, I took up Country and Western dancing at a local Malibu hangout. My dancing partner's twin sister left her six-year-old son at my house while we all went out to drink and two-step. My older children and their teenage friends were assigned babysitting duty. A couple of hours passed before Darcy, the oldest, called in a panic. "Mom, lots of cops here. Come quick!! I don't know what to do."

Apparently, the child had jumped up on a toilet seat, naked. Jerking his erect weenie, he'd screamed, "Look at me! Look at my cock! I'm going to fuck all you bitches!" One of the visiting girls reported this behavior to her mother, who happened to be a shrink. Understandably, she called the police and Child Services.

Another time, I was horrified to learn that one of Alex's classmates at Malibu High School was living with his mother in the bushes along PCH in Santa Monica. I invited them to stay with us for a few days. What a mistake. She was extremely well-spoken, pushy, and 300 lbs. She settled in for a free and as-lengthy-as-possible stay (she especially loved the food). The woman artfully eluded all my attempts to find proper shelter for her and her son. None of the charitable and civic service operations I contacted on her behalf would raise a finger. They'd already been there with her. I had to pay a week's rent in cash to a nearby motel to finally get rid of them.

I've learned to look at terrible situations twice as hard — you can't save people from themselves. My mother, on the other hand, never stopped until the day she died.

Sister Anne and Sister Mary were members of the Fountain of the World, a religious group that lived just a few miles from our house. It was a scruffy compound up in a place called 'Box Canyon.' From time to time, a few of the women, sometimes with children in tow, would come to visit my mother at our Carlson Circle ranch. Although my father absolutely refused to have anything to do with them, my brother, sister and I joined my mother in spending quite a bit of time up in their canyon with the whole "family."

Mother would sit and chat while we ran wild with the other kids, playing hide and seek and exploring the giant rocks and caves.

All kinds of buildings were scattered throughout the 25-acre property. Most of them had been built by the members using stones, cement, a few wooden beams: all without virtue of a single building permit. The main house was where Krishna Venta, their master — their Messiah — lived. It stood three stories tall and featured large, beautifully proportioned rooms with medieval-looking windows: small, lead-lined diamond-shaped panes. The whole place made a lasting impression on me.

Beside this imposing edifice stood a slightly smaller building that served as a dormitory for the children of the cult. All of them. The rest of the followers lived in low-lying one-story huts, each with a couple of rooms. All of them opened onto a central earthen area.

It is difficult to reconstruct their social structure. According to mom, it was very fluid. All the members took care of all of the children, not just their own. Although there were many marriages, there was also sexual freedom, and (not surprisingly, in retrospect) the Master reportedly had access to all the women.

When we walked into the outdoor common, many children would be playing in groups on the bare ground. The scene reminded me of pictures I had seen of African villages.

There were mandatory rules and dress codes. Everyone had to be barefoot at all times and in all weather conditions. No one could shave or have a haircut. The men wore monk-like robes with rope sashes, and the women dirndl-type dresses with the *WKFL* (Wisdom, Knowledge, Faith, Love) crest sewn on the front. White, frilly short-sleeved blouses were worn under the dresses; on their heads, Mother Teresa-style scarves.

Specific colors denoted different assignments. Door to door solicitors always wore grey; yellow was reserved for Krishna Venta; artists donned lavender; pregnant women all pink; students wore green, and kitchen workers, brown. Hierarchical titles were bestowed by the Master: *Brother, Sister, Cardinal, Priest, Priestess,* etc.

Krishna Venta's version of his early days was a little hard to believe. According to him, he was born 244,000 years ago, and later led a convoy of rocket ships from the planet Neophrates to Earth, landing on Mount Everest. He spent time in Rome, AD600 (and also previously lived in the Garden of Eden). He was the Messiah, thus would never die. He predicted that in 1975 he would lead a group of 144,000 to assume leadership of the United States, followed by the rest of the world. His wife, Bishop Ruth, swore he had no navel...

There were many positives about the group. The press called them "angels of mercy" for fighting the brushfires common in those dry hills. "The barefoot boys of box canyon" was the name given by grateful local fire companies. In fact, barefoot women also participated. On one occasion, they became famous for rescuing the survivors of a nearby plane crash. More than 45 people had been on board; cult members tended the survivors and helped carry out the dead.

Their motto was *Dedicated to Peace through Love and Service*, and they did in fact visit and help those in homes afflicted by illness, take in destitute people, and assist the authorities following earthquakes and floods. By allowing the media generous and frequent access to the compound, these acts of kindness were well publicized. The grey-robed solicitors took in a lot of donations as a result.

There was a dark side, of course. How could there not be? Four younger members of the Fountain of the World were convicted of murdering two young girls who had hitchhiked to the Topanga Canyon Plaza to go shopping. It was only a few blocks from our house. The two couples picked up the girls, took them to an empty house on the beach, got high, had sex, and then brutally killed them.

Charles Manson didn't appear on the scene until a decade later, but spent a couple of weeks at the compound living in what were called the Skull Caves. He adopted some of the Krishna's ideas, and is said to have toyed with the idea of taking over the property for his "family."

Entering disciples were compelled to surrender all worldly assets to the group. Although the Master preached the evils of money, he was frequently spotted at the racetrack and gaming tables. He was accused of misusing funds and of forcing himself on other men's women. Eventually, it all caught up with him.

On December 10th, 1958, two men, both of them former members, confronted him in the main house. They tried to force him to admit he wasn't the Messiah. That failing, they accused him of molesting their women. Then they blew themselves, the house and dormitory, the Master and nine others to smithereens. The firemen who responded said that one of them had strapped 20 sticks of dynamite to his body. They said just one would have done the job. It was a horrific scene.

Fifty or so members rebuilt the complex and stayed on into the '70s, but gradually their numbers diminished, and the cult eventually disappeared entirely. The widowed Bishop Ruth, who had been sent with a few children to open up a center in Alaska, returned to take over with Brother Asaiah. My mother and we kids were still frequent and naive visitors well into the '60s.

The final time I set foot in The Fountain of the World came in late 1964. Starting my senior year at Occidental College, I finally caved to social pressure and agreed to join a sorority: Delta Omega Tau. Part of the initiation was to attempt to conduct a successful "ditch." Because I had put off joining for so long, my 'ditch' had to be a solo effort.

A ditch started with the abduction of a standing member who would be held at a secret location. The trail of clues that would lead to her had to be fair: solvable through sufficiently adroit detective work.

But nobody said the clues had to be easy — one of mine was taped to the median fence in the middle of the Ventura Freeway.

My ditch was the first in years to be declared a success. The secret location was, naturally, the Fountain of the World. The cultists, who had known me for years, were thrilled with the adventure (things around the place had grown a little grim). If anyone showed up, they vowed to hide us just as the nuns had in *The Sound of Music*. They didn't have to.

FRIENDS DENNIS POWERS AND TIM NEWMAN, co-creatives at Y&R, once wrote and produced a big budget, unusually elaborate two-minute ad for Gulf Oil. It was titled "Spindletop."

The commercial opened in the ancient Arabian desert. A camel howled, the sand started to blow, and the sky darkened as a shadow crossed the Sun. The commercial won multiple awards.

The project came into being after the two read about an upcoming 'once-in-a-century' solar eclipse, and thought it would be neat to see it in person.

Now...if only they could figure out some way to get there...

Chapter 24

Sir Paul, Sir George, and Randy

———

THE POOL AREA AT THE BEVERLY HILLS HOTEL was damned hot under the blistering California sun. We sat there in street clothes, baking and sweating amidst the frolicking bikini-clad guests, awaiting the royal summons from Mr. & Mrs. Paul McCartney. We were to join them in their upper level private cabana when it was convenient. That took more than an hour.

I was in the company of a few representatives from Young & Rubicam, the giant New York City advertising agency, but I really only remember the great Lou DiJoseph: in my book, one of the best creative bosses ever. We were there to discuss Paul's musical contribution to a new campaign for Dr Pepper. The team had come armed with all manner of presentation material: big storyboards of the proposed commercials; explanations of the new line; ideas about how Paul would appear in the commercials...

Despite the discomfort of the moment, we were all thrilled he had signed onto the project, and filled with anticipation of meeting and working with this musical genius/icon. *One of The Beatles*, for God's sake!!!

Negotiations for this major talent coup had begun a few months earlier in the New York offices of Lee Eastman: renowned show business attorney, father of Linda Eastman McCartney, and lawyer/manager/father-in-law of Paul. Herman Edel, my boss at the time, and

I entered Eastman's gorgeous brownstone on West 54th Street just off Fifth Avenue. We were shown into his office. It filled an entire floor of the building which he obviously owned. Elegantly and tastefully furnished, there were numerous *objets d'art* on display: paintings, sculptures, antiques and oriental carpets. It was clear that this man was a major collector — I recognized some of the pieces. (For the umpteenth time, I thanked those art history classes at Occidental). We were shown to comfortable leather-upholstered chairs facing Eastman's French antique Louis XIV desk.

The conversation began with friendly chit-chat between Herman and Eastman. I kept quiet; I hadn't expected to be included much, anyway. I was there to learn how to conduct myself in high-powered negotiations, but also because I was the one who had the strongest relationship with the people at Y&R. I knew what they wanted and needed out of the deal.

As the two men made small talk about Eastern Europe (Herman was Romanian by origin), I let my eyes wander the room to feast on the surrounding beauty. I snapped out of my reverie as I heard Lee Eastman ask, "While you and your family were in Bucharest last year, did you get a chance to enjoy some Brancusi?" I glanced sideways at Herman's face, and recognized the blank look of incomprehension. Before he could open his mouth to speak, I actually leapt up, stomped on one of his shoes as I exclaimed, "Oh! Constanin Brancusi, one of my *favorite* sculptors of all time! I remember now that he's Romanian, even though he did most of his work in Paris. I would love to be able to go there and see his work, especially that famous trio of outdoor sculptures. Isn't it somewhere outside of the capital?"

I knew I was babbling, but Mr. Eastman took the bait and replied with an indulgent smile, "Yes, yes, you're talking about the *Ensemble at Targu Jiu*: 'The Table of Silence,' 'The Gate of the Kiss,' and 'The Column of the Infinite.' One of the most important outdoor displays of all time." I sat back down and breathed a silent sigh of relief.

Herman later told me that he had guessed that a Brancusi was some kind of sausage and was about to respond accordingly. He thanked me for saving his ass. The rest of the meeting went quite well, and we came out of it with a signed contract that pleased all parties.

Back to the Beverly Hills Hotel. At last, the summons came. We were ushered up steps and down the narrow flowered path that ran alongside the row of upper cabanas until we reached the McCartneys' private area. Once in, we arranged ourselves awkwardly on the ends of a couple of the BHH signature-patterned chaises and a chair or two.

Paul and Linda sat facing us in bathing costumes. Not surprisingly, they were both pale as sheets. They lived, after all, in England. But most striking — even mesmerizing — was the scene of her constantly applying sunscreen all over him as he tried to talk with us. She even worked on his nose and face despite his attempts to wave away her hands. It was embarrassing. She treated him as I would treat my squirming six-year-old son. Frankly, I was appalled.

The Y&R team worked their butts off presenting all the material, one or two holding up the big storyboards while others explained each scenario in detail. The line/slogan "The Most Original Soft Drink" was presented on its own, and also appeared in the last frame of each proposed commercial. Paul smiled and nodded throughout the show-and-tell session, but Linda hardly glanced at it.

After the last spot had been presented, Lou looked at Paul and asked, "So, what do you think?" Paul grinned and said, "They're good and I really like them, but I have a wonderful surprise for you. I've already written your song, and it's a hit! Would you like to hear it?"

Nobody, not a single one of us, had any idea of how to respond to this unexpected and worrisome statement. After a throat-clearing pause, I piped up with, "Sure. Of course. We'd love to!" What else was there to say?

Paul whipped out a portable cassette player and pressed the button. The song was simply done; it was classic McCartney; it had a great hook, but it had absolutely nothing to do with our campaign. It was mainly focused on the "Dr" in Dr Pepper. There was no relevance to all of the spots that had been tailored for the campaign — the precious campaign that had been worked on for months and (more importantly) sold to the client.

We all took turns trying to explain the problem to him. And we all failed miserably. I'll never forget the puzzled expression on his open and innocent-looking face. He really didn't have a clue. In his mind, I'm sure, we had asked him to write a hit song for Dr Pepper, and he'd delivered. He had been genuinely enthusiastic about doing it; had jumped right on it.

Then I made a gigantic, memorable mistake. After the guys had fallen all over themselves at length trying make Paul and Linda understand why the song had to be rewritten to fit the concept of the campaign, I said quietly, "We do have a signed contract."

Well, well, the mother lioness showed her claws. Linda leaned over Paul, picked up the copy of the contract that was lying on a side table next to him, stared at me with open hostility, held it up in front of my face and hissed, "Contract? You want to see how much your contract means to us?"

Then tore it in half and let it drop to the ground.

Obviously, the whole deal was equally torn apart. Everyone backed out of the cabana mumbling little white lies: *We'll be in touch...Sure we can work things out...Great meeting with you.*

We never had any contact with them again, which really was a loss. I had learned a valuable lesson: never challenge the person who holds all the cards. Very similar situations came up in later years later with both Chuck Berry and Marvin Gaye. With Chuck, I worked things out. With Marvin, I tried, but...

So now I had to come up with 'Plan B' for Dr Pepper. Even though everybody was greatly disappointed and annoyed, including me, the clock was ticking. Filming was scheduled to begin in a few weeks and we needed the song before we could set up anything. I racked my brains for another star singer/songwriter. We needed a celebrity — a regular jingle writer, no matter how good, just wouldn't do. I thought of Randy Newman.

I didn't know Randy personally, but I knew a lot about him through Tim Newman, who happened to work at Y&R. Tim and Randy were close: he was Randy's first cousin. I ran the idea past the agency and got a guarded okay. Tim put me in contact with Randy directly, and I sent him all the material. I can't remember if some of the creatives went out and presented it; I don't think so. In any case, I worked with Randy over the phone. That was when I made my second huge mistake on this project, but one that worked out in my favor. Sometimes you roll the dice and win.

The agency people were understandably gun-shy about working with another celebrity — now they refused to guarantee anything. They insisted on a competition for the jingle, and even hired a couple of other companies to do demos. But Randy refused to participate in any kind of competition. So I lied. Baldfacedly lied. I knew in my heart and in my gut that if Randy wrote something, it would be great, and it would win. And it did, hands down. (*Whew!*)

Randy's song was charming, catchy and quirky. In other words, typical Randy Newman. He sang the demo personally with a simple piano accompaniment. These are his priceless original lyrics:

> *We are television actors*
> *Who are paid to appear.*

We sell cars and toys and toothpaste

We sell milk and cheese and beer.

We dance if we have to

And sing to prove that we're sincere.

Now we work for Dr Pepper

And that's why we're here.

It's not a root beer,

There are root beers by the score.

It's not a cola,

It is something much much more.

Drink Dr Pepper

The joy of every boy and girl,

It's the most original soft drink ever

In the whole wide world.

I mean, really! How far from the typical jingle lyrics can you get? And of course, they include the undeniable comedic sting of truth. Granted, our ace writer, Jake Holmes, had to come in and write other verse lyrics that were later used in many of the radio commercials. But Y&R and Dr Pepper actually shot a *Chorus Line* type spot to Randy's lyrics. I'm still trying to find a copy.

This was one of my personal Top Five campaigns. The classic *Be A Pepper* is right up there, too, but this campaign was different from all of them. The first flight of ads consisted of mini-Broadway shows. I got involved in all aspects of the productions — casting, shooting, recording the actors for playback: the whole deal. I was in heaven. All of the things that were my passions.

And Barry Manilow sang solos on some of the spots. He worked for me during that period, both as a singer and writer. He became a friend, too, before his amazing rise as a solo artist. Barry included this jingle and one we did for Kentucky Fried Chicken in the commercials medley on his first album. Barry's producer, Ron Dante (lead singer of The Archies), was and is a close friend who sang on many of my sessions.

These were the early 70's: the years of fat budgets and pliable clients. For the most part the creatives and I got free rein to do what we wanted. Y&R even shot a wacky *Punch and Judy* ad for the campaign based on an idea from my childhood. As a music vendor, I was supposedly just a supplier, but I wasn't treated that way. I became part of the team, a contributing creative force. J Walter Thompson under the supervision of Jim Patterson; N W Ayer with Pat Cunningham; Leo Burnett with Rob Nolan, and Campbell Ewald with David E. Davis were other American agencies in those years who, among others, called on me regularly in that capacity. But that era of unguarded co-operation, mutual respect and admiration was short lived. It was heady and great fun while it lasted.

I met Paul McCartney again briefly in a London studio, only because I was meeting Sir George Martin there for a lunch date. Paul was most polite, but I doubt he made the Dr Pepper connection. God knows, I didn't mention it. I was in London working on some ad campaign or another, and took the opportunity to meet up with George once again. It was a continuation of our casual but sustained friendship that had started a few years before. He had come to the States to canvas and research the New York studio scene before building a studio complex of his own. It was to be in the center of London, and he wanted it to be both inviting and comfortable for American record producers and jingle people. His liason in the states was Herman Edel, who made me George's personal ambassador. Herman and George later founded a jingle company in London similar to HEA. Air Edel still exists and is doing very well.

George had sometimes followed me around from session to session and studio to studio, nominally to observe the recording studio layouts and equipment. But he was also taking in my dealings with the advertising people. At the end of some days, we would meet up at the historic Algonquin Hotel in the west 40's. We'd always stop to say 'hello' to Matilda, the hotel's Ragdoll feline mascot. She roamed free in the comfortable, elegantly appointed area that was and is a fabled meeting place. We would sit in the tiny bar that used to be located to the right as you came in the lobby (it's now the coat room), drink Scotch, and ramble on about everything.

Of course I asked him many questions about the Beatles and his contributions to their records. I was most interested in the harmony — the chord structure of their songs that was so unusual and haunting, (e.g., "Eleanor Rigby"). I had always been certain that a lot of it had to have come from George with his classical background. Not so. He gave

100% of the credit to Paul. He told me that Paul was simply a natural musical genius who found his way on the piano to these masterpieces without the need for formal training. George just executed what Paul created. Okay, but I wouldn't call the string quartet arrangement on "Eleanor Rigby" 'simple execution;' nor, for that matter, the orchestrations on their albums.

To his credit, we didn't gossip about the Beatles at all; we pretty much stuck to music and production. George is a lovely English gentleman, and I cherish the memories of the time spent with him.

It's odd how memory works. I can recall every detail about that day we met for lunch in London. I can't remember anything I have eaten at 99% of the über-fancy, three-star Michelin restaurants I've visited all over the world. Yet how clearly I remember sitting with George Martin at that plain cafeteria-style eatery in downtown London, enjoying that simple salad of mesclun greens, crispy little pieces of duck confit, slivered almonds and mandarin orange slices...

THE TONE LOC SESSION was even scarier than the Ike and Tina experience.

His studio was so filthy I couldn't find a place to set down my purse. As he worked on the track, he drank straight gin out of a plastic cup while his scantily clad lady companion flounced around the room, heaving sighs of impatience. He ignored her.

We were working on his rap version of the Burger King jingle, "Sometimes You Just Gotta Break the Rules." David Buskin and I were proud of the lyrics we had written for him. He hated them. All but spat on them.

For two hours, I was on the receiving end of an angry tutorial on rap.

The finished product impressed everyone. I could hardly bear to listen to it.

Chapter 25

When in Rome

NEWS OF MY FULBRIGHT SCHOLARSHIP came just as we were finishing a two-week international tour. The Occidental College Glee Club was under the direction of Dr. Howard Swan, a truly world class mentor who turned a glee club from our small college into an international success. I had just graduated from Oxy, and relished this last chance to tour with my college friends. I knew I probably wouldn't see many of them again.

You might get the wrong impression here, so let me make one thing clear. I am not a good singer. My tone is dreadful. I have no vibrato at all. I also have the range of a tenor. They only tolerated me in Glee Club because I had perfect pitch, could sing in tune, and, when called upon, made a damn good accompanist.

After the tour was over and we had said our tearful goodbyes, Marti Rolph, Pamela Hoiles and I went on our merry way. Marti was a Junior, headed to a year abroad in Strasbourg, France. Classmate Pamela was going to come with me to Rome to pursue her career as an opera singer. She was then as now extremely wealthy and a powerful singer. We are still close friends after more than 50 years.

In Brussels, we picked up Pamela's pre-ordered Volvo, and backtracked for a tour of London, the rest of England, and Scotland. We had a ball. I drove most of the time because I was able to adjust to driving on the wrong side of the road better than my companions.

As my Fulbright start date drew near, we dropped Marti in Strasbourg and continued on to Rome. I checked in with the Fulbright people: an oral exam was sufficient to free me from the otherwise mandatory two-week language orientation program. After that earlier summer in Siena my conversational Italian had become passable. The unexpected free time allowed Pamela and me to concentrate on finding a place to live. We rented a big two-bedroom apartment not far from the *Piazza del Popolo* and a half block from *Il Tevere*. It was a postwar 'modern' apartment with little character, but we decided it would do.

We set about looking for a roommate. Pamela and I could share the master, and our roomie could have the little spare bedroom. We found Gabriella working in the modest beauty shop on the ground floor of our building. She was a blonde with big green eyes in a heart-shaped face and a sexy little body. I was horrified when she told me she'd recently shed over a hundred pounds. In Rome, they bake delicious rolls (*panini*) with a crisp crust and soft, elastic inside with the kind of big holes you find in real Parisian baguettes. Gabriella told me she used to eat five or six of them with every meal.

She also talked about her year in Paris. She was a licensed beautician, and had found a job in a fashionable salon on the left bank. After looking at all of the svelte, stylish French women, she went on a strict diet and lost the weight quickly. It wasn't long before an admirer came calling. He was tall and thin, always elegantly dressed. They took long walks along the Seine, made out on the park benches late at night, and spent hours talking in cafes. He even read poetry to her.

Now, Gabriella was a practical sort of woman. Although she wasn't madly in love with her new admirer, he was a true gentleman who treated her very well. The thought did cross her mind that maybe he was a little *too* much a gentleman. After a few months together, he had done nothing more than kiss her. His hands never strayed. She didn't think he was a homosexual, their kissing had been too passionate, but his restraint seemed a bit strange. She was tired of being on her own, though, and convinced herself she was ready to settle down.

One night he told her he wanted to spend the rest of his life with her, whereupon his hands did roam. Gabriella was a very passionate woman and reciprocated with some of the heat she had been holding back for so long. Unfortunately, she got a shock when she finally reached her hand down between his legs. There was nothing there. He was a she. Gabriella didn't want to hear another word, never wanted to see that face again, and was so dismayed that she ran off to throw up into a trash basket. She moved back to Italy the following week.

Gabriella spoke French and Italian, but not a word of English. My first new friend in the building, Mario Franco, an 18-year-old Dominican student with sexy, heavy-lidded latin eyes, spoke only Spanish and some Italian. I made it a point to speak no English at all, paying particular attention to Italian grammar in an effort to sound as much like a native as possible. I even started dreaming in Italian. By the time we left, I could fool most Italians for about a half hour before I'd make the slip that would give me away. (When I got back to the States, I would sometimes stumble mid-sentence, searching for an English word that had escaped my memory).

I do believe that Italian is the easiest language of them all. Sure, there's the rolled *rrrrr* thing to master, but the written words are spelled phonetically, and all of the letters are sounded. The nightmarish rules and exceptions in French and English don't exist. Italian is also the prettiest language — to speak, and (especially) to sing. It has all open, pure vowels, and none of those pesky diphthongs. Have you ever noticed how pop singers never really hold long notes on "you?" They sing a drawn out 'yoh' instead.

I settled into a routine. I would get up and practice for a few hours (Pamela was nice enough to rent us a decent grand piano). Most days I'd then set off and walk to Rosati's Cafe, right on the *Piazza del Popolo*. I'd sit outside at one of the little tables, nurse a cappucino, read the paper, and people watch. The waiters all came to know me; didn't try to shoo me away, even when it grew crowded.

One week I noticed a tall, silver-haired gentleman who had been sitting at the same table for a couple of mornings. We struck up a conversation. He was from London and told me his name was Anthony Steel. It didn't mean anything to me. He was quite friendly in an avuncular way, and we chatted the next few mornings about America, England, traveling, etc. I told him about my scholarship and studies, but since he never brought it up, I didn't ask him what he did for a living.

The last morning I saw him, we were suddenly set upon by a horde of *paparazzi*. All at once a blizzard of flashbulbs were popping in my face; the photographers were jostling each other and peppering me with all kinds of puzzling questions about me and my friend. I don't think Mr. Steel spoke Italian, and I had no idea what was going on. Finally they left, and so did I.

The next day my picture with him was plastered all over the front pages of the major Roman gossip rags. Italian headlines screamed, *"Who's the Girl?"* *"Tony's New Flame. Who is She?"* *"Does Anita Know?"*

The Fulbright people were not pleased. Maestro Agosti was not pleased. I was mortified and confused. Gabriella explained everything. Apparently, Anthony Steel was a big deal in Europe. He had been a top-tier movie star, though his career was starting to fade. He had also been married to Anita Ekberg. Wow. I shielded my face for a few days, but the fuss died down quickly enough. I never saw Anthony again.

I was supposed to be attending *Il Conservatorio di Santa Cecilia* for lessons with Maestro Guido Agosti, but he soon changed our venue to his elegant apartment. He had arranged the same set up of side-by-side grand pianos as in Siena. I expanded my repertoire and made satisfying strides refining my interpretation. My teacher deserved his reputation: I was now able to understand subtleties in the music I had not noticed before. He worked with me as James Levine had worked with the singers in Aspen, and also corrected my Italian grammar and pronunciation.

I put in my due diligence, but wasn't all that happy with the isolation that went with hours of practice every day. I had always combined the piano with other activities. But here, there wasn't much else to do. For the first time in my life, I grew bored with the piano. Life's excitement was out on the streets of Rome, not sitting inside on a piano bench.

I flew back to the States for Christmas to visit my parents and sister at Aunt Helen's house in Scotch Plains, NJ. There I began to worry about my mother: she looked tired, down in the dumps, and, all of a sudden, older. It scared me. I knew she didn't like living with Helen and Uncle Charles, but there was nothing I could do about it at that moment. I stiffened my resolve to make something of myself. I would save my mother.

That Christmas I also took a trip out to Golden, Colorado to visit my college boyfriend, Chris Shelton. That didn't go so well. He confessed to seeing someone else back at Oxy, and we decided to break up. I neglected to tell him how shamelessly I had carried on with studly David Taylor throughout the whole Glee Club tour.

During my visit, I traveled with the Shelton family to Vail, where I took up skiing for the first time. I loved it. Once back in Italy, Pamela was nice enough to take me on a road trip to Zermatt, where I got to ski by myself for a couple of days while she hung out in the lodge.

Pamela was always very generous. Often when she bought something nice for herself, she would buy one for me, as well. My wardrobe improved immensely.

My Roman social life started to pick up. I also began to cook in a serious way. Gabriella taught me the dishes she knew, and I bought a couple of cookbooks written in Italian. The interest soon developed into a major passion. Today, semi-retired, I whip up at least something nearly every day. I love exploring new cuisines, discovering how to procure their exotic ingredients, then trying to replicate some of the most famous dishes. The latest two have been Puerto Rican and Persian.

By early springtime I had two boyfriends. Eugenio was a surgical intern at the teaching hospital up on *Monte Mario*, close to the Cavalieri Hilton. He was a nice young guy: kind, earnest, intelligent, and dedicated to his future profession. We went out frequently, mostly with his group of medical student buddies. We'd dine at the cheap places in *Trastevere* across the river, drink wine and talk the night away. In bed, Eugenio was considerate and thorough, if a bit awkward. I don't know (maybe it's my hang-up), but great sex with a doctor seems like an oxymoron. The word clinical comes to mind. I don't know how the wives of OB-GYNs get past it...

Nino was older, hot-looking, more experienced. He was a bad boy. We didn't socialize much. We spent most of our time together in his apartment, naked. Even after the glorious hot and sweaty episodes, he would go over every inch of my body with his hands and lips while we chatted about this and that. Europeans. I learned to accept nudity and appreciate the body I had (always wanted longer legs, though).

Nino did take me on a driving trip down through the boot of southern Italy. We stopped first in a little town in *Apulia*. This was a step back in time; starkly beautiful white buildings in brilliant sunshine. No electricity, no phones. Warm in the day. Frigid after sundown. Eerily glowing all-white buildings in moonlight.

We stayed with some friends of Nino's. They would set a brass bedwarmer full of hot coals underneath the covers at the foot of my little bed so I wouldn't freeze to death at night.

Then we motored over to the port city of Bari, where I made a big mistake. On a dare from Nino, I went all macho and ate raw mussels from a fishing boat docked at the pier. They were gross, but I swallowed a few anyway. A foolish move.

Back in Rome a week or two later, I noticed my skin was turning yellow. It got worse. Within a day or two, the whites of my eyes were a glittery orange. That night, Eugenio and his intern friends took one look at me, stuffed me into a car and drove straight up to their hospital. Diagnosed with hepatitis, I was admitted immediately and put into a little isolation room.

I called the Fulbright office to leave word that I would be in the hospital for a while, and asked them to notify Maestro Agosti. I also asked Pamela to inform my mother.

That night, alone in the tiny room, I began to freak out. This was a very Catholic hospital. Prayers were regularly broadcast over an intercom system. Mumbling pairs of faceless priests in black robes and cowls shuffled past my room, chains and crucifixes clanking at their waists. They were harbingers of my death, I was sure.

The nurses gave me a valium to calm me down. It had the opposite effect. I became hysterical, inconsolable. I bounced off the walls until dawn.

The next day, they moved me to the isolation ward for hepatitis patients. This came as a relief: a big sunny room with plenty of company. At once I began to feel much better. Actually, I had not been feeling that bad physically — just tired. The treatment consisted of nothing other than a special diet. I rallied quickly.

What I had no way of realizing was that I had created an international incident. Nobody knew exactly where I was. My mother was having a fit trying to find me. Pamela was out of town, and hadn't relayed the hospital information to her. The Fulbright people were embarrassed because they hadn't written down the name of the hospital when I had called. My mother contacted the American Embassy — they got involved in the search.

Finally, my mother managed to recruit a Roman telephone operator. She was her usual persuasive self and somehow got him to call every damn hospital in Rome until he found me. He even came to visit me so he could give an eyewitness report back to mom. The Fulbright Commission sent a representative, as did the American Consulate. The hospital personnel were impressed; I was amused.

My time spent in the hospital was actually not bad at all. The days were routine, but pleasant enough. There was only one incident that strained belief.

It was Easter Sunday, with a service planned for midday. Hundreds of chairs were placed in the wide corridor facing a makeshift altar. Every patient in the whole isolation ward who could get out of bed was forced to attend. It didn't matter what damn infectious disease you had that could spread to others, you were going! Seemed weird to me: TB next to Hepatitis, Meningitis next to Measles, etc. I have to assume the Catholic hospital believed that a service held on Easter Sunday would guarantee invulnerability to all.

It was at that amazing service that I met a delightful little Brazilian boy, also recovering from hepatitis. Marco was nine, and small for his age. A beautiful child. We became fast friends, even though he spoke only Portuguese. Between French, Italian and English, I could understand enough. Especially in the middle of the night, he took every opportunity to sneak out of his room and climb into bed with me. Most of the time the sentimental, sympathetic nurses didn't have the heart to shoo him away.

After we were both released, I visited him and his parents in their grand apartment. His father was a famous polo player, his mother, a Brazilian model. These were certainly the "beautiful people," but they didn't seem to have much time for their little boy. I took him out a few more times, but then polo season was over and they jetted off home. I felt sorry for him, but knew he had the kind of indomitable spirit that would see him through.

One day in late April, as I was crossing through the *Piazza del Popolo* on my way to Rosati's, a car screeched to a halt in front of me. A man jumped out and followed me into the café, leaving the engine running and the door open. I know it's hard to believe, but he told me he was producing a movie, and I would be perfect for it. *Yeah, right!*

But he was for real; he pursued me with phone calls and meetings. I eventually asked the Fulbright people if I could work on a movie for the next six weeks. They said absolutely not.

Even so, he did introduce me to some of the luminaries of *Cinecittà* (the 'film city' created by Mussolini in the '30s). I'll never forget two separate trattoria evenings with Italian biggies: Mastroianni (gorgeous), Fellini (always in black), Masina (intense), and Cardinale (breathtaking, even without makeup). One of the hangers-on let me drive his Lamborghini all over the streets of Rome late one night. Heady stuff.

As all good things must, my scholarship came to an end in June. Pamela and I scheduled a voyage on the *SS Rotterdam* with a bunch of other returning American students.

Our last night in Rome was one to remember. I had given up the master bedroom so Pamela could finally spend the night with her Italian boyfriend Bepe. He was a fisherman from the town of Gaeta who spoke no English. Since she spoke only little Italian, their conversation was limited. But they loved spending time together, and this last night was going to be a first time event for her.

I had my own problems. I had to say goodbye to two boyfriends who didn't know about each other.

Eugenio came and left fairly early, responding to my pleas for rest before the next day's journey. We were just finishing our lengthy farewells when I heard Nino's whistle from the courtyard. With a final kiss for Eugenio, I sadly turned, head hanging, and softly closed the door one last time.

Once inside, I had a knuckle-gnawing moment, considering the possible outcomes a chance meeting of the two might bring. But I'd timed it well.

Nino came up in the second elevator and was his usual chipper self. I didn't sleep much after Nino left. Gabriella and I stayed up talking, and I had to reassure Pamela around two in the morning that all was well. I also left Gabriella my diaphragm. In Italy, in those days, it was almost impossible for single women to come by any kind of birth control.

For the last few months in Rome, I had struggled with a major life decision. In the end, I chose to give up the pursuit of a career as a concert pianist. It was not for me.

I was filled with terrible guilt at the thought of all of the money and effort that had gone into giving me my chance to become a famous artist. I had the talent and the work ethic — but I didn't have the chip on my shoulder that would compel me to shut myself off from the rest of the world to prove the point. Without the distractions of the well-rounded life at Oxy, I might have caved to the pressure and stayed the course. But that hadn't happened. I was deeply saddened to disappoint all of those greats who had believed in me: James Levine, Rosina Lhevinne, Guido Agosti, Robert Gross at Oxy, Mr. Voorhees, my teacher through high school. But the life didn't suit me. It was too lonely. I knew it wouldn't make me happy; and if I weren't happy, nothing much would come of it.

I figured it was better to act now, rather than as a burnt-out 40-year-old whose career had gone nowhere. I made the choice to be true to myself — who I really was — not who people expected or wanted me to be.

Unexpectedly (but, actually, true to form), my parents didn't care much. They understood when I explained to them, and were eager to support me in whatever my next endeavor might be. They weren't the kind of parents who live vicariously through their children. They also must have respected my judgment, believed that I knew myself well enough to make such a life-changing decision about what was best for me. What was best for them never entered the picture.

ALESSANDRO INVITED ME to have lunch with him at a lovely restaurant overlooking a lake just north of Rome. Spring lamb, a Roman specialty, was in season. We had dated a couple of times. Although I was fond of him, I *loved* his Alfa Romeo convertible.

The drive was beautiful; the lunch was fabulous. As we were having espresso, the proprietress came over and said, "Your rooms for the siesta are ready."

Not wanting to offend, I sat on the bed of the charming room, twiddling my thumbs and wondering what I was going to do for an hour. (I am not a nap person).

The interior door to the adjoining room slammed open to reveal a grinning Alessandro hopping back and forth from one foot to another. He was stark naked.

As he jumped me, I put my hands on his shoulders and pushed hard. He fell back on the bed and I escaped.

The atmosphere in the Alfa on the way back was no longer friendly.

Chapter 26

A Gordian Knot

I HAD NO IDEA WHAT DANGER I WAS IN. This was just a late afternoon meeting at Young & Rubicam. Mike Slosberg and I were comfortably seated in his spacious office on one of the upper floors of the Agency. He was a top creative director, and I knew him pretty well.

Rays of the setting sun slanted through the tall windows onto his elegant oriental carpet. We were discussing the jingle that needed to be written for their upcoming pitch — to win the Keds sneakers account. As usual, Y&R had waited until the last minute to call me in.

The situation was a bit odd for my company, but the same thing had occurred several times in recent years. Sometimes it would happen that two different advertising agencies, both of which worked frequently with HEA, would be participating in a competition for a new account. In some cases they would agree to let me and my people work on both campaigns. There was always a tacit agreement of nondisclosure, so I never worried about it. My people were trustworthy. The first time this happened I felt a little weird about the situation, but I became more used to it as HEA became more successful. Nothing bad had ever happened.

In this case, we had already finished all the work for N. W. Ayer's pitch. Done and delivered. So I listened patiently and attentively as Mike went through his whole spiel. The rationale, the backstory, previous failed campaigns, the market share, demographics, etc. Usually, I appreciated being let in on an agency's 'work platform' — all the inside information about a company and the agency's thinking behind the proposed advertising campaign. It was important stuff, and Mike was a smart man, but I had heard most of it before from the N. W. Ayer people.

It was time to cut to the chase. It was a Friday afternoon. I needed to know what the line was. I needed to hear Y&R's slogan for their Keds campaign. Mike got up and strode purposefully to his back wall where a large piece of foam board was leaning against the bookshelves. With a dramatic flourish, he spun it around.

I almost died on the spot. It was N. W. Ayer's line. The very same words, only in a different order. I don't remember either line exactly, except that they both used the same stupid pun dealing with 'feet' and 'feat.'

I was speechless. I had no idea what I could say, but I did know one thing for certain: I was truly fucked no matter what happened. If either of them won, the other would certainly blame me somehow and assume I had spilled the beans. Or accuse me of favoritism, of doing a better job for the agency I liked better.

It didn't matter if I opened my mouth and tried to discuss the predicament I was in. It didn't matter if I kept it shut. I was doomed. In a flash, I understood what it felt like to be under the Sword of Damocles.

I wouldn't even be able to ask mentoring advice from other ad bigwigs who weren't in the competition. There was no time. I couldn't very well say, "Uh, Mike, let me get back to you on this." I had to react to the line. I realized I had been silent for a long time. Mike was staring at me.

I don't know where the idea came from. Maybe there is a God, after all. I looked earnestly into Mike's eyes and cleared my throat.

"Mike, this is a really good line, I know. It's clever, fun and memorable and I'm sure we could come up with a catchy song for it." (*long, deliberate pause*) "But there's something else you said about 20 minutes ago that resonated with me. I mean, deeply resonated. It had a lot of emotional punch, and I can't stop thinking about it.

"It was when you were talking about the moments when ordinary people make impossible-seeming shots, moves, dunks, hits — whatever — while they're in their Keds. Just like the pros. So what do you think about a line something like: *Keds. For all those moments you feel like a pro?*"

I sold it hard. And it happened: slowly, miraculously, he came around. He told me he loved it. Said he would present it in the morning to his team and to the account people.

They bought it and loved it, too. Jake Holmes wrote a great song; I produced a great track. Y&R won the account.

The cards fell my way that day, but I don't even want to think about what would have happened if N. W. Ayer had won. We probably would never have worked for Young and Rubicam again...and they were our biggest clients.

By the way, I have never told this story to anyone on the agency side of the business. I'm not sure I even told my people at HEA — at least not until we had won.

DAVID BUSKIN AND I attended a secret evening meeting at Y&R. We were in Frazier Purdy's huge executive office with a bunch of bigwigs, and the two of us were in a wacky mood.

We had decided to count the times the agency people said, "in any way, shape or form." After the third time, we couldn't even look at each other.

But when Frazier told me, spitting with intensity, "Susan, we're talking *serious deoderancy* here!" David and I both lost it.

Chapter 27

Walter

————

WHEN HE CAME TO WORK AS A WRITER for my boss, Herman Edel, Walter Raim was at the top of his game. To me, he was an irresistible alien creature with his red goatee, granny glasses, beret, leftist philosophy, cynical humor and altogether super cool attitude. I was hooked. Within a few months, we were dating, and I was spending weekends at his vacation house in Bondville, Vermont. He was an accomplished skier, and especially because I'd had an earlier taste of the sport, I was determined to become one, too.

I've been skiing ever since. Took hundreds of lessons and paid my dues, going up on the mountain every day I could (even the 20-below ones), howling wind or not. Eventually, I could handle nearly any trail — years later, I was even offered a low-level instructor position with the Aspen Ski School.

In the Vermont summertime, Walter and I rode motorcycles: enduro style, off-road biking. I soon had my own Honda 90; then a Bultaco 125. It was the most exhausting sport I ever took up. Dragging your bike through rivers and mud, changing the spark plug by the side of a hot dusty trail, picking yourself and your bike up after a fall on a rock-strewn trail (or an encounter with a tree); I ate more dirt and injured myself more often than with all the other sports combined. But after a ride, I learned to love the miraculous effect of an ice-cold beer.

I even entered a couple of real 26-mile enduro races, with checkpoints and everything! Sure wouldn't be able to do it today...

On the weekends, we had a true and wonderful hippie scene going. An assortment of a dozen or so regulars populated the house every weekend, including my best friend, Sherry Reaser, who worked with me at the office in Manhattan. She eventually married a local Vermonter, and still lives happily there. All the friends hung out on the back deck, smoking weed. I spent a lot of time in the kitchen, cooking.

There was the time I happened upon a magazine article with the headline, "Buffet for Sixty." I said to myself, *I could do that!*

Walter and the boys built a long, massive dining table for me. I heated up the sauna and put it to use as a holding oven. It was late fall, so I was able to use the outdoor deck as an extra refrigerator. I invited all the townspeople whose names I could remember, cooked for days — and pulled it off!

My relationship with Walter was complicated: probably doomed from the start (as so many of the others were). He was nine years older than I and much more sophisticated. I was infatuated, slightly in awe. When we met, we were at opposite points in our respective careers. I was at the bottom, at the beginning of a swift rise. He was at the top, starting what would become a slow decline. As time passed, there was a definite shift of power. Walter was an intellectual: emotionally (much like my father), a withholder. As a result, I felt compelled to please him, impress him. But over the years, I became less compliant. More rebellious.

A good friend of ours, Jane Christopherson (a former love of Walter's), and I took a girls-only weekend ski trip up to Stowe. It was at the end of my first full year of skiing. She was an instructor with impeccable style. I trained my eyes on her and followed in her tracks for two entire days.

We hung out in the bars, flirted with the local guys, drank beer and talked a lot. She encouraged me to get out from under Walter's influence. Symbolically, we hung the lumpy, dark blue, warm-up ski pants Walter had bought for me up on a tall fencepost along the highway, and never looked back. I bought a sleek matching outfit the next day. It cost a fortune: I didn't care.

Four years into the relationship, Walter insisted we get married. For tax reasons, he told me. Not the most romantic proposal. I felt uneasy about it, tried to ignore a vague sense of dread, but reluctantly caved to his plan. I wasn't sure I loved him, but I did love our lifestyle in NYC and in Vermont: working intensely together in the studio, tra-

veling and skiing together, and the whole upbeat scene with our
Bondville crowd. Besides, somewhere in my head there was the
optimistic notion that I could always get a divorce if things didn't
work. Great way to start a marriage...

We were married by a Justice of the Peace in the living room of
Walter's Vermont house with a few close friends attending. After the
brief ceremony, we went out to a local restaurant. No big deal. We
were living together following the "interpersonal relationship" philosophy of psychiatrist Harry Stack Sullivan: an 'open' agreement in
which dating other people was encouraged, as long as the 'primary'
partner was kept informed. I'd hated the concept from the beginning,
but was forced to become accustomed to it. Subconsciously, perhaps, I
contemplated revenge. And in the last year or two of our marriage, I
took full advantage of the rules: those Stratton Mountain Austrian ski
instructors were most attractive.

Things between us got worse. It turned out that Walter didn't
like my carryings on with the Tyrolean Boys (or random rhythm
section players in the City). He couldn't really say anything. After all,
he had been the one to pressure me into the dumb, unsustainable arrangement.

Meantime, money was rolling in. I hadn't been spending much,
but now, I started buying things. I bought my first car: a BMW Bavaria.
I hated it almost immediately, and got rid of it in favor my beloved
Mercedes 450SE a year later.

I decided to buy my own Vermont house just down the road
from Bondville, in the little town of Jamaica. I told Walter it was for
investment purposes. To my shock, even though I had no debt and a
high-paying job, the local banks wouldn't give me a mortgage unless I
produced a co-signer. The manager, an avuncular New Englander,
soothingly explained that I was attractive and of childbearing age, so of
course they couldn't trust that I would be able to pay off the debt —
especially in just 15 years, as I was requesting.

I was furious. It was the first time I was made to understand that
I was a second-class citizen living in a man's world. I swallowed my
pride and allowed Walter to co-sign the loan. The experience sealed
my determination to become totally independent.

I started restoration work on the old farmhouse within hours of
the closing. I was working with a talented young architect/builder. The
day before, the area had suffered major damage from the remnants of
a hurricane, so we had to ride in on motorcycles to get to the property
— most of the highway had been washed away. We spent that after-

noon smashing the old plaster walls with ball-peens and sledge-hammers, pulling out years of stinky rats' nests, and drinking beer. Yes, predictably, this turned into a hot (though short-lived) affair. He turned out to be a little shaky, ethically. When I discovered some financial monkey business (he'd used my money to save his ass from the consequences of some previous bad judgments), I threw him out. It would not be the last encounter of this kind.

Walter was slowly disappearing from my personal life, but we were still working together all the time. It was sad for him, I think. He knew the writing was on the wall for our marriage. I overheard him tell a friend, "Well I hope I get to spend some time in her new house." It had a happy ending: Walter ended up spending a lot of time at the house after all. Just not as my husband.

We worked out the divorce amicably; in fact, it was the only one of my three that ended without the least bit of rancor. More surprisingly, we stayed friends. Not just business associates, but actual close, confiding friends. We socialized on weekends; he asked my opinion on all of his girlfriends (I hated the NY lawyer one).

I finally set him up with my former college roommate, my good friend, Marti Rolph. They were married in my co-op on East 64th Street. Eliot Scheiner, my second husband, was the best man, and I, the matron of honor.

Walter died of Parkinson's disease a few years ago. Marti and their two kids are doing just fine, and she and I are back in touch. When I think about Walter, I miss him. Good and true confidantes can never be replaced.

WALTER BOUGHT ME a beautiful antique pink-gold, spring-cased Patek Philipe pocket watch, strung on a long 18 karat chain. He'd purchased it at one of the little booths you find in stores in the Diamond District on 47th street.

One day Walter took me into the back room of that jewelry store to introduce me to an old man named Bernie. He sat in a big wooden desk chair, wearing the same dirty light blue cardigan sweater he always wore. His dusty office was tucked behind locked doors. I could never tell exactly what he did there.

He took quite a fancy to me. He told me to call him "Uncle Bernie." I would stop by to visit sometimes (A&R was just down the street).

One time he told me in his heavy Yiddish accent, "You're a pretty girl and I like you. If any of your boyfriends give you any trouble, you just tell your Uncle Bernie, and I will see that they don't walk so good anymore."

He was serious. After that, I was, too. It was my last visit.

Part III

BIG TIMES

Chapter 28

Berry Mansion

———

I SIGNED MY LIFE AWAY one cold rainy afternoon in a lawyer's office in Manhattan. Or so I thought at the time. It was 1974, and I had just bought out my boss, Herman Edel. I was now president and owner of HEA Productions.

It had been a contentious negotiation with threats of criminal action on his side countered by the *I'll just walk away and hang out my own shingle* attitude of mine. It was a five-year payout, and I signed all the papers in red ink with a rebellious flourish. My worries that I wouldn't be able to make the payments were short-lived. Company profits would soon skyrocket, and I paid him off early.

Eliot Scheiner, engineer extraordinaire, was waiting outside. We headed straight for La Guardia, on our way to St. Louis to record Chuck Berry for a Dr Pepper radio campaign.

At the gate we met up with the team: Dennis Powers, freelance producer and former Y&R employee; Jim Desmond, cinematographer for *Monterey Pop*, straight man on TV's *Candid Camera*, and successful actor/comedian; Jim's new sound guy, (a source of worry because he had never before flown on an airplane); and suave Bernard Drayton, salesman and producer at HEA.

The film crew was an unusual component for a radio campaign. They were creating a documentary that would be screened at the upcoming Dr Pepper Bottlers' Convention. They had been filming and interviewing every Dr Pepper artist as I recorded them. There had been more than 20 already: legends like Loretta Lynn, Muddy Waters, Doc Watson, Ike and Tina Turner, Eubie Blake, B.B. King — the list went on and on.

For this session, Bernie had handled the personal communications with Chuck and his people. We felt honored: they had arranged for us to stay at Berry Mansion. Apparently, Chuck had insisted we stay there instead of a more conveniently placed hotel in downtown St. Louis, where his studio was located.

Bad weather, heavy turbulence and a major backlog on the runways caused us to be thoroughly late to St. Louis. We also had to deal with the weird freak-outs our sound guy pulled. I'm surprised the pilots didn't make an emergency landing somewhere. He wasn't violent, just scared, standing in the aisle mumbling, stumbling, and flailing about. We babied him, got him calmed down, and everyone managed to survive the flight.

It was close to midnight when we finally landed. The airport was deserted: not a soul in sight. Amazingly, we retrieved every bit of luggage and equipment from baggage claim. At the Hertz counter, a sleepy, uncooperative agent professed to have no reservation for the two large station wagons we had requested. In fact, he had no cars at all.

Perfect. We were thoroughly screwed. I looked down the long empty concourse and spotted two distant figures. One looked familiar. Leaning against an escalator wall lounged the tall, lanky black man with his arm draped across the shoulders of a blond waif of a girl. I don't think she could have been much more than fourteen.

We hurried toward them. At the last moment he straightened up, flashed the familiar Chuck Berry grin, and said, "Howdy, I've been waiting for you folks."

The blond waif had on tight jeans, a tie-dyed shirt, tall shoes, and almost no makeup. She was very shy. She kept turning and burying her face into his shoulder. He was dressed like a lounge lizard and slouched appropriately: shiny slacks, polyester semi transparent short-sleeved shirt, little black hat. Clean-shaven, he looked amazingly young for the years I knew he had to have on him.

All smiles and charm, he took us back to the Hertz counter and, after a few words with the clerk, we had our station wagons. Chuck told us to follow him out of the garage. It wasn't long before a giant pink pimpmobile Cadillac exploded out of the tunnel. We pulled out behind it, and sped off into the night.

We drove on and on for the better part of an hour. Mostly on an expressway, or interstate; whatever. I was exhausted. After the confrontational day I had endured in Manhattan and the endless flight, all I wanted was a semi-decent hotel room and a bed without bedbugs. But no, no, no; we had to stay at Berry Mansion. I cursed Bernie in my mind.

All of a sudden, the pink monstrosity screeched into a Denny's parking lot. Chuck jumped out. "Thought you folks might want to eat. God knows I'm hungry for something tasty." With a wink, he led us into the restaurant. It was filled with young people out after some kind of sports event. The boys wore uniforms with colorful sewn-on corporate logos and embroidered names. Bowling, Baseball?

They were all white people, and we certainly got the steady stares as we sat down. We received zero attention from the wait staff. Other customers around us were being served promptly. It didn't take long before Chuck got up; he must have had a word with the right somebody because suddenly waiters were stumbling all over themselves to get us whatever we wanted.

I was beside myself. It was now almost two am. All I needed was a bed. But no — off we went into the darkness. This time on side roads. It was another 10 minutes before we got our first glimpse of Berry Mansion.

Now, I had envisioned rolling green lawns and tall alabaster pillars in front of a gracious plantation manor. Instead we saw hundreds of feet of cyclone fencing topped with triple barbed-wire strands under a peeling billboard sign which read *Welcome to Berry Mansion, Summer Camp for Inner City Children.*

We followed the Caddy down the long driveway and pulled into a deserted parking lot. Chuck and his chippie disappeared immediately. We never saw her again, and didn't see him until the following morning.

Piling out of the station wagons, we found ourselves in a dark, unlit wasteland of broken glass and cracked asphalt. Poking up through the cracks, stalks of dead weeds topped by dried seed pods rattled in the night breeze. I had been thoroughly pissed at our situation, but now I was also a little scared.

We were startled when a strange figure appeared out of the black. In all my life I have never encountered a weirder-looking person. Very slight, with short black hair and wearing mismatched disco clothes, she held her head down and off to one side whenever she spoke, never once making eye contact with any of us. Asymmetrically formed, she had a pronounced limp and sideways crablike shuffle. Sneaking a glance at sexy Bernie, she exclaimed, "ooh la, la!" The name 'Igor' came to mind, but we settled on 'Lola.'

Lola ordered us to follow her and led into one of the dark buildings. When she turned on a light, we were greeted by a line of rusted, open-lidded freezer chests, broken soda machines, and ancient cracked Formica counters, all set before a full-sized, decrepit stagecoach on exhibit behind a wrecked stretch of corral fencing.

Lola led us down a motel-like corridor with numbered doors on one side only. She said, "You can have whatever rooms you want" and left.

The rooms were filthy and appropriately hideous. They had deep shag carpets and long-haired, fuzzy lime green bedspreads with the kind of stains you wouldn't want to think about. I'd rather not describe the bathrooms. Use your imagination. Eliot and I just stood there and looked at each other. What was there to say?

Before we had time to gather our wits and figure out where and how we were going to get some sleep, there came a *rap, rap, rap, - rap, rap, rap, - rap, rap, rap* on each door in succession. Everyone yanked open their doors. *What the hell now?*

Lola stood sideways at the end of the corridor. "Just wanted to warn you guys. Don't open any windows. Don't leave your rooms. I've let the dogs out."

Chuck's Cadillac pulled up beside our rent-a-wagons about nine a.m. There was no sign of the waif. With no coffee, no showers, and no food, we were all sleep-deprived, grouchy and jumpy. But it was a sunny, beautiful Friday (and we were all professionals).

It took well over an hour before we swung into the parking lot of the warehouse that held his studio in downtown St. Louis. As we rolled to a stop, Jim Desmond jumped out with the big Arriflex camera on his shoulder to get an establishing shot of Chuck's arrival at the studio. That didn't go over well. The resulting footage shows Chuck leaping from his car and charging the camera with snarling ferocity. His huge hand reaches forward to cover the lens and wrench the camera away. He is yelling, "*No pictures! No pictures!*"

I was new: still quite naive about the business of dealing with celebrities. I couldn't believe Chuck was pulling this stunt. I had personally negotiated the filming as well as the recording details with his manager. I had a *signed contract*. Yeah right. Meant nothing. Live and Learn.

We followed Chuck into his studio complex. Eliot and the rest of the team went about trying to figure out how to record or film anything. The place was dark and dirty. In the cramped control room, there were no faders, just left-to-right knobs. A few of them didn't work at all. I guessed it had originally been a radio station studio.

At his request, Chuck and I settled down on a couple of wooden crates for a talk.

At the time I was not yet familiar with the infamous Chuck Berry '$5,000-more-at-the-last-minute' rule, but that's what was in play. After a couple of calls back to New York, I managed to get agency approval for the extra money.

Further negotiations then proceeded.

In pencil, I hand wrote the new contract he dictated to me on the backs of several blank envelopes. There were no regular sheets of paper around. We both signed it. His signature was about three times larger than mine. I never bothered to discuss this development with either the agency or Dr Pepper. I figured the contract was probably non-binding. I certainly was no lawyer, and we already had a signed contract from his manager that bevies of Y&R lawyers had gone over with fine-toothed combs. Now I just wanted to get the damn job done and get home.

Chuck's smiles now returned and the legendary charm was switched on full force. We had already recorded tracks, so we only needed to add his guitar and vocals.

When he started playing his guitar, I suggested a bit of tuning up. He didn't like that. He pretended to agree and fiddled with a peg or two, but when I asked for a little more, said, "Look lady, that's part of my sound. Live with it." All with another toothy smile and a wink. (He was always winking.) I lived with it; and in truth, I was dead wrong. In the end it sounded great. Definitely authentic.

The vocals were a pleasure to record. The guy was really a pro. Tons of personality and attitude, and he knew the song cold. We got a bunch of takes and in a very short time. I knew I had plenty of material to be able to compile a great performance. Of course it was a little difficult to judge because we didn't get to hear some of our previously recorded instruments. They just wouldn't play from the 24 track machine through the broken faders. Oh well. We just imagined them.

The on-camera interview was also a breeze, and just terrific. His face had a Jim Carey kind of elasticity, and he oversold the product with humorously broad grimaces and lots of winks. It was highly amusing. I knew everybody — including the bottlers — would just love it. And they did.

It was late afternoon and we all wanted out of there. I thanked Chuck profusely while Eliot and the film crew packed up. We were ready to head for the airport. As I turned to go, I felt a hand on my shoulder. Chuck held out his free hand, palm up. He said, "Where's my money?"

I laughed because I thought he was joking.

He wasn't.

When I realized that he was deadly serious, I explained that, as was customary, the monies would be sent to his manager's office within a week or two.

That was not going to do it for Chuck. Patiently, he explained he was only talking about the extra $5,000. He wanted it now, and he wanted it in cash.

He explained further. "You're not leaving here until I get it. The tape is not leaving here, and your people ain't leaving here, neither."

I was dumbfounded. *What the fuck?!*

I thought fast. It was late on a Friday in St. Louis, even later back East. I wouldn't be able to find anyone at Young & Rubicam. Explaining the situation to the client — Dr Pepper in Texas — was out of the question. On the bright side, at least I didn't have to run it past Herman Edel anymore.

I picked up the phone and dialed my office. God was merciful, and someone was there. I had them wire the money out of our account to the Western Union facility in downtown St. Louis. I told them it was ransom money. I was serious.

Chuck ushered my people and the tape into a back room of the storage building. Pulling out his key-ring with a flourish, he locked them in.

I'm not kidding.

Given the circumstances, they took it in stride. They probably thought it was a charade, a joke. I was a lot more nervous than they were. What would happen to them if something happened to me? No magic cell phones in those days...

Chuck and I rode Downtown in style in the pimpmobile. He waved to quite a few local fans as we went. He was certainly well known in this city.

I had to wait at least 30 minutes in the grimy, run-down Western Union office with its barely moving line of beaten-down customers —

but eventually, the money arrived. I came back to the car where Chuck was double-parked. He wanted the money right then, but I wouldn't give it to him until I had the tape and my people.

I got to count it out into his hands with them watching, wide-eyed and open-mouthed.

It wasn't over. He absolutely insisted that we all go out with him for some soul food. I was toast; no fight left in me. Just gave in, so off we trooped in the station wagons and the pink Cadillac to a cafeteria in one of the scariest parts of town. There he was treated like the rock star he was, a true icon, a symbol to everyone of aspiration and extraordinary success.

And damn, the food was good!

THE FULL ORCHESTRA TOOK UP nearly every square inch of the biggest studio at A&R. I was producing a 60-second score for a Chuck Jones-like animated commercial requiring scads of musical sound effects. A goodly amount of the studio floor was occupied by the percussion instruments. In addition to the larger items like tympani, xylophone and a snare drum, all the little sound effects paraphernalia (including mandatories like the slide whistle and vibraslap) were carefully laid out on two folding tables.

The challenging, complicated composition took much rehearsing. The two percussionists had to work out their choreography. They had to quickly jump from one instument to another, criss-crossing each other in a kind of manic dance.

We were three-quarters of the way through a perfect take when the recording was interrupted by horrible gagging sounds. I looked up to see that one of the percussionists had made a disastrous move. They were audibly choking on the headphone wires hopelessly wrapped around each others' necks.

I called a break.

Chapter 29

The Big Sound

———

IN THE EARLY '70s, a new kind of jingle began to emerge. We were entering two decades of widely accepted excess: more and more, most expensive, bigger and bigger grew into virtues that were seldom challenged. The ad agencies were quick to catch the wave. More often than not, music for advertising sought to emulate hit records, usually after a six-month or so delay. I don't even want to think about how many times I was asked to rip off this record or that movie score. *Chariots of Fire*; Toto; *Shaft*; ABBA, *The Mission* and The Beatles come to mind. No single style was favored: if it was a big hit, it qualified.

But the Big Sound movement was different: more defined and unique. It lasted for more than 12 years. Perhaps because it reflected the era's Zeitgeist instead of any particular chart-topper in *Billboard* magazine.

The 'Big Sound' should not be confused with 'The Wall of Sound' famously created by genius, madman, and convicted murderer Phil Spector. True, both systems used the layering of sounds. But Spector relied on recording countless numbers of tracks: mostly different kinds of guitars playing the same part over and over, then mushing them all together with obscene amounts of echo that often buried the lead singer. Yes, he used some orchestral instrumentation, but it was never featured — it just slurried into the reverberating, glorious messy mass of The Wall.

In those days, echo or reverb was created through the use of actual physical echo chambers: usually basement rooms or wooden compartments set up with speakers, microphones, and, sometimes, plates. Even bigger spaces like an empty staircase or large bathroom might be used. The signals from the studio microphones were sent to the chamber and reverberated throughout. The newly echo-laden sounds were sent back up to the control room to be recorded on tape. Sometimes the engineer would have to stop a session and run down to adjust something in the chamber. There were lots of creepy-crawly stories about the various creatures that lived in the dim light down there.

The 'Wall of Sound" approach wouldn't do for jingles. It was too 'dirty' and overwhelming. Creative elements in the advertising world needed clarity, definition, and cleanliness. Almost always, our jingle cakes were made with white or yellow cake layers, vanilla butter cream frosting, with perhaps a few multi-colored sprinkles of triangles, finger cymbals, orchestra bells, or a celeste.

In the late '60s and for the first couple of years of the '70s — before the onset of the Big Sound — jingles (especially supposedly rock 'n roll ones), were done with a small group of rhythm section players and a few singers. I remember that Charlie Calello and Artie Schroeck were occasionally allotted a few extra dollars to add a small (no more than seven) compliment of violins on their sessions at Olmstead. Full orchestral sessions were generally reserved for dramatic underscores composed for TV ads. These would be recorded with a conductor directing all of the players at the same time.

For the new Big Sound sessions, though, my process was very different. I would start with just the rhythm section: drums, electric bass, a couple of guitars, a keyboard player and often a hand-held percussionist. Many of these boys were up-and-coming stars in the wider music industry. They were featured players on major movie scores and records, often performing with the most popular groups on live concert stages. Many went on to become solo artists themselves. That all-star list would have to include drummers Steve Gadd and Rick Marotta; bass players Tony Levin and Will Lee; guitarists David Spinozza and Elliott Randall (who could forget his solo on "Reelin' In The Years?"); keyboard players Richard Tee and Don Grolnick; percussionists Ralph McDonald and Crusher Bennett.

Those rhythm section musicians would lay down the foundation: the basic structure of the tracks that established the 'feel,' the 'groove.' After the best takes were chosen, another rhythm guitar part or electric solo would be added on another track, possibly followed by an additional percussion overdub of small stuff like a shaker, tambourine or triangle (the sprinkles on the musical cake). We now had 24 tracks at our disposal — numbers way beyond our dreams only a few years before.

Next to arrive would be the horn section. Generally, a couple of trumpets, a trombone, an alto or tenor saxophone, and a bass trombone or baritone sax. These were the hip cats, the wild boys. Slightly older and more experienced than the rock 'n rollers of the rhythm section, these guys (they were all guys) were the bad boys I would have to watch. In certain years, I had to check them all for white residue under their noses as they emerged from the restroom. Most often they included some of the following: trumpeters Randy Brecker, Alan Rubin and Jon Faddis; trombonists Billy Watrous, Tom Malone and David Taylor; saxophonists Lou Marini, Michael Brecker and Ronnie Cuber. All of them were already (or well on their way to becoming) jazz icons. They would perform their parts, maybe double them, and leave. ('Doubling' or 'stacking' is playing the same exact parts — the same notes in the same rhythm — on a separate track. It creates a fuller, bigger sound).

Then came the mice. Yeah — that's what we called the string section. Actually, it referred mainly to the violin players. Most of the viola players and the cellists were talented classical musician oddballs just trying to survive in NYC. They played in the pits of Broadway shows, jingle sessions like mine, and filled the limited number of seats in local orchestras whenever available. My sister Janet was a cellist for Broadway and the studio scene (she once got to go on a world-wide tour with Paul Simon and his band).

Because there were so few of them, the classical upright bass players (the ones who usually play with a bow) were stars in their own right. They were longhairs: very different animals from the fabulous jazz players of the upright bass, like Buster Williams or Ron Carter.

But the violin section was special. Although they were all well trained musicians (it is harder to create anything that actually sounds like music on a violin than on any other instrument); they had an odd, herd-like mentality — at least in those early years. During the '60s and '70s, most of them were heavily invested in the stock market, smoked cigars, and wore toupees. Before each session (especially the morning ones), they would sit in their assigned chairs, puffing on their Monte Cristos and reading their deftly folded newspapers with the Dow Jones page on top.

The violinists also bickered, feuded and sniped more than any other group (even more than the background singers). Prominent members of their section would sidle up to me when I was momentarily off guard to whisper in my ear (too often with terrible halitosis) of the treachery, betrayal and disloyalty of their fellow players. It wasn't so much that they were vying for the position of first-chair violinist (in the good old days, the concertmaster was often awarded double scale). No, the acrimony was more personal than financial. It went beyond jealousy. They truly hated one another, and regularly tried to knock each other off my booking lists with various vicious (likely apocryphal) stories.

While producing these marathon sessions, I would sometimes begin to feel like Cecil B. DeMille. As I would call in a new group of players or singers, I'd be tempted to yell out, *Bring on the camels!* (or elephants, or whatever)...

The noisy arrival of the background singers would come next. This component of the Big Sound was the most glamorous. These people made huge amounts of money in residuals. Apparently, back in the '30s, the Screen Actors Guild negotiated a contract establishing the premise that since singers (even group singers) could be identified by their voices, they should therefore be paid like actors. Soloists were paid more, but still, background singers earned a lot of money: then as now, commercials were everywhere on television and radio.

As the era of the Big Sound got going, a relatively new, younger roster of popular singers was also emerging. These newcomers were gradually supplanting an older group of consummate professionals — people like Marlene VerPlanck, Bob Ragaini, Helen Miles and Arlene Martell, whose musical roots were in jazz rather than the newer sounds. The new girls dressed in up-to-the moment, casual high fashion (designer shoes, matching handbags, and jewelry were important accompanying statements). The guys dressed in jeans, khakis, shirts and sweaters (nothing like street-cred low-rise pants, hoodies and t-shirts of later years). To check out how well anyone was doing, I always snuck a look first at the shoes and the watches.

These singers were a disciplined, professional lot. They could read the most complicated arrangement, sing perfectly in tune, harmonize, blend, credibly mimic many different musical styles, and when chosen to be a soloist, pour their heart into the performance:　earn your trust with their sincerity. Yet they were not particularly distinctive or identifiable. They weren't supposed to be: as stand-ins for an ideal everyman or woman, they were meant to connect with the everyday housewife and breadwinner. A short list would have to include Lesley Miller (my favorite), Florence Warner, Jerry Keller and Kenny Karen.

In the beginning, they were frequently late. Very late. I couldn't blame them. Most of my competitors scheduled them too early; then, if there were client problems in the control room, the singers would have to wait around endlessly. That could make them late for their next booking, or worse, they might miss out altogether on a potential big moneymaker.

I insisted on running my sessions like clockwork. It became a major source of pride. In the process, the singers had to be retrained to trust my booking times. It took a bit of yelling, screaming, and embarrassing them in front of their peers, but eventually we all got along.

Once the backing or group vocals were on tape, it would be time to record the soloist. Ninety-nine percent of the time, the soloist would have been chosen in advance, and would have already sung in the group (a way to earn even more money). Making the decision long before the session started was a whole lot easier than auditioning soloists in front of clients in the studio: a nightmare scenario sure to embarrass everyone. For the most part, these soloists came from the most elite group of jingle singers and performed effortlessly. It wasn't until later, after tastes changed to favor individuality and idiosyncrasy, that soloists with distinctive character rose to the top.

That change started in the mid '80s, and snowballed quickly. The glossy, homogenized productions with their layers of orchestration and generic singing gradually slipped out of style. Simultaneously — for money reasons — synthesizers started replacing flesh-and-blood musicians. The string section players were first to go...

It was sad. Soon, many musicians were no longer able to make a decent living playing on jingle sessions. My sister went back to school to begin a new career as a massage therapist (she continues to be in high demand in NYC today).

As a stubborn survivalist, I turned the page, found new talent, adapted, and carried on.

Change may be inevitable, but this one was hard on many talented people. And many friends. And I really don't know that the jingle business ever again reached the heights of that era of the Big Sound.

WHEN GRACE SLICK and The Jefferson Airplane agreed to do their version of "Be A Pepper," I was thrilled. I loved her voice; "White Rabbit" was an all-time favorite, and her indomitable female spirit and Dorothy Parker wit made her seem a kindred spirit. And the group even loved the tune!

About a week before the session, I got a personal call from Grace.

"Susan, I just can't do it. I love you, the campaign and everything, but I figured I had to taste it before the gig...and I can't *stand* the stuff!"

I thank my lucky stars that I've always loved the taste.

Chapter 30

Haitian Divorce

————

I STEPPED OFF THE PLANE at the Port-au-Prince airport and into an alien world. I had visited Caribbean islands before, but never experienced anything like this. I thought I was in Africa. The lush landscape looked like the jungle movies from my childhood: *Tarzan*, *Mogambo*. The tarmac steamed; the air was hot, wet, and heavy with the smells of decaying vegetation and jet fuel.

Despite forceful expressions of worry from friends and family, I had chosen to travel alone to Haiti. It was the quickest way to settle my divorce with Walter. I was young and brave — didn't know enough to be scared. My lawyer had assured me it would be both legal and perfectly safe.

The waiting room in the quonset hut was packed with humanity. Darker-skinned and with larger, stronger features than the other Caribbean peoples I recalled, they also dressed in brighter primary colors. I began to understand I was in a more alien place than I had supposed. I also began to realize that mine was the only white face in the crowd. I had started to wonder if this was going to become a problem when I noticed a thin, dapper man dancing and weaving through the crowd toward me. He sported a pearl-tipped cane, a three-piece white suit, and a fedora — reminded me of Joel Grey in *Cabaret*. He bowed and introduced himself as a "tourism director." He had been expecting me. He led me into a tiny side room where two profusely sweating lawyers in tropical suits were waiting. They set out papers for me to sign, explaining that they would present the documents to the court first thing in the morning. The official divorce decree would be issued the following day. Then I could go on to Jamaica to meet up with Eliot. There would be no need for me to appear before the Judge...

My self-appointed guide put me in a cab for the ride to my hotel. It was a bouncing, lively trip: brightly colored, over-packed mini-buses crowded the noisy, traffic-choked streets, their sides covered with hand-painted voodoo symbols and sayings. People and animals hung out of the windows and doors yelling, bleating or barking at passersby and other vehicles. There were an amazing number of chickens, goats and dogs both inside and outside the buses. It was all but overwhelming.

The El Rancho hotel was owned by Albert Silvera, multi-millionaire racecar afficionado and the actual Director of Tourism for the country. Sited on a bluff over the center of town, it was perfectly fine (and tame). I settled into my room, but quickly grew bored, and took off on foot to explore some of the shops down the road in the tourist part of the city.

The scene on the streets was colorful and lively, but on closer examination, it was also disturbing. So many people everywhere, jostling and bumping into one another as they tried to make their way. It wasn't that the streets were small: they were broad and fairly modern. There were just too many pedestrians, too many cars and trucks, and too many obstacles. There was also a mixture of good and very bad smells; what seemed to be raw sewage water ran down the gutters. Even in the middle of the afternoon, many people lay resting or sleeping in rows along the streets, wrapped up in sheets or light blankets. I found out later that almost every day, some of them never got up. They had to be carted away. This reality, so calmly stated, rattled my easy-going American confidence and naïveté. I had never before been so close to death, and the indifference with which these people accepted it was startling.

I wandered through the shops, sipping Coca-Cola out of a bottle I'd bought from a street vendor. I had been told that Coke was safe to drink...what I didn't learn until later was that after you pried off the metal cap, it was mandatory to thoroughly wipe clean the rim and top inch of the bottle. The price for my slipup came a couple of days later: a nasty case of dysentery.

I had just crossed an intersection when my eye was caught by a painting in an art gallery window. I had already seen scores of similar

Haitian "primitives" with their strong primary colors, black lines and squished-together images. They were everywhere, and cheap.

But this painting drew me in. Soothing pastel acrylics created a simple but finely drawn rendering of a village marketplace as a few sellers are seen putting out their meager wares on scraps of cloth laid over bare ground. Just arriving on the scene, two other women balance woven baskets on their heads...

I had to have it. Later, I found out it was painted by Antoine Obin (one of two famous artist brothers from Cap-Haïtien, a city on the other side of the island). I paid what at the time I considered a fortune for it, and it does turn out to have become quite valuable (both famous brothers have passed on). I still treasure that painting. It hangs in my bedroom — I get to look at it every day.

After returning to the hotel, I had a quiet dinner by myself, then slept well.

The next morning, I took a cab over to the Hotel Oloffson. I'd read about that gothic, gingerbread monstrosity in Graham Greene novels, so I had to see it. It was everything you could hope for. Away from the chaos of the capital city, it overlooked its little valley, perched on the side of the hill surrounded by lush tropical gardens. It was enormous: a sprawling white wooden structure with pinkish-red trim. On the covered open-air porch, faded chintz-covered wicker furniture and giant potted plants radiated an aura of proud history and now-shabby elegance. There I was served a fine English breakfast (with tea, of course). I sat sopping up the atmosphere, imagining myself surrounded by distinguished guests from the old days: Charles Addams, Harold Pinter, Sir John Gielgud, the fictional characters from *The Comedians,* and naturally, Greene himself.

I spent the afternoon at the pool of El Rancho. After dinner, having no better plan, I drifted into the cocktail lounge.

About 10 o'clock I was joined at the bar by two men. Both were impeccably turned out: tall, fit, well spoken...and in impressively decorated military uniforms. They told me they were colonels in the Haitian Air Force. Realizing that could only mean that they worked for Baby Doc Duvalier may have caused a momentary frisson of fear, but I chose to ignore it. They were such nice guys.

It didn't once occur to me that I was being incredibly foolish as I merrily accepted their invitation to head off into the night with them. I was bored, ready for adventure — and they seemed like perfect gentlemen. Maybe it was my youth; maybe it was those neat uniforms with so many colored bars and medals...

First, we stopped at a deserted airfield. It was pitch black as they opened the locks on the gates and pulled the Jeep alongside the dark outline of a parked helicopter. We climbed aboard; I sat behind them as they treated me to a swooping 20-minute spin over the twinkling lights of the capital city and beyond. I felt breathless; I'd never *been* on a chopper before.

Then we drove down into the heart of Port-au-Prince to an underground music club where (you guessed it) *the band was hot so, we danced*...but I'm not sure it was the merengue. *Now we dolly back. Now we fade to black...* True — but there was no chance of a baby nine months later. My two new friends were perfect gentlemen to the end.

So despite (or because of) my rash behavior, I was rewarded with an adventure I couldn't have made up. The next morning I picked up the official papers and flew off to Jamaica. I ended up liking Haiti a lot more than I would have guessed from that first impression.

Even today, most people find it hard to believe that I set off to Haiti by myself in that era. But I was never genuinely afraid of anything or anyone on that trip. Sure, the voodoo undercurrent was palpable. But it was sexy — fun-scary — not threatening. I planned to come back soon for a true vacation. *This place was cool...*

Shortly after my return to the States, I stopped by A&R 799 to say hello to Eliot and the Steely Dan gang: Donald Fagen, Walter Becker and Gary Katz. They were mixing a track for *The Royal Scam*. We got to talking about my Haitian adventure. Donald, especially, was intensely curious, and pumped me for all the details I could remember. Needless to say, the first time I heard their hit, "Haitian Divorce," I was amused (and flattered).

THE GREAT RAY CHARLES SANG a version of "Remember the Dream" written by the incomparable Bill Eaton. I produced it for the UNCF's *A Mind Is A Terrible Thing To Waste* campaign. Glenn Berger engineered.

I was thrilled to the bone. The band was perfect. Ray performed brilliantly and was very complimentary to me.

But the image I can't get out of my mind is the one of Kenny Loggins, Donald Fagen and Walter Becker, all lined up and kneeling on the control room floor, watching their idol through the glass.

Chapter 31

At the Office

———

WALKING EAST ON 49TH STREET from 3rd Avenue, you might easily miss the little black door with the number '219' on it. You would first be distracted by the ever-popular Smith & Wollensky's Grill, and then delighted by Amster Yard: a charming gated courtyard with lovely gardens and attached brownstone. But you might also notice the next building — a stunning example of Bauhaus architecture, partially faced with those signature glass bricks. It was in this building, behind the unremarkable door, that my company HEA rollicked its way through 23 years of creating original music for advertising.

Before we built our own recording studio (we called it "Ground Control") in the early '80s, you had to climb three flights of stairs to get to our office, a triplex at the top of the building. As you entered through the propped-open door, you faced a smallish waiting area and its lone couch. To your left, the room opened onto the larger space that was my domain. One of its most appealing features was its lack of any sharp angles. Cabinets, the plaster walls that held the interior staircase, my built-in marble desktop — all were gently curved. I sat in a rolling chair in front of a desk that ran the entire length of the room. Shelf after shelf of tapes, vinyl LP's, books of sheet music, awards, speakers and playback equipment hung above the marble expanse.

In an alcove across from me was the "hot seat," the nerve center of our operation. Here sat the person I depended on most. I suppose their title could have been "office manager" or "head of production." More accurately, both. He or she had to know everything that was happening, preferably before it happened.

The center of my area held a comfortable seating arrangement for clients as well as our battered old upright. Oh my: if only that piano could talk! To think of all the great ones who sat on that bench, working out a new song with me or demonstrating their composition for an underscore. There was that time when Mel Torme took over the bench from David Buskin, the writer, to demonstrate a much better way to handle the passage David had just played. And then did exactly the same thing to Dick Behrke, the arranger. All in a most gentlemanly fashion.

I'm happy to report that the piano now lives with Gerard McConville, the last and best of my office managers.

A good New York color scheme of hip grays, blacks, and creams dominated, but with the exception of the startling red couch and chairs for the clients. The front of the room was a glass brick wall that provided soft filtered light from the outside. There was also a door that opened onto a narrow balcony overlooking 49th street.

Off to the right of the waiting area was the other half of our main floor: the two desks for secretarial assistants, and lots of equipment: typewriters with special billing arm attachments, a primitive foregoer of a fax machine used to send personnel sheets to the booking services; multi-line phones and rows of filing cabinets. Every inch of any flat surface was perpetually buried under stacks of paperwork from recent sessions: lead sheets, typewritten lyrics, W-4's, W-9's... You could tell a lot about the nature of the session they belonged to by their condition. Some were neatly stacked; others had food stains and footprints all over them.

To the right of this space was the better-than-adequate kitchen, at all times fully stocked. Frequent trips to Gristede's were necessary. I always kept lunch provisions on hand for the office workers as well as any writers, singers or musicians who happened to be around. Needless to say, we also maintained an admirably stocked liquor cabinet including beers and wines for later in the day.

I am a foodie, and only took clients to the best places in the city. Our neighborhood was peppered with fine restaurants: The Box Tree, Smith & Wollensky's, The Palm, Lutece, and Chin Chin — the last, a Chinese eatery and gourmet's delight right across the street. Chin

Chin's owner, Jimmy, was a good friend. After Ground Control was built, he supplied us with extraordinary late night take-out for years. Other favorite haunts were La Cote Basque and La Grenouille.

I deliberately kept the entire first floor space open. There were no doors to close anywhere, ergo, no closed-door meetings. It discouraged keeping secrets or whispering behind others' backs. Everyone could hear everything, and that's the way I wanted it; in practice, the instantaneous communication and immediate intake of information was necessary for the company to function properly. Things could move pretty damn fast around there. A memo system would have been out of the question.

We had two spacious rooms on the second floor. The one in back was Bernie's office (and in later years, Nick DiMinno's also). The bright, airy front room was for working. We had a grand piano, a Movieola with two sound heads, film and tape splicing equipment, a more extensive tape and vinyl record library, and a small deck for simple recording and tape duplication. It was there that we held auditions, took timings, put together demo reels, and recorded very rough scratch tracks.

The third floor was actually more like half a floor. Up there was where Sherry Day, my friend and office business manager for every one of those years, had her office. People who have to deal with numbers all day need more peace and quiet than could be had anywhere else in the place. Across from her office was a little door that led to the roof. Amazingly, we never did anything with that large outdoor space, and very few people hung out on it. I did hear much later that there were a few who occasionally retreated up to the 3rd floor for some recreational smoking...

Being in the loop, having up to the *second* information was terribly important for what we did. But to the person in the hot seat, it was mandatory. Gerard writes:

You might overhear plans to record a demo for a spot being composed a few feet away, and so then you'd know to start looking for studio time. Or maybe during the course of a phone conversation with artists' service, you might hear that the vocal session you're in the middle of booking is being delayed a week. You needed to develop an omni-directional way of listening to EVERYTHING going on around you at ALL TIMES whenever the boss lady was in the house. Because you were responsible for knowing everything that was going on, even if you hadn't been told directly. And that wasn't easy, given the environment.

The atmosphere and mood of the office could go from library calm to cacophonous mayhem in less than a minute and stay that way for hours. Phones ringing off the hook; cartage companies delivering road cases of musicians' gear to both studios; messengers coming and going with agency memos, tapes, videocassettes, and music contracts; producers yelling at Gerard (or his predecessors) for estimates *NOW!* before their meeting; and then the dreaded call — *the bass player didn't show for a session!*

At the same time, piano meetings with two sets of clients might be going on both upstairs and down. R&B would be blaring from Bernie's office, and one office assistant would be trying to explain procedures to the new girl. At times, the din forced every one of us to run to the kitchen wall phone to complete a phone conversation.

The piano meetings could get heated. I remember one in which Tarlow Advertising (one of our favorite clients) had brought along their client, Ralph Lauren. The CEO and owner of his global conglomerate had a 'used to getting my way' attitude. He chose to directly challenge Dick Behrke, my prickliest composer, as he demonstrated his underscore at the piano.

Now, there was an ironclad rule for HEA meetings and sessions: no one spoke directly to a composer or arranger except me. All questions and comments were directed to me, and me alone. Mr. Lauren wasn't familiar with the rule. Dick Tarlow and his lovely wife, Sandy Carlson (who handled the Lauren account) were embarrassed, but they were in no position to say anything. Mr. Lauren got snotty; Behrke's face turned red, and I watched his lips disappear into a thin line. He threatened to walk, at which point I had to jump in and play defense. I firmly explained the rules of the game to Ralph, but was deferential and complimentary enough to smooth *his* now-ruffled feathers. We got through the rest of the meeting and the final product was most successful.

One of my favorite employees and good friend Rachel Margulies (now Rachel Smit) summed up these scenes:

I'd watched other producers, but her style was smooth, tight and focused. Nothing got past her. She had a solution for everything. I never saw anyone make a juggling act look so easy...

A few random memories:

Many early mornings watching a determined Kate Hepburn, in headscarf and long coat, sweeping fallen leaves or shoveling snow in front of her brownstone down the block. I was thrilled and inspired. What an indomitable Yankee spirit.

#   #   #

The years when Mendl, my Alaskan Malamute and Grok, Sherry Reaser's German Shepherd, spent their days in the office taking turns terrorizing clients and interns alike.

#   #   #

The morning Connie Boylan pushed open that little black front door to come face-to-face with an armed robber who ordered her into the hallway. Instead, she turned tail and ran for the corner phone booth to call Kathy Brega upstairs and warn her to lock our doors. Kathy called 911; the cops came and caught the guys. The next day, we installed a remote camera over the outside doorway.

#   #   #

Monday mornings, I would drive my new Mercedes 500SE down from the Vermont farm, honk the horn, and idle in front of the building. Connie or Gerard would rush down to take the car to the garage, and I would shepherd little Alex upstairs and keep him entertained until his nanny came to pick him up.

#   #   #

Coming back to the office after a good session, 15 ips tape in hand, I would thread it on the downstairs machine, turn the volume up to 11 and yell, "Wine!" with an outstretched hand before pushing the 'play' button.

#   #   #

I stole my best employees from other people. I'd spot an on-the-ball secretary at an agency, or an assistant engineer who quickly and correctly anticipated what was needed in the studio. After sufficient observation, I'd pounce. Nobody ever turned me down. I wasn't the easiest person to work for, but the good ones stayed for years.

Gerard writes:

When [as an assistant engineer] *I first met you, you used to give me nightmares. I lived in mortal fear of rousing your anger. One flash of your eyes across the control room at a missed punch was enough to turn my stomach to ice water. If somebody had come up to me then and told me that I would someday work for you, I'd have walked away laughing. But it came to pass. And I've never regretted it. You could be a little difficult to please, so whenever I'd do something that met your approval, it would make my day. As time went on and I became more confident with myself, I came to realize that your demanding persona brought my game up.*

There are many tales about the differences between HEA and other jingle companies (as there are between me and other producers). I firmly believed that producing an outstanding product was the single path to success. In practice, that meant that sometimes in a prep meeting there was no way to avoid telling an agency client he was wrong; that what he was suggesting wouldn't work; to educate him or her in demographics; to let them in on what kind of music their customers really liked. And, in the worst of cases, to say aloud that their line or campaign idea sucked.

I was convinced that what I was doing was right for both them and us, and it made me fearless. I had no problem saying "No!" (I'm told that it became a somewhat well-known industry visual: the image of me swinging my long straight hair back and forth like a curtain in front of my face: *No!*) I would not bend over for some asshole client, nor give in to a foolish one with dumb ideas. But I did understand how my nicknames became "the terror" or "the dragon lady" of Madison Avenue. In a kinder light, I was also sometimes called "an external creative director" of such and such agency...

In the studio, I behaved brazenly. When circumstances warranted, I defended my arrangers, musicians and singers like a she-wolf. Any criticism of what was happening had to be directed at and handled by me. It was part of the reason so many of the HEA writers chose to stay instead of striking out on their own. Who wanted to deal with constant agency bullshit?!

And I *was* completely focused on the job at hand — on the music — not on kissing up to clients or paying attention to agency politics. If a client got too out of hand, he or she would be banished from the room, or the session would be canceled on the spot. I actually did that twice.

So I wasn't the most loved music supplier in the biz. But HEA had a hell of a track record, and a great deal of respect. I was content with the tradeoff.

I THINK I WAS ALREADY IN COLLEGE when my friends began to label me "android." It continued into my first decade in NYC. Why?

My brow would furrow and I would be without a clue when someone would mention an American icon everybody in the world knew — except me.

It happened often enough that eventually someone came up with the explanation: I really wasn't human at all — a convincing android, likely from another planet.

From then on, whenever one of the frequent slip-ups would occur, one of my friends would offer a helpful suggestion like, "Check her wrist box, it seems to be malfunctioning again..."

(I never told them that we had had no TV set during my formative years).

Chapter 32

The Dynamic Duo

T hat's the nickname people in the biz gave to Eliot Scheiner and me. It's quite appropriate: our whole relationship was based on "doing."

Don Hahn, my number one engineer, was sometimes unavailable for sessions at A&R, so I started working with Eliot, an acolyte of Phil Ramone. A few years later, Don left for the West Coast to work with Herb Alpert and A&M studios, but it was not a problem. It had been immediately clear to me that Eliot was an extraordinary engineer — he made my tracks sound amazing. Plus, sessions with Eliot were upbeat, fun, and relaxed.

There was one summer in the early '70s that turned out to be particularly jammed with sessions. It became one of the busiest of my career. Eliot and I ended up putting in day after day of long hours in the studio. We laughed and joked our way through the gamut of challenges. I remember one that took 108 mixes to get a Eubie Blake Dr Pepper spot right.

We would unwind from the marathon sessions with lunches, dinners, drinks. No surprise that we bonded; besides, he was a looker: his body was wiry and toned; his dark hair set off brilliant blue eyes. He always wore pressed jeans, tight-fitting shirts, clean white sneakers. Eliot was light on his feet; I would watch his hands as he moved with swift, graceful precision over the width and length of the console —

tweaking knobs here; adjusting settings there. It could be mesmerizing. And like me, he radiated energy.

I'd been separated from Walter for a couple of years, and was about to travel to Haiti for the divorce. It was a quick route many people were taking. Although I'd had dalliances in the interim, I was not interested in — nor had I time for — a serious relationship.

I also knew Eliot was married, which made it easy to keep my distance. But I couldn't deny that I wished he weren't. I would have thought he was the perfect man for me at the time.

Then, in October, I remember how my heart leapt when he told me that he had asked his wife for a divorce. So the stirrings had been mutual. It's not hard for me to understand why so many of Hollywood's ill-fated marriages are forged on movie sets. When you work side by side for extended periods, on high-stakes projects, it's hard to resist the strong attraction that can develop. Unlike my occasional dip into the "bad boys" pool, all of my marriages were based on work relationships and mutual respect. Every time, I got the work part of it right. And failed three out of three on the other parts.

That fall, Eliot and I endured a couple of difficult months as he attempted to extricate himself from his marriage. We had some serious make-out sessions, but nothing more until the matter was settled (I thought) with his soon-to-be ex-wife.

That year, Christmas fell on a Wednesday, and I didn't have any extra days off. Eliot called to tell me that he and his brother Chuck had to make an emergency trip to Miami to be with his mother and stepfather. He explained that she had contracted a weird sleeping sickness disorder: she was in the hospital being attended to by his stepfather, who was a doctor.

Eliot called regularly to describe the hospital visits he and his brother were making. He told me about the piano his stepfather had given her for Christmas.

When he returned, our relationship continued to deepen. I left for my Haitian divorce, solo, while Eliot worked with Steely Dan on *The Royal Scam* album. Then we reunited in Jamaica for our first vacation together. I had rented a house complete with servants.

Immediately, there were problems. Days of steady hard rain in a house with a tin roof made it difficult to hear each other; hostile locals actually yelled, "Go home, Whitey!" There was practically no palatable food in the supermarket (I remember the goatdogs in particular), and I had dysentery (thank you, Haiti). After a couple of days, we retreated to the Bahamas — and finally enjoyed at least a few days of blessed re-laxation.

For the next few sunlit years, Eliot and I spent most of our time together: happy-go-lucky, always busy with sessions, always having fun. We skied in Aspen and St. Moritz; we gambled in Vegas and Monte Carlo. We vacationed at least once a year at La Samanna on the French side of St. Martin, our favorite Leeward Island in the Caribbean.

One particularly riotous HEA boondoggle took place there. La Samanna is now an impeccably manicured big-time resort with lush landscaping, path lights and patrolling security guards. But in those days, it had just been built by a local architect for a New York busi-nessman and his French designer wife. It was named for their three lit-tle girls (one of whom is married to the tennis great, Ivan Lendl: he swept her off her feet when she was only 15). Today, hotels just like it can be found in Hawaii and Florida, but back then, it was exotically charming. The palm trees, bougainvillea, and hibiscus were newly planted — so at first, the place felt more like desert than jungle. No air conditioning, just ceiling fans; no TV's or phones in the rooms; little whitewashed buildings reminiscent of the Greek Isles scattered down the three-quarters of a mile of perfect private beach (complete with a shipwreck at the far end). The open-air terrace restaurant served world-class cuisine, and the intimate round bar was enclosed in a tall, richly colored Moroccan-style tent.

Included on the HEA guest list were Jake Holmes and his second wife, Marguerite; my own ex, Walter, with his new wife Marti (my old college roommate); Nick and Teri DiMinno (Nick had joined me at HEA as a second producer); Al Gorgoni (a talented composer/gui-tarist who had been brought into HEA by Walter), and his wife Camille; and a favorite client and wife, Mark and Linda Goldstein.

We would roll out of bed and jump into the warm turquoise sea for a quick swim before heading up to breakfast with the 'jelly birds' (their curved black beaks fit perfectly into the little opening between the lid and jar of the confiture containers). Afternoons were spent sipping tropical drinks at the Olympic-sized tiled pool terraced into the hillside above Baie Longue beach, or visiting the French capital town of Marigot to shop for Parisian goods. Then dress up for gourmet din-ner, laughs and nightcaps at the casbah, and off to a sleep lulled by the sound of the gentle surf — then up early to start all over again.

One funny memory: Teri DiMinno would suddenly leap into her husband's arms when we walked down the stone paths. She was ter-rified of the cute little lizards that scurried back and forth (and they were everywhere). More universal was our fear of the palmetto bugs that loved to hide in the warm towels we found placed over the shower rods each afternoon. Those suckers could fly, and would actually energetically chase you across the floor or through the air.

All in all, I remember that trip as one of the high points in my life: one of those times when things go completely right...

It was on a later trip to St. Martin that Eliot proposed to me. Once more, vague misgivings stirred in the back of my head. I'd known he was going to ask, but didn't want him to. If only everything could continue just as it was: free and easy, unencumbered. But I said yes, anyway. I didn't want our storybook life to end. It was so perfect...

We moved into a two-bedroom co-op apartment in the East Sixties. The real estate agent suggested I use my name alone in our interview with the Board (and also on the deed). I was the one buying it, so that was fine, but still... shocking to believe that there were remnants of what could only be anti-semitism still lingering in Manhattan. But at least this time around, I wasn't required to provide a man to cosign for me.

Eliot was engineering most of my sessions not just in NYC, but all over the world. His star was rising with the solid success of the Steely Dan records. When we flew to L.A. for the Grammys, he won for their album, *Aja*.

He was also recording with Jimmy Buffett and his producer, Norbert Putnam. Eliot and I spent one wacky weekend in London with Jimmy and his wife, Janey, along with Norbert and Dan Fogelberg. We overindulged at an incredibly elegant restaurant in Surrey...I'd never before had a $700 snifter of cognac...

Now we bought horses; and before long became deeply involved in Morgan horse shows all over the country. We worked on my Vermont house together: taming, clearing and fencing the 55 acres. Then we needed to raise a barn for the horses, chickens and Nubian goats. A French Canadian team of six builders was recruited; they finished it in a couple of weeks. I watched in awe as they nimbly danced across the beams, somehow carrying 4'x 8' sheets of ¾" plywood. By the time it was finished, the barn also included a big two-car garage and a two-bedroom upstairs guest apartment. We finished renovating and decorating the inside of the main farm house, then added an all-weather tennis court, then a riding ring.

Dinner parties in Manhattan — as well as gourmet weekends at the farm — became a constant. Colleagues from the City and local friends came in droves. Cooking and entertaining weren't chores for me: in fact, they were relaxing. Organizing a meal was a whole lot easier than setting up and producing a session. And I loved to cook. Life was great.

We planned a picture-perfect outdoor wedding around the trout pond in the woodland backyard. The guests would stand on the wide grassy perimeter around the pond. About 150 people came. The music people from New York carpooled. Our friends from Bondville, Londonderry and Stratton Mountain helped us set up. David E. and his new wife, Jeannie, were there. Even Herman Edel and Buddy flew in from Aspen (we had mended fences). My friend Sherry — now married to Vaughn Clark — did the flowers. A local restaurant owned by friends catered. Area construction guys built a huge raised platform at the far end of the pond; they set up an array of big lights, amps, electric keyboards and microphones to accommodate pick-up performances from the celebrity-studded crowd.

So, on a perfect summer afternoon in late July, with a string quartet to start, a witty speech by my father, and a very nervous young Justice of the Peace who barely got through the formalities, we were wed. The late afternoon sun slanted through the trees, sending a golden tinge over everything. The purposely brief ceremony was over quickly, in appropriate dynamic duo style...

As the wedding crowd started to break up, a sudden, violent thunderstorm struck. Booming and rumbling, there were fearsome lightning strikes all over the place. It poured sheets of water on the scattering crowd, sending one and all scurrying for shelter.

After the worst had passed, Eliot and I decided we'd better make a sweep of the house, property and outbuildings to make sure everyone was safe. Tucked into corners of every building, we found couples having wild, wanton sex (a not altogether unexpected post-wedding phenomenon). In the hay loft, in an empty horse stall, in the sauna, in OUR bathroom shower, in the greenhouse... But even in a Port-A-Potty? *Really?*

Later, after the feast, many, many musicians and singers got together in different ad hoc groups and stepped up onto the rough stage to perform. The rest of us danced on the grass until 4 in the morning. Thankfully, we had no close neighbors — but I kick myself today for not having recorded the whole thing.

The dynamic duo careened on through a few more years. We honeymooned in Paris. Then we rented a fast car and embarked on a three star Michelin tour from restaurant to restaurant, working our way through the countryside to the Riviera. I, in true over-achiever style, had painstakingly booked us for both lunch and dinner in two or three star dining establishments all the way down. That plan lasted about a day and half, after which we couldn't even look at one more creamed *anything* in a puff pastry shell. We went in search of pizza and peasant food.

Our whole relationship was based on action: *doing!* We glided and romped through the years, never discussing much of anything in depth. No politics, no religion, no philosophy (just the work, and *who was coming up for the weekend?* or *should we buy another horse...*)

I guess for my part, I was rebounding from being married to an emotionally withholding intellectual. Screw that. I didn't want to deal with deep dark important issues. I was now content to bask in the glow of unbridled material success. It seemed limitless: the business, the music, the farm, the Morgans.

There was one dark cloud. Eliot and I both wanted children. Years before, as soon as the relationship started, I'd had my IUD removed. Year after year, nothing happened. As was our way, we didn't talk about it. I assumed the problem was mine.

HEA ALWAYS CLOSED between Christmas and New Year's. But in 1975, I made a business trip to Chicago to attend a mandatory meeting on a big campaign.

After the meeting, I took the clients out for cocktails. We were having a great time, so I decided to postpone my flight back to LaGuardia by an hour or so. I called Eliot to let him know.

The plane landed around 6:45 pm, yet when I came out of the boarding gate, the concourse was completely empty. Not a soul in sight. *Strange.* I started to walk toward Arrivals when I spotted Eliot racing toward me. His face was ashen.

A deadly bomb had gone off in the lockers next to Baggage Claim. Eliot had been crossing the street in front of the terminal just as it exploded. He was thrown off his feet by the blast, but was okay.

We ran out of the nearest exit and rushed to the garage, passing carnage along the way. It was horrifying. As I hurried past spattered jeans and boots lying along the curbside in rivers of blood, I couldn't help thinking, "*So many of my friends and clients dress exactly like that...*"

Chapter 33

The King of Pop

———

I WAS SET UP AND HOODWINKED by the Jackson family, although I didn't realize it until six months after the fact.

I had been thrilled when they agreed to do their own version of the "Be A Pepper" jingle for the very successful ongoing radio campaign. Why, they had even promised to feature Michael as the lead singer.

So I was pretty psyched as I headed to Los Angeles. I mean, Michael Jackson, for goodness sake! I was going to work with THE Michael Jackson.

When I arrived at the studio (Westlake, I think), everything seemed very professional and under control. Five of the brothers were there: Jackie, Tito, Marlon, Randy and Michael. Neither of the girls, nor Jermaine. The Jackson Five had changed labels to CBS, and Jermaine had decided to stay with Motown. Anyway, when Marlon introduced me to Michael, I started to worry a bit.

The King seemed really out of it. Very pale, visibly sweating, kind of rocking back and forth with his eyes half-closed. When I shook his hand, it was clammy, soft, limp, oddly small. I'll never forget the feeling of it. Michael was wearing normal, nondescript casual clothes, and sported an afro. After he drifted off to lean against the back wall of the control room, Marlon explained, "Don't worry. He'll be fine. He's just got a touch of the flu."

Marlon seemed to be closest to Michael. He spoke for him, led him around in a protective, almost parental way. In those days, he even looked like him. The Great Greg Phillinganes was the keyboardist/arranger for the session (boy did I forever wish he was located on the East Coast), but Marlon was the leader. I was of course in the booth, observing, listening, and keeping my mouth shut. And as they ran down the tracks with the band, I couldn't have been happier.

They were great! Tight as hell, and the funky groove was making me want to get up and shake it. (Come on—that's how you talked in 1977, the height of the disco/r&b craze).

In short order, we had final takes on both the 60 and 30 second versions, did a couple of overdubs, and were ready to move on to background vocals.

All the while we had been recording, I'd been singing along with the tracks, making sure everything fit properly with the tune and lyrics. It all did, perfectly. So it's easy to imagine my shock when the brothers, who were doing the bg's, opened their mouths at the first chorus and sang:

"Sunshine, Moonlight, Good Times, *Oooh, Aaah!*"

I almost fell on the floor. The chorus, you understand! They were messing with the *chorus*! The very keystone of our super-successful "Be A Pepper" campaign!

When they started to do the same thing at the second chorus, I had the engineer stop the tape. It was time to walk into the studio to have a little meeting. I didn't feel this could be handled with proper delicacy over the talkback.

I pulled Marlon off to the side and asked him why they had changed the lyrics of the chorus. (I was polite, so I didn't say *"fuckin' chorus"*).

He looked at me with completely lifeless eyes and replied, "You told us we could have creative license with the arrangement. This is our personal, creative interpretation of the song."

I took a deep breath, then tried to explain what the agency and client reaction would be to this variety of "creative license," but I could see we were headed for a battle royal.

Here I must digress a bit. For the first time in this kind of situation, I was completely alone, completely on my own. No musicians or singers I knew, no husband-engineer, no agency music director, no agency creatives, no agency account people. Not even an uninvolved, detached documentary film crew. Nope, just me to figure out this bizarre development.

To top it off, I couldn't understand it. Why would they want to change "I'm a Pepper, He's a Pepper, She's a Pepper, We're a Pepper" to inane, bland, vanilla words like "Sunshine, Moonlight, Good Times, *Oooh, Aaah*"? It made no sense. Also, it was already late in the evening in L.A. It would be impossible to call anyone back on the East Coast who could possibly help. I had to solve this stalemate or just cancel the whole session — and *that* choice wouldn't make anyone happy...

I called a break and sat down to have myself a *let's think about this* time out. I don't quite know how I came up with a solution, but it happened. It's a mystery — creativity. Most of the time I believe ideas for lyrics, melodies, creative solutions to problems all come into the brain the way radio waves are pulled toward an antenna. Maybe we all have invisible antennas on our heads and just have to be receptive to the incoming information. At least it feels like that when suddenly something good pops up, seemingly out of nowhere.

So it was with confidence that I marched back in the studio, gathered up the brothers and suggested, "How 'bout you guys sing the words you've been singing and we let Michael anticipate the down-beats of each one with 'I'm a Pepper in the....', and then finish up with 'Wouldn't you like to Be A Pepper too?'"

This was certainly a stretch on the lyrics of the chorus, but it did seem to work in my head. And after all: this was a Michael Jackson showcase, wasn't it?

The Jacksons bought it.

A crisis averted (or at least postponed). I had no idea how the Agency and client would react to the lyric changes. But what else could I do? And the whole track had an upbeat energy I knew they'd love.

We were ready for Michael's solo. If anything, he seemed in worse shape. Behind the mike stand, he was weaving back and forth, his eyes closed, barely able to stand up. My heart was in my throat as the intro played.

But dammit if he didn't blow me flat back against the wall on his first take. It was unbelievable! He knew the verse perfectly. Clearly, his brothers had explained the change of plan with the choruses — he knew those perfectly, as well.

I could have got down on my knees and bowed to him, but I restrained myself. He really *was* the King! I don't know if the whole sickness thing was an act to protect him from crazy advertising people or pseudo music producers, but whatever — he delivered in spades. Two or three takes and it was all done.

I walked out of the studio a couple of hours later with the tapes under my arm, happy and exhausted. What a ride...

Back in New York at Y&R, I played the finished tracks. Everyone loved them. I didn't even catch much flak about the whole 'sunshine, moonlight' thing. The client didn't care, either. So I'd dodged a bullet. Maybe I had misjudged the seriousness of changing the chorus lyrics; maybe my solution was on the money. Who knows?

About the "hoodwinked" part. Six month later, The Jacksons released their new single, their first for Columbia Records. Guess what the background lyrics of the chorus were? That's right, good ol' "sunshine, moonlight" etc. The name of the record is "Blame It On the Boogie." Check it out on YouTube; you'll have to laugh, too. The savvy Jacksons had used the Dr Pepper Company to get six months of free subliminal advertising to promote their new album and single.

But that's not all. The real kicker was still on the way, arriving when the Jacksons' publishing company later sued Dr Pepper for ripping off their song lyrics. I wanted sooooo much to testify, but the agency just paid the money. It wasn't that much.

It's entirely possible that a turning point in the world of celebrity endorsements for advertisers was reached right about then. During the 60's — and even well into the 70's — there was a perceived stigma attached to any reputable recording artist who stooped to selling the rights to his or her song, voice or name for financial gain. Especially to endorse some idiotic product.

But slowly and surely, the times changed into today's reality where top artists in all categories of the record business vie to be the next celebrity spokesperson for a Pepsi or McDonald's. It has become an honor, a feather in one's cap. Even the holdout of all holdouts, John Mellencamp, who railed very publicly against the use of hit songs in commercials, has caved. I like to think my 40 years of producing and recording famous artists helped change the tide. I didn't keep count, but there had to have been more than a hundred.

I saw Michael a few times after the Dr Pepper session. First, about a year later at A&R's 799 Studio A when Tom Bahler, a good friend of mine and associate producer for Quincy Jones, asked me to both recruit talent and sing in the chorus for the movie, *The Wiz.* Michael dropped by the studio with Diana Ross — both had starring roles in the film. His appearance set me back for a moment. I had heard he'd had some work done: but these were radical changes. A completely different thin aquiline nose, more pronounced cheekbones, much paler skin and straightened, oily long hair. I had heard that he was trying to look like Diana Ross. He was getting close, and the result was almost macabre.

Coincidentally, I had just spent an afternoon with her at the Sunset Boulevard clothing store of designer Holly Harp. We were trying on clothes in adjoining dressing rooms, and Holly introduced us. We talked quite a bit about the music business, mutual friends etc. I found her to be both intelligent and really friendly — at odds with the usual rap on her.

The last time I saw Michael was with Brooke Shields in L.A. It was in the early '90s. My friend, songwriter/producer Desmond Child, had asked me to produce some of Brooke's vocals on song demo tracks he'd produced for her. Astonishingly beautiful Brooke and I did become good friends, and hung out for a few months after that. She brought Ray Liotta to one of my dinner parties in Malibu. We talked a lot about her difficult relationship with her mother, Teri; the men in her life; and her longtime friendship with Michael Jackson.

Once, before one of her vocal sessions, Michael dropped Brooke off at my studio in Culver City. He popped his head in for a second. Michael seemed incredibly frail; he barely glanced at me, and left quickly. She later showed me the large diamond friendship ring he had just given her...

It seems that the artistic flame in some geniuses burns so brightly that it cannot be dimmed by any kind of abuse. At his lowest point, just before he passed, Michael Jackson's incredible talent was still undeniable. It showed throughout the rehearsal film for *This Is It* as brilliantly as it had when he recorded the Dr Pepper spot so many years before.

CISSY HOUSTON SANG on many of my sessions. Often she would be accompanied by her husband and her young daughter, Whitney.

Whitney would lie on the carpeted floor of the control room, dipping into her box of crayons to color in her church-sponsored religious books as her doting father looked on.

One time she couldn't help herself. She sat up and belted out a phrase she liked from the song we were working on. Needless to say, I sat up and took notice.

She blew me away at 9, and I never forgot it.

Chapter 34

Pia Zadora

WHAT AN ENTRANCE! We were all sitting around, waiting for the winner of the widely advertised "Find the Dubonnet Girl" contest. She was scheduled for her first rehearsal with the arranger/composer of the jingle we were to produce. The lookout had already reported the arrival of a stretch limo three stories below, but it took a few minutes before the little white poodle came in, followed by his mistress. She let his leash drop, and he immediately ran over and lifted his leg on the newel post at the foot of our stairs. She didn't notice; we pretended we didn't, either.

Pia was a tiny thing; she couldn't have been much more than 5'2". She shrugged off the big fur coat (maybe silver fox, maybe coyote), and one of my guys scooped it up before it could hit the floor. She was dressed in white stretch leggings and a low-cut, long sleeved purple top. They were her signature colors. The workout style, fine for Vegas or L.A., didn't seem to make sense for a business meeting in midtown Manhattan; but boy — it sure did show off her perfect little body.

The rock on her finger was large enough to make Lloyd's of London nervous. She also managed to drop the fact that the jewels on her dog's collar were real. Her blond bouffant hairdo framed a kewpie doll face with a mouth to make a man fantasize. She spoke and sang in a husky, whispery voice: it reminded me of Marilyn Monroe's "Happy Birthday, Mr. President."

We soon learned that she was no dummy. The jazzy tune we had created for Dubonnet was tricky. There were a lot of chromatics and rhythmic upbeats to handle, and she performed them well. The rehearsals (I think there were three before we set foot in a studio) were completely unnecessary, but they fulfilled her need for all the attention she could get, and god knows our client was willing to pay for it. We were all amused.

As soon as I met Pia's husband, I started to understand the cheesy, suggestive lines the agency had insisted be included in the jingle. I also understood why, out of all the hundreds of contestants, she had won. She had just turned 23; her new husband was 53-year-old Meshulam Riklis, the Israeli multi-billionaire who just happened to own the distributing company for Dubonnet. *Duh.* For all I knew, he could have bought the company and then had them create the contest just for her (the way it was rumored later that he 'bought' her a Golden Globe). He was utterly besotted and didn't mind showing it.

The actual recording session was a breeze. She performed "du, du, Dubonnet, anyway you like" with the perfect amount of superbly blatant sexuality for the microphone. Also later for the camera. Her pitch was good; her rhythmic sense was better (I think because she was a dancer), and the tune demanded neither sustained notes nor bravura technique. The spot had a good run.

For whatever reason, both Pia and Meshulam took a shine to Eliot and me.

A few months after the Dubonnet experience, we were invited to be Meshulam's guests at the opening of Pia's nightclub act. It took place at the Rainbow Room on the 65th floor of the Rockefeller Center building.

We sat at a front row table with Meshulam. I swear: I was more taken with watching him watching the show than with the actual performance itself. He sat there beaming and smoking a cigar while at least 20 or more shirtless male dancers pawed his wife. True, she sang and danced in her barely legal Vegas showgirl costume, but mostly she was thrown around and mauled by the men on stage. Her husband kept turning to us and asking, "Isn't she *something?*" During intermission, Pia came over to the table and cuddled in his lap.

I heard later that after the couple bought "Pickfair" (the Beverly Hills mansion of Douglas Fairbanks and Mary Pickford), Mr. Ricklis commissioned a large nude oil portrait of Pia and hung it to greet visitors as they entered the foyer.

One of Pa's typical crazy contraptions allowed me to reach the pedals with my stubby little legs.

Days of innocence — Pa, me, and Girlie

My mother

Rutherford is Home of American Foils Star

Miss Carol Alessandroni, of 71 Donaldson avenue, Rutherford, ranks among the world's best foils artists. She is considered best among American women despite the fact that she has engaged in foils competition but three seasons.

At the New York Fencing Club matches recently she placed behind Miss Helen Mayer, of Germany, last year's Olympic champion and the latter's third straight win of the championship.

Zoomerang factory,
Rutherford, New Jersey

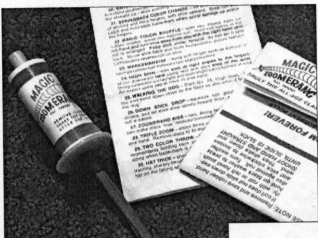

Magic Zoomerang
(31 magic tricks and
games included)

The Dinosaur's Night Out

The Zoomerang Gang in uniform

Grandma
Etta:
'Good Witch'

Il Travatore:
Grandpa Cesare

Grandma
Lilian:
'Bad Witch'

Not As A Stranger, 1957. I did love looking up at Robert Mitchum with my mouth open...

'50s child actress

A sign said 'aura pictures'...

With Won Mo Kim, headed home from Aspen

Performing in Siena at the Count's Palace

Herman Edel

Bela Sigetvari: avalanche expert

The 'Mod Squad of Madison Ave': Bernie, Herman and me

In the studio

...on the warpath!

George Martin at the office

Eliot and Walter at Walter and Marti's wedding

Brother Rollin

Five of the seven dogs in Vermont

Dr Pepper extravaganza at the Jamaica house

La Samanna boondoggle

The morning of my second wedding: Pa writing his speech

Sister Janet
Mother Carol

Jingle belle:
Susan Hamilton
is called the
Clive Davis
of the industry.

New York magazine profile, 1979

242

In studio with
Bobby Short

Chuck at the
Dr Pepper session

Rob Mounsey

"Radiance"

Okalahoma City: Winning Grand National
Championship with Appleton Radiance

Steve Sohmer:
client, mentor,
friend

Doug Katsaros
('Dougie')

Outside House of David with David Briggs, Will Lee, Vince Gill

Bolton

"David E."

Sue Read

Clewsy!

Malibu: the '90s

Julian with
John McCurry

Malibu dinner party: an "oddly prophetic" snapshot

The Kids:
Joscelyne, Alex, Scott, Darcy, Dexter...and Samson

I ran into them a couple more times in later years. Once flying home to New York on the Concorde, and once after a sitting at the 95th Street studios of Al Hirschfeld, the revered caricaturist whose line drawings of celebrities with their hidden "Ninas" (his daughter's name) frequently graced the pages of the *New York Times*. Hirschfeld's drawing of them nailed my impression of their relationship perfectly. Pia was sitting on Ricklis' lap: his hands were disproportionally huge as they grabbed various parts of her body.

ON THE SET OF A KFC SHOOT, I got to hang out with the other Colonel in my life: Colonel Sanders.

There he was, in his signature white suit, goatee perfectly groomed and walking stick in hand.

Also on hand was a gorgeous redheaded nurse in uniform, complete with the little white hat. She sat next to him, only occasionally pushing away his roving hands.

Chapter 35

Justin Morgan Had a Horse

———

I ONCE OWNED 45 OF THEM. What was I — insane? The answer is yes.

It all started so innocently, just the typical 'pre-teen girl becomes horse crazy' syndrome. I have read that in earlier times, mothers frequently introduced their daughters to horses to preclude their interest in young men. I get it. That sense of being one with more than a thousand pounds of powerful, living, beautifully muscled machine — one that you control by having it between your legs — is much more exhilarating than getting kissed by some pimply-faced boy.

One year my parents finally managed to scrape together enough money to buy me my own horse for Christmas. I was 10. The year before, I'd had to settle for a Nubian goat, but that didn't work for long.

"Brandy" was a Morgan/Quarter Horse mare, and she lived in our backyard in a single stall hut and small corral. I have no idea why my parents allowed it, but I often rode her by myself over the thousands of untamed acres that stretched from Canoga Park up into Chatsworth. This was the Warner Ranch: rolling hills, scrubby oaks and about a million sheep. One time I rode out to find hundreds of them lying dead amidst the grazing herds. I never knew what killed them.

No cell phone, no way of calling for help out there in the middle of nowhere, lots of mountain lions around...most of the time I had no idea where I was. I just let Brandy find our way home. But I guess things were different in those years. More often than not, people operated on blind faith that nothing bad was going to happen (at least not to them).

I also rode with a girlfriend at a ring on the part of the Warner Ranch that ran along Canoga Avenue. Judy and I did all kinds of crazy circus tricks with our horses, like riding them standing up on their backs, barefoot. Even worse, we sometimes rode as a pair, horses in step next to each other while we each had one foot on our horse and one on the other. I came out of those years unscathed, but Judy broke her pelvis when her white horse reared up and fell over backwards on top of her. My Brandy once made the same mistake in a show ring, but I managed to jump off in time. I later successfully taught her not to do that by smashing a plastic bag filled with warm water on her head when she reared: horses think it's their blood streaming down over their face.

When I decided to compete in local horse shows and gymkhanas, we bought a broken-down horse trailer and hitched it to the back of our old station wagon. My mother and I would get up early and drive to Thousand Oaks, Camarillo, or Oxnard. She learned to back the thing up and turn around like a pro. Of course we did all the grooming and tacking ourselves.

At first I entered Trail or Western Pleasure classes, taking home a lot of ribbons of all colors (but not too many blues). Then I graduated into gymkhana classes, which proved far more exciting: barrel racing, flat racing, roping horse technique (neck reining, skids, spins, rapid backing up). I won more blue ribbons, but it took its toll on Brandy: made her buzzy and jumpy enough that I quit the whole scene.

I was growing older anyway, increasingly caught up in school and all its activities. When my parents got into their usual money trouble, they sold Brandy without telling me. I was furious and outraged. When my father made some snotty comment about my lack of attention to Brandy, I slapped him in the face. I don't know if our relationship ever recovered fully after that.

Many years later, after I had bought my country house in Vermont, Eliot decided to buy me a Morgan horse for my birthday. He thought he would also rent one for himself. We had idyllic visions of trail riding through the woods together. That didn't pan out. After one too many misadventures (his horse definitely had the upper hand in their relationship), Eliot wisely decided that riding was not for him.

But by then we had Dream, a lovely young mare who needed more training. We found a young woman trainer who did a terrific job. All could have been perfectly fine, had it not been for what she said one day. It sealed our fate.

"You know, Susan," she said, "this is a really nice mare. I think you should show her."

We entered Dream in a conformation class at a local show. There were maybe a dozen other horses in her group, but by damn, she won! What we didn't know was that this particular judge had a definite bias toward the old type of Morgans. Dream wouldn't have had much of a chance to win under any of the other judges. We found that out when she came in dead last at a big regional show at the fairgrounds in Northampton, MA.

But the bug had bitten, so we decided *we just needed a better horse* to show!

That decision led me into a 15-year immersion in the Morgan horse show world. Buying, showing and breeding horses became a consuming passion. For years, I experienced the extreme highs and lows, victories and heartbreaks.

My involvement with Morgans turned out to be the ultimate money throw. Just like campaigning a dog in the show ring costs big bucks, running a breeding stable on your own farm and having an 11-horse show string out on the road for half the year costs a fortune.

For starters, buying expensive stock was necessary if you hoped to win in the big shows. Then there were trainers, vets, blacksmiths, farm hands, etc. — not to mention transportation, insurance, equipment, tack and clothes. A hand-tailored saddle suit cost close to a thousand dollars, and at least five or six were needed for the different classes — including a formal, tuxedo-style one for evening finals.

I became truly crazed. I often chartered a twin engine Cessna with a personal pilot to fly me and a trainer all over the Eastern Seaboard to check out horses for sale. I also attended major auctions. One time I bought the highest-priced horse instead of the Porsche I had been looking at. But I made the money; I had the money, and I spent the money with no regrets. Thanks to the jingle business, I had come a long way from the days of bread and milk for supper.

Every July there would be a 10-day period when the big New England Regional show was held, causing me to fly back and forth from Teeterboro to Northampton. I needed to produce music sessions during the times my horses weren't showing or I wasn't riding or driving them myself.

I was a hands-on, participating horse owner; had to get in there and perform in all of the amateur classes. I rode saddle seat in both pleasure and park classes, but never entered hunter/ jumper or western events. I also drove the two-wheeled carts in pleasure classes and the big four-wheelers in park events. Naturally, for driving classes, I needed a whole additional wardrobe.

On the fairgrounds, a rented RV with A/C is a must. Events start early and end late. The hotel's too far away, and the miles of walking in the heat, dust and dirt — plus the smells and constant noise— make having such an oasis a life-saving necessity. There I could change in and out of all the required outfits; Alex and his nanny (they were always with me) could take breaks there, and I could serve cocktails and sit around to chat with any and all.

The number one cocktail on the circuit at that time was the "seperator": a concoction introduced to me by the grooms (always my best friends). It's made with equal parts of brandy, Kahlua, and half-and-half, poured into one ice-filled red Solo cup, and shaken using another. They're delicious, taste like coffee milkshakes, and live up to their name: deadly at separating your mind from your body.

I met scores of interesting people over the horse years and made a few good friends. My favorite was quite a guy. Tall, dark and handsome, a take-charge kind of man with superior intelligence, devilish charm, lots of money and an absolutely gorgeous blond wife. We had a strong connection, not at all sexual: two equals whose philosophies on life and how to live it were similar. Rick told me of his rebellion against his powerful Utah family, his time as an FBI agent, his return to take over the world-wide construction business. He described spotting his future wife at a bar when she was with another guy. It was love at first sight, but it was also determination to take her as his wife. His choice was a lovely and charming woman — but we didn't have much in common.

Once, while spending time with them at their home, I noticed the dozens of nail polish bottles she kept in the refrigerator. It made me stop and think. It led me to ask him whether they challenged each other in conversation or talked about his professional life, successes, failures, problems — as he and I had done so often.

He looked at me quizzically. "God no, Susan. The last thing I want when I get home at night is a complicated conversation. I get all the intellectual stimulation I can handle from work and friends. It's a pleasure to sit, relax and hear my wife talk about what she did that day."

That was a revelation for me, and helped me understand what many strong successful men want from their female partners. Not all men — but a lot of them.

Another friend and icon from the industrial world was Herbert Kohler. The headquarters of his famous plumbing fixture company was located in Kohler, Wisconsin. There I visited his home, his stables, and stayed at his beautiful American Club Hotel on several occasions. I bought horses from him, competed against him, and verbally sparred and joked with him at the shows.

The side of Herb Kohler that always kept me on the alert was his penchant for control — not just for the women in his life (I was definitely not one of them), but for just about everything else. Don't get me wrong: he was brilliant, and I admired him greatly — but resisted being included among the things he controlled. I was always a little wary: he once put me on a horse that broke its bridle and bolted through the Wisconsin woods, scaring the shit out of me until I got him back under control. I'll never know if it was some kind of test of my mettle.

Other interesting Morgan horse friends were Leslie Blanchard, his partner Miguel, and an older couple, John and Rose Schemmer. In the '60s and '70s, Leslie owned a beautiful four-story brownstone just around the corner from my apartment on Madison Ave. It housed his famously successful hair coloring and styling salon. In those years, he was regarded as one of the stars in his field. The three of us hung out at horse shows and in the City drinking our gin and tonics. I went to his salon; so did my mother; and I visited his elegant, manicured horse farm in Connecticut. He, Miguel and I gossiped and gabbed about everyone and everything. Gay men make the best girlfriends...Leslie's life was tragically cut short by AIDS in the '80s.

John Schemmer was a renowned litigator in Manhattan. Flowing grey hair, leonine good looks and a flair for the dramatic made him a favorite on the horse show scene. Being a showman at heart, he also rode and drove in the amateur classes. I visited John and Rose often at their Pawling, NY horse farm. He and Rose were always talking to me, trying to interest me in their son, Tony who was a physician, but fascinated by music and the music business. I resisted. As the owner and president of a successful music company, I had to fend off many similar attempts by well-meaning parents and relatives of people who were interested in getting into the biz.

Many years later, I was with Michael, my current soulmate and partner, at his college reunion. He introduced me to his good friend and fellow Yalie secret society member, Tony Schemmer. I was getting to know Tony and his accomplished and witty wife, Ann, when I suddenly made the connection. We all had a good laugh; and they became very good friends of ours. Although he is a Harvard-trained doctor, Tony is devoting his life to his music. Once again, the world is very small place.

For two weeks every fall, the Grand National Morgan Horse Show is held in Oklahoma City. It was there that the dramatic high point of all the horsey adventures came to pass.

I had competed in the amateur pleasure driving qualifiers against a hundred other entrants. With Appelton Radiance, my dynamic, classic bay mare, we had made it into the finals.

Then, the night before the championship class, my trainers and I were horrified to notice a two-inch gash just below one of Radiance's eyes. It was open and bleeding.

Something had to be done, but our vet couldn't use a general anesthetic: if we won, she would be drug tested and disqualified. I watched in disbelief while she let him stitch her up with only a mild local shot. Slowly, patiently, allowing his hand to follow the bobbing of her head, he got it done. After the class the next night, she was immediately put under for the more extensive operation.

Radiance was an amazing horse. Powerful and big for a mare, she almost drove herself. She knew instinctively when it was time to pass another horse and show off her stuff. She helped me maneuver through the congested, wheel-threatening traffic of carts and horses like a top NASCAR driver.

That night, as we waited in a lineup after the class, my hard-boiled ex-cop trainer, Jim Anderson, stood at her head with a hand on her bridle and mumbled something like, "I think we may have won this."

When my number was called as the winner, he whooped "*Holy Shit!*" and jumped a couple of feet in the air. After the ribbon and flashbulb-popping trophy presentation, Radiance and I were called to take the winner's lap as Grand Champions. I was wearing Holly Harp: a long lavender Victorian dress with jet beading. Elbow-length black satin gloves completed the costume. My hair was long at the time, so — with hair blowing back from my face and goggles, and with the crowd now standing and screaming — we trotted speedily around the open ring in what was, simply, the thrill of a lifetime...

Later reflection on this whole period of my life doesn't exactly make me proud of myself. Granted, I had some fun, but was it really worth all that time and money? Probably not...It was such an ego trip. Somehow I thought I had "the eye," the expertise to pick out winners and sponsor them to greatness. Ironically, I have that gift in the music business: finding extraordinarily talented people and nurturing them to fame and fortune. But these are people, not bought-and-sold animals.

The horses became extensions of me and my ego. Any criticism of my horse was a personal attack on me. If my horse won, I was great. If my horse lost, I was a loser. Yes, it's stupid, but true. In reality, it had little to do with me. I once saw two Presidents of major corporations worth billions get into a bloody fistfight on the show grounds over a championship cooler (a blanket with the title of the class written on it). The cooler cost maybe $25.

And the judging can become purely political. Unlike racing events where winning is based on time, and unlike jumping classes where fault points are included, ribbons in breed classes are awarded based solely on personal opinion. Who would ever be the wiser if some cash or other favors affected the decision?

There is also a gigantic fallacy at the root of the horse business. Every owner fantasizes about breeding champions and making a lot of money. It is pure nonsense. Even the biggest, most successful and wealthiest Morgan farms would probably do well to break even. This is not the arena in which a Secretariat or a Seattle Slew could arise — not even close. For the most part, the only people who eke out a decent living are the trainers and handlers. But we owners are universally foolish and greedy. I had many offers for my good horses. In fact, someone offered me $10,000 on the spot for a filly foal that had just won her class at the New England Regionals. Did I take it — or any of the others? No, of course not! There's always the hope that she might be worth much more as she grows up. Never mind about how much it costs to raise, train, and show her.

Eventually I held a huge auction and sold all of the Morgans. I lost a ton of money that day, but on the bright side, at least I was out of the business. Later, even when we had a perfect, gorgeous 12-stall horse barn on our property in upstate New York, I didn't succumb to temptation. We left the barn empty — and turned the large fenced riding ring into a vegetable, berry and perennial garden.

I ONCE SWEET-TALKED the American Morgan Horse Association, a group of tight-fisted New Englanders, into forking over $250,000 to produce a docudrama that would promote our breed.

I had come up with an outline for the script, but had no time to produce it. So I set up the horses, the farms and the cast, and turned the project over to my friends Tim Newman and Dennis Powers, a couple of pros from the real world.

The film was a huge success and won an award at the Cannes Film Festival. (I earned a lot of brownie points).

Chapter 36

Divine Intervention

I WAS DRIVING IN A BLIZZARD, and not happy about it. The two-wheel drive rental was slipping and sliding all over the Interstate as I made my way from Salt Lake City down to Provo. And all on a fool's errand. I'd flown out to have a meet and greet with Donny and Marie Osmond, and to take a tour of their newly built production facility. It was a multi-million dollar project designed to attract valuable TV, motion picture, and recording business from L. A.

Some background information: HEA had once again won a jingle competition: this one for Hawaiian Punch. The spots were to feature the brother and sister team of Donny and Marie. The catchy tune had been written by Bill Eaton, and the track was infused with an infectious r&b groove.

It had been the Osmonds' choice to record the final tracks in their studios in Provo; thus my visit. They insisted on using their own band from their TV show, and probably also would have liked to film the spots there as well — but that was purely wishful thinking on their part. The ads were going to be shot in L.A. with a hotshot director.

I found the facility to be shiny, spotless, and empty. The rooms were cavernous, completely outfitted with state-of-the-art equipment, all apparently unused. Even the dressing rooms were theme decorated, squeaky clean, but there was no feeling, no personality, no history to any of them. They were DOA. Nobody home. The place was truly cold.

Donny and Marie did put in a token appearance, but the tour was conducted by a clean-cut guy who didn't know very much. I left fairly spooked by the whole experience. I couldn't imagine recording there.

We soon heard from the Osmonds' people that the recording session for the tracks had to be moved to California due to their schedules. We would do the tracks one night, and they would record the vocals the next.

Needless to say, I was relieved.

So off I went to L.A. once again. The studio turned out to be in some strip mall in the Valley. And cheesy-looking.

Donny and Marie weren't there when I arrived, but we started with the band anyway. It was rough going at first, but I figured it would all fall into place eventually.

It never did. The guys in the band had as much soul in their entire bodies as I had in my little toe (and I'm white and a classical music chick). The track felt like shit. I worked and worked, suggested this and that, but it was no dice.

By the time it got to midnight, I was tired, frustrated, out of ideas. The musicians were friendly, willing to take direction, and completely hopeless. I considered my options. I couldn't just cancel the session. What could I give as a reason? *It just didn't feel right. It had no grease, no soul.* Yeah sure, I was going to explain that to a bunch of agency people — much less the Osmonds?

I know this is going to be hard to believe, but it is the absolute truth. At that moment, I looked over at my also-clueless engineer to see a big *poof!* of grey smoke rise from the middle of the console. The little green and red lights went off row by row, and we were finished. Shut down by the hand of fate. The engineer looked like he was about to faint. Maintenance came in, and the guy just shook his head sorrowfully. I did a big internal fist-pump "YES!" and feigned disappointment. There was nothing to be done; the session was cancelled.

Donny and Marie ended up having to sing and shoot to the original feel-good demo. And that is what ended up going on air.

I didn't regret not being able to record their vocals personally. Frankly, I'd had enough of Provo. The whole town gave me the creeps. I don't know why, exactly, but I kept having visions of bad things happening behind those white picket fences and super neat yards.

I didn't read Marie's tell-all book until much later.

My other encounter with a brother-sister act took place in Canada. I met Richard and Karen Carpenter at an expansive studio complex in Toronto. The mission was to record their shortened versions of "We've Only Just Begun" for a bank commercial. They seemed like a couple of farm kids. Their clothes could have come from a J.C. Penney catalogue: the antithesis of rock and roll garb. Khaki pants and skirt, button down-shirts and penny loafers. She had a pageboy with bangs; his hair, short and neatly trimmed. I was surprised. They didn't look like big time celebrities. And that they certainly were.

The song had a unique history. It was originally written as a jingle for Crocker National Bank by Paul Williams and Roger Nichols. Richard Carpenter happened to hear it on air and realized its potential. He turned it into their best-selling single, ultimately their signature song — it has probably been performed or played at more than a million weddings.

Years later, the Bank wanted a couple of advertising-length versions performed by the stars who had made it such a hit. It was a very long (and sort of dreary) session. Richard was a perfectionist and the tracks didn't have a single flaw. Every note was in tune, every beat in the perfect place, every lick very tasteful... but boy, it sounded and felt completely sterile. I got bored, frankly.

Everything changed when Karen finally stood in front of the microphone and started to sing. Her voice was magic.

The tone was a deep rich velvet to rival Mel Torme's, but without the fog. Just pure lusciousness. She projected complete sincerity, but underneath, a very discernible sense of wistfulness and sadness. That pervasive undertone comes across in her records too. And I don't believe it's just the choice of songs. I felt it from her personally, as well. She obeyed every direction her brother snapped at her, almost robotically, whether she was playing drums, doing background parts or performing the solo. She was quiet, pleasant and childlike, but displayed little emotion. Yet her vocals were full of feeling. Quite remarkable.

I saw her again many years later, a short time before she passed away. She was recording an album with my friend Phil Ramone in the big studio A of A&R Recording. I immediately noticed how unnervingly thin she was. Off and on during the following couple of weeks I did a few sessions of my own next door in Studio B, and chatted with the New York musicians Phil was using on the album. They liked her all right, but bitched and moaned to me about the absolute prohibition against any words stronger than 'heck' or 'gosh darn.' She was always such a good girl.

If there is a heaven, I bet she's finally happy, singing somewhere with a real band. She deserves one.

THE MUDDY WATERS session for Dr Pepper was recorded in Chicago at Chess Records Studio, and it was a nightmare.

The studio was in disrepair. When mixing the spots, we found the harmonica and the electric bass on the same track. Worse yet, Muddy and the band hadn't a clue how to handle Randy Newman's charming, chromatic shuffle tune.

I had to somehow wrangle it into a 12/8 blues song. It took a while...

Bernie had to sit next to Muddy on a piano bench and whisper-feed him the words just before he spoke/sang the lyrics.

The choruses were fine, but the word "originality" in the verse was mangled almost beyond recognition. Eliot and I ended up piecing it together, syllable by syllable. The client bought it anyway.

Chapter 37

The Pineapple

———

ONE OF THE MOST CREATIVE people I ever worked with in the advertising business was Tom Figenshu. Tom was a senior writer at N W Ayer — but he was much more than that. He was a collaborator who was always willing to think outside of the box, if not sideways to the box. The ideas he came up with never sounded labored or off the wall. They made absolute sense and resonated with just about everyone.

We worked together on accounts that included Pan Am, AT&T, General Motors and Citibank, among others. But the name Tom Figenshu is most often associated with the "Be All You Can Be" campaign for the Army. Tom told us he wrote the line and provided some of the lyrics; Jake Holmes wrote the music and most of the lyrics, and I produced all of the tracks for years. It was probably the most lucrative account HEA ever had, and definitely one of the most admired. Odd but true: this long-running, most successful, super-macho campaign was conceived and supervised by a strange gay guy, and the gutsy music tracks that accompanied it were produced by a young Manhattan woman. To their credit, none of the four-star generals who visited us in the recording studio ever batted an eyelash. There was never any sense of discomfort.

Tom became good friends with everyone at HEA and would frequently appear at the office just to socialize. He had great taste in music and literature offset by a somewhat bizarre taste in art and films. We would sit around after hours and drink and talk into the night. We all loved him.

Sadly, as the years went by, his mind began to crack. I guess the best way to describe it is that his personality started to fracture little by little. First, odd sentences would come out of his mouth; words that made no sense at all. Then there was the occasional jumping up from the couch and rushing off abruptly with no goodbyes. Absences from meetings and sessions followed.

All of us grew increasingly worried about what was happening with him. But we also had no idea what to do. It all culminated with his bringing a flagrant male prostitute up to the offices of N W Ayer right after lunch. He allowed his companion to tag along as he went from agency meeting to client meeting. The two of them deliberately paraded up and down the halls on several floors. The bigwigs at the Agency loved Tom too, but this behavior was the last straw. They fired him on the spot.

A few days later, some of us were having lunch with Tom at a restaurant on East 57th Street. I remember that it was very cold outside. Tom was strangely upbeat and philosophical about his situation. Quite cheerful, actually. We ate, joked around and discussed nothing serious. At some point, he got up and excused himself to go to the restroom.

He emerged many minutes later dressed in Bermuda shorts, a Hawaiian shirt, and combat boots. He also sported a pineapple lifted from one of the fruit displays, strapped right to the front of his head. He came over to our table, bowed at the waist said, "I gotta go now," and left the restaurant. The last we ever saw of him was as he sauntered past the front windows, headed west on 57th Street.

A month or so later, I was sitting at the King Cole Bar in the St. Regis Hotel, gabbing with Bob Cox. He was another great client and friend, and we got to discussing the strange sights one sometimes ran into on the streets of New York City. He told me, "One of the oddest things I ever saw happened just a few weeks ago. In the middle of the day I was walking from the agency to a meeting on 57th Street. I was in a hurry because it was freezing and had my head down, but I looked up just in time to see a guy walking toward me with a fuckin' pineapple strapped to his head!"

I guess New York City really is a small town, after all.

Tom Figenshu was rolled, mugged and murdered on West 42nd Street later that year, but his body wasn't identified until literally the day before he would have been buried in Potter's Field. Thank God for that.

CINDY CRAWFORD, LITTLE RICHARD, and Richard Gere. I had quite a struggle producing that combo for Charlie perfume.

Mr. Gere, husband to Ms. Crawford, was on his best behavior. He tried to take over only a few times.

Cindy was spunky, cheerful, and worked long and hard to perfect her singing lines.

Little Richard, a ghoul up close, scared me with his ¼" thick greenish makeup and wild eyes. But he played and sang with his signature energy and, after many takes, the track came out great.

It's amazing how natural, effortless, and *normal* the finished commercial looked on-air.

Chapter 38

Things Fall Apart

The decay crept in through little things. On the surface, everything about our marriage seemed perfect. The work Eliot and I produced together was more and more successful. The money rolled in, and we spent most of it. One weekend, we jetted off to London on the Concorde simply to attend an Oscar Wilde party given by my TV network client, Steve Sohmer. We were back home within 48 hours.

Eliot, in particular, had become accustomed to our increasingly extravagant lifestyle. He loved the limos, the first class cabins, the personal attention from the maître d's at our favorite restaurants — so much so that he threw a mini-hissy fit and pouted if we ever found ourselves having to fly tourist. I didn't care as much; I figured I would be able to go back to being poor if that ever came to pass. After all, I hadn't felt terribly deprived when money was so scarce growing up or starting out in Manhattan.

Work was still being done on the Vermont farm. Eliot asked me if he could supervise and direct the carpenters, electrician, plumber and painters. I had been managing the projects until then. I agreed: it would serve to establish his 'man of the house' status.

This was a disaster. Within two weekends, friends who had worked for me for years were threatening to quit. Ordering them around imperiously and finding fault with minutiae weren't serving to encourage excellent workmanship. I had to step in. I tried explaining to Eliot that these were proud, independent contractors — not intern assistant engineers who might benefit from the 'boot camp' treatment. He retreated in a huff with, "Fine, you do it. They don't like me anyway."

Uh oh. I started to worry. What could possibly be going wrong? This was nothing like the disparity of career arcs that had affected my relationship with Walter. Both Eliot and I were on the rise in the biz, his accomplishments more glamorous than mine.

Other changes were happening. I grew concerned and bewildered. With absolutely no reason for it, jealously reared its ugly green head. When we were alone, Eliot began to accuse certain clients of having feelings for me, and became uncharacteristically rude to them in the studio. If I needed to go out to dinner with one, he would sit on the sill of our seventh floor living room window, staking out the street entrance below until I got home. A quick embrace and peck on the cheek of my dinner companion at the door would trigger an intense, uncalled-for interrogation.

I hate public displays of affection. Always have. No clinging, petting, making-out for me when I am out and about. Not with anyone. Holding hands on the street is about my limit. We had always had an understanding on that score, but now, for the first time, Eliot changed. Hanging out with friends, he would put his arm around me, or start playing with my hair while I was trying to make a point in conversation. Sometimes I'd get pulled around the neck for a supposedly spontaneous kiss on the mouth. I guessed that these actions were meant as a show of proof of our togetherness, or possibly of his proprietary rights. Whatever. It freaked me out. I felt choked, smothered. Where was the easy-going, happy-go-lucky Eliot I had married?

It got worse. I was genuinely shocked and upset when he announced he wasn't leaving for L.A. to work with Steely Dan on a weeklong project. He said he didn't want to leave me alone in New York. In retrospect, it was at this point I should have suggested counseling, but didn't. I never even considered it. I was upset, reluctant to air our dirty laundry in front of anyone (so much so that I didn't even tell my best friend: my mother).

Eliot started hiding things from me. We both had quit smoking, but it became obvious that he'd started up again. I could smell it in our bathroom, on his clothes. When challenged, he vehemently denied it. I grew sadder and sadder.

Then the worst happened. It came at his brother's wedding reception in Brooklyn. We were sitting with his whole family at a long table, eating dinner and telling stories. Chuck Scheiner was right across from me. At some point, I brought up the lost Christmas from years before when the two brothers had to go to Florida to be with their sick mother.

I got it in a nanosecond. The totally blank look on his brother's face made me shut my mouth instantly. Eliot's entire story from years before had been an out-and-out lie.

We were both silent for a long time on the ride back to town. Then blurting out sentence after sentence, he tried to explain and make excuses. "I had to, Susan. Denise insisted that I at least spend Christmas with her and her parents before she told them about the divorce. I felt bad for her, so I gave in. I didn't tell you because I was so afraid I would lose you. I couldn't let that happen. I wanted to be with you so bad."

He pleaded with me to forgive him. To understand that he did it for us, so we could be together. It was as though I had been kicked hard in the gut. I could feel the fabric of my world being torn into rags. In my head, I started to question many other things. I had already discovered that despite telling me his birthday was February 29th, his passport showed the actual date was March 6th or 7th. There was a tale from the time he was a drummer in a band. He'd described sitting at a bar after a show, suddenly seeing a look of fear cross the bartender's face. Before he could react, Eliot said he was jumped by a couple of mob guys. They broke all the fingers on his right hand one by one because he hadn't gone along with some shakedown. He had explained that it was the reason why he had turned to engineering as a career. Now I began to doubt: was this another story? Why would he need to dramatize and aggrandize his past? Everyone, including me, loved and admired him. It made no sense.

I threw myself into my work. Pushed away my worries, put my head down and just did, did, did. That was my normal reaction to any kind of trouble.

And I was busy. The jobs were pouring in, and I was back and forth to L.A. at least once every other week. I had also started working with a new keyboard player and writer. Rob Mounsey was (and is) a true genius. Not only musically, but also through power of intellect. He had started composing his own symphonies at seven. His older sister, against direct orders from their parents, had filled his ears with recordings of classical masters. They feared their only son would fall victim to the arts. She had also slipped him books on composition and orchestration, as well as actual scores. His work for HEA was stellar. All of the other writers were jealous — mostly because I was so blown away. Not only by his talent, but also by his startling brain power.

The inevitable happened. Rob and I were spending a lot of time traveling, talking, and working together. I was dispirited by the situation at home, and so yes, we began a secret casual affair. Oddly, only six months before, Eliot and I with Rob and his girlfriend had all enjoyed a pleasant, drama-free vacation at La Samanna. Just before things started falling apart.

That fall, Eliot and I took my parents on a mini 'grand tour' of Europe. He and I were to travel with them in France and Italy, and then send them off for a week in London with a chauffeur/guide at their disposal. We all boarded the AirFrance Concorde for Paris at JFK. A little less than halfway across the Atlantic, at 66,000 feet, the plane began to shudder violently, then rapidly drop. My father turned to my mother, patted her hand, and said, "Just a little turbulence, my dear." I knew better. I thought to myself, *Glad my boots are off if we're going into the water.* There were no screams or prayers from any of the passengers, just eerie stillness and silence. We leveled off at 33,000 feet before the pilot finally came on the p.a. system. He apologized for the lack of communication and explained that we'd lost one of our two engines and could no longer fly at supersonic speed. Also, since we hadn't quite reached the halfway mark, we had to turn around. Thinking to comfort us, he related how he had decided not to land in Greenland, but to try and get back to JFK - he felt confident we had enough fuel to make it.

We didn't.

We made an emergency landing at Logan in Boston. No Concorde had ever attempted to touch down there because of the shorter runways. From our tiny little oval windows, we could see more than a hundred emergency vehicles lining both sides of the runway.

They weren't needed; our French pilot made a perfect landing. The airline put us on an overnight Delta flight to Paris. Not quite the Concorde, but at least the plane was almost empty, and we were able to sleep stretched out across the tourist seats in the tail.

The near-death experience woke me up. I resolved to make a concentrated effort to fix my crumbling relationship. It didn't work.

We spent four days at the Plaza Athénée, then five days at the Hassler in Rome. Eliot's behavior toward me became steadily worse. Now my mother noticed it. His almost constant need for attention and physical contact was oppressive. I felt like I couldn't breathe. It was like he was devolving into someone I didn't know. He even looked different. He had a slight trace of fear on his face most of the time; his features seemed pinched. I reacted in my normal way — scheduling so many outings and activities that I didn't have time to think about anything else.

The whole scenario affected me physically. I felt logy, slightly nauseous, and more tired than usual. Late one afternoon, my mother and I sat on the Spanish Steps, discussing Eliot's uncharacteristic behavior in the soft golden light of Rome. She looked into my eyes and quietly said, "Susan, you're pregnant; I can see it in your eyes."

It took a full week of agonizing before I made my decision. I would have an abortion; it seemed the only way out. I was nearly certain the baby would be Rob's, but I also couldn't be sure. What if it were Eliot's (even though we had failed to get pregnant for five years)? What if I had been wrong about my assumption that my appendectomy had made me infertile? I went to my wonderful ob/gyn on Park Avenue and poured my heart out.

Dr. Zuckerman was genuinely annoyed with me for failing to mention my assumption that I couldn't get pregnant. He had been my doctor and friend for years and let me know that he would have seen it and told me if I had been dysfunctional. Then told me I could have ten children if I wanted to — even after an abortion. So I scheduled it for a Friday.

The irony depressed me. Wanting a child for so long, now this... But I thought it was the only way: I had decided I had to make one more try with Eliot or disentangle myself. A baby on the way (a baby that he thought was his) would have complicated the situation irredeemably. I wouldn't be able to live with the lie. And what if the baby had brown eyes? How would I explain that when it is incredibly rare between two light-eyed people? If it were possible for me to get pregnant fairly easily, I wanted to start being a mother with a clean slate.

Early in the morning on the day of the procedure, Eliot burst into our bathroom where I was getting ready, and literally bounced off the walls. He'd gone through my purse and found the doctor's instructions for the prep. He was screaming and crying at the same time,

"I knew it was me! I knew I couldn't have a baby. Now I know for sure you *have* been carrying on with someone else. Tell me who is it, dammit? Who is it? Oh wait, of course, it's Rob, Rob fuckin' Mounsey."

He collapsed on the bench inside our big steam shower. I merely said, "Eliot, I have to do this. I have to go now. We'll talk about it later." But I realized I couldn't leave him like that: I was beginning to worry about what he might do. I called Walter and quickly explained the situation.

So it was my ex-husband — long-suffering Walter — who came, picked up Eliot, and took him away to some bar where they got very drunk. He babysat all weekend. That is a true friend...

I fled to the Vermont house that same night. I got into my car and drove the four hours. Late that night, I fell apart, too — by myself, in the bathroom, away from my parents. I cried and cried (for the baby, for Eliot, for me). Then I vomited. Then I slept for 14 hours.

Saturday and Sunday I wandered around the property, facing my thoughts. I returned to the City Monday morning, and sat down with Eliot. I felt terrible. He wasn't even angry anymore; just beaten down. But he wanted to work it out between us. I had to give him and us a chance; so I did. I supported him when he went to a reproductive specialist and found out his sperm weren't very motile. One question answered.

We tried and tried — both of us — to revive the magic of the past, but it was gone. Eventually, Eliot moved out. Although we continued to work together for a while, that, too, faded away.

I had a hard time figuring out what had happened to our marriage. I thought it must have been equally my fault, but couldn't understand what I had done wrong. I did hear that Eliot told a mutual friend, "Whatever you do, never let your own self disappear when you love someone. You can lose everything."

Glenn Berger, first the top assistant engineer at A&R, and later a senior engineer in his own right, worked very closely with Eliot and me for all of those years. He writes,

Els was completely caught up in Susan's world. I use that phrase because that's really what it was. There was the place the rest of us lived, and then there was Susan's world. Els was a pretty energetic guy, and he wanted to keep up, but I always got the sense that when Susan crossed the finish line barely breaking a sweat, Eliot was running a few steps behind, carrying the bags, and panting out of breath. Sometimes he'd look at me with a small amount of desperation in his gaze, thrilled to be there, but a bit freaked at this lady's energy.

I don't think any of us thought the relationship would last forever because it was hard to conceive that he would be able to hold Susan's interest, and it was impossible to imagine that he would be able to keep up. Eventually he would get exhausted, pissed off, and act out in some moronic way. One did not get the impression of the deepest level of integrity in Els.

Glenn was right, in a way. It was the lack of integrity — or moral fiber — that most likely finally did us in. The big ancient lie, surrounded by all the little ones, ate at me. I couldn't forget or forgive them. His suffocating downward spiral into insecurity completed our undoing. It was over. So sad.

(Eliot's spectacular career continued for many more years than mine. He met and married a wonderful woman, and eventually – they had a son! Maybe we weren't meant to be together forever, after all.)

FEEDING FRENZIES have always been common occurrences at my country houses.

I cook. Seriously. I love it, and have been working at it since I was seven. When I have guests for the weekend, I go all out.

Problems arise whenever my diet-conscious, highly disciplined friends lose control and gorge. At 3 am I find them standing at the open refrigerator door, stuffing cold *spaghetti alla carbonara* and Belgian chocolate cake into their mouths.

Sometimes they leave early, mumbling, "Gotta get back to my primary care physician..." Sometimes there's a trip to the local emergency room.

But in the worst cases, they call 911. An ambulance and other emergency vehicles fill my driveway, and I have to explain to the neighbors that yes, it happened again...

Chapter 39

Music City, U.S.A.

———

A T FIRST I WASN'T THRILLED with the idea of producing music in the South. Hillbillies in the studio? A Manhattan broad telling 'real' men what to do?

I couldn't have been more wrong. I ended up falling in love with Nashville and its people during the 20 years I worked there. In fact, I did seriously consider moving there permanently. What nixed the idea is the absolutely dreadful weather that can envelop you any time of the year. Tennessee produces just too many hot, humid, thoroughly oppressive days. Then there's the beauty of the hanging Spanish moss (and trying not to think about the chiggers that live in it). I love winter — but *real* winter: crisp frosty mornings with mounds of pretty fluffy white snow everywhere. This does not happen in Nashville. A typical winter there consists of heavy ice storm attacks that scare the shit out of everyone. The trees break, the power lines go down and the roads become impassable. Not for me. And I won't even mention the deadly tornados, scariest of all...

My jaunts to Nashville started sometime around 1970. The memories are slightly sketchy when it comes to who I recorded for whom in those early days. I remember the artists clearly; the products not so much. I do know at first I was working on Kentucky Fried Chicken and McDonald's campaigns, followed by Dr Pepper, among others, from 1973 on.

The first legendary performers I produced in Nashville were Mother Maybelle Carter and Bill Monroe. Mother Maybelle and her three daughters (including June, who was married to Johnny Cash) were billed as The Carter Family. They were beloved fixtures at the Grand Ole Opry. I remember looking at them through the glass wall of the control room, all sitting around casually in front of the drummer and bass player, smiling and nodding to each other as they strummed and picked their guitars and autoharp.

Maybelle was a notably skilled guitarist. She developed a revolutionary style of playing which became known as the *Carter Scratch* or *Carter Family Picking*. It required being able to play the melody lines on the bass strings with her thumb while rhythmically strumming with her other fingers. This groundbreaking technique was partially responsible for the guitar's ascendance from rhythm-only to lead instrument.

The girls did the vocals, with June singing the solos, and although I don't recall much else, it was a warm, friendly, relaxed session, quite different from the chillier studio scene in NYC.

Bill Monroe, on the other hand, was a grumpy old man who never smiled. But he sure played a mean mandolin. This "Father of Bluegrass," who almost single-handedly created the whole musical genre with his band the Blue Grass Boys, led a successful career for over 50 years. In its formative years, his band included both Earl Scruggs and Lester Flatt.

When I worked with him producing his version of "The Most Original Soft Drink," he was tall, slim, trim and grim, dressed in black pants, cowboy boots, a fancy white shirt with a string tie, and cowboy hat. I don't think he liked me (probably didn't cotton much to taking direction from a city girl). He barely acknowledged me, reluctantly answering my requests with "Yes ma'am" and a tip of the hat. He sang in a thin, reedy nasal voice, but played his Gibson 1923 F5 model signature "Lloyd Loar" mandolin at blistering speed with total accuracy. The performance was professional and suck-the-words-out-of-your-mouth brilliant.

I went on to record and produce many country artists and groups in Nashville (Memphis, too) including Lynn Anderson, Alabama, the Oak Ridge Boys, Tom T. Hall, Dave Loggins, Vince Gill, Loretta Lynn. But it's Nashville that stole my heart: the place, the feeling of it and my relationships with its very special people. During the '70s, and especially the '80s, it became a home away from home for me, both professionally and personally. Another draw to Nashville was the presence of Toni Wine and her new husband, legendary producer Chips Moman. Toni, a best friend and bridesmaid at my wedding to Eliot, wrote many hit songs, sang with Ron Dante for The Archies, with Linda November for the Tony Orlando records, and, of course, for me on many jingles. She and Chips helped a lot during my early days of producing there.

Nashville is small. The music scene is happening, not only for country (both old fashioned and modern), but also for rock, rockabilly, pop, r&b, and soul. The jazz scene in those years couldn't come close to what was going on in the Big Apple, but the rest of the music business seemed fresher, less jaded — and more relaxed, for sure.

When working there, I felt like I didn't have to watch the clock as much; didn't have to play politics as much, could let my guard down, joke around, and in general, have a good ol' time with the boys. There was a whole lot less ego on display from the musicians, singers, arrangers and engineers. Much less competitive jockeying and bickering, less worrying. As a result, I didn't have to be so careful in what I said or how I gave constructive criticism. I was always treated with the utmost respect, but at the same time allowed to feel I was one of the guys let in on the jokes, a member of the club, and welcome at their after-session hangout joints.

I had to learn a new musical language to work with them. Charts (the music sheets handed out to players) in Nashville were like none I'd ever seen. There were no notes on even a single staff, (never mind a double one); there were no named changes (chords). There was just a sequence of numbers written within slash marks (denoting bars), usually scribbled on any old scrap of paper. It was generally left up to the musicians to make any rhythmic notations they might need to jog their memory about of some particular pattern that needed to be precise. This system was fairly easy to learn, but it made producing more difficult — at least it did for me.

I have perfect pitch, and have used it throughout my career as a communications shortcut during production. A side note about 'perfect pitch.' It's an inherent skill one is born with: you either have it or you don't. You can't acquire it through any amount of practice or training. To someone who is born with it, identifying any particular note or chord is as simple and effortless as distinguishing red from blue. Each note or chord with the same name identifies itself to my ears and brain the same way each color does to my eyes and brain. Yellow is yellow; a "c" is a "c."

So when directing or correcting during a music session, a quick way of finding your place in the score, or pinpointing the beat, bar, or section you want to fix, is to locate the particular chord. For example, you hear that there was a wrong note in a G major chord, so you glance down at the score, spot the nearest G major notation, get right on the talkback with, "*Hey Joe,* (Joe is the guitar player) *there was a clam in bar 54: that's a G major chord, not G minor.*" It can make you come off like a genius to the players — but in all honestly, that particular wizardry is a whole lot easier when you have perfect pitch and most of the rest of the world doesn't.

My perfect pitch system was not as effective in Nashville, where I had to use their simple but screwy numbers method. I understood, of course, that their system referred to the numerical names of the chords in any scale or key. One was the root chord, five the dominant, four the sub-dominant, etc. It was a practical method because it could be employed for any key or any change of key without involving all the machinations of transposing.

But for me, it required a whole extra step in my thought process. *Now let's see, we're in the key of A major* (my perfect pitch told me that) *so therefore the 4 chord is D major.* Those extra mental steps meant extra time wasted. Even worse, I couldn't refer to a D major chord, I had to refer to the "4 chord" for the musicians to understand me. Terrible at first, but I got used to it soon enough.

Perfect pitch can have other drawbacks. I cannot transpose at the piano to save my life. Or, if I'm singing in a chorus, reading my part in the score, and the director decides to change the key, I'm S.O.L. In my brain, the notes I have to sing don't correspond to what's on the paper.

I once had a shocking experience in an L.A. studio. I was working next door to the cavernous Studio A where Guns N' Roses were recording an album. They weren't there during the day, so on a break, I visited their studio and sat down on the piano bench to try out the beautiful Bösendorfer. I struck a loud chord and jumped back off the bench in terror. I may have even shrieked. I couldn't play anything. Apparently, the band was known to tune their guitar strings down a half step for a richer, deeper tone. It was also good for the horn players, who always prefer to play in the flat keys — but not so great for a rock n' roll piano player who found those keys more difficult. Solution? Tune the piano down like the guitars - problem solved! Most pianists would never have even noticed the difference. For me, it was like being zapped with a cattle prod.

There are a lot of other fabulous things about Music City. Besides all of the famous country music attractions, there are also historic plantations like Jackson's Hermitage, Vanderbilt University, stately old architecture in downtown, and of course, Music Row: an area centered on a couple of blocks of parallel side streets that house the major players of the country music business. Publishing houses, record companies, talent agencies, booking agents, a few studios, managers' offices: the buildings all look so quaint, cozy and unassuming. *Yeah, right!* Southern-style genteel cutthroat wheeling and dealing was going on at all hours.

And oh my, the food. In NY studios, it's bagels and bialys; in L.A., Roscoe's chicken and waffles; but in Nashville, it's fluffy hot biscuits and Tennessee country ham: those addictive salty, tangy pink chunks, sometimes soaked in red-eye gravy. Other specialties include country fried steak, fried green tomatoes, turnip greens, fried okra, and hushpuppies — but you haven't lived until you've sat around on folding lawn chairs in a gravel parking lot next to the studio drinking cold beers and eating fried catfish straight out of the big barrel filled with boiling oil.

Something else that tempted me to consider moving to Nashville is its proximity to the exquisite Tennessee countryside. Real country. Rolling hills of blue/green grass, gorgeous old trees and scattered wooded copses are less than 10 miles from the center of the city. Manicured horse farms with miles of white three- or four-rail fencing line both sides of the road. And very little traffic. People in New York City have to travel at least an hour through heavy traffic to get to the country, and even then, much of it is so gentrified you could really call it suburbia.

One time after we had done a session for Diet Dr Pepper, I spent a lovely afternoon with Lynn Anderson at her elegant home and horse ranch just a few miles out of town. She raised and showed cutting horses. So we talked horses and the horse business, music, musicians and the music business, and what it is like to be a woman in the South and in show business. She seemed to have it all.

As the years passed, I looked for any excuse to record in Nashville. As luck would have it, at that time the popularity of country music was growing exponentially, so I found them. The whole Miller Beer campaign, *My Beer is American Made,* based on the Oak Ridge Boys song, was recorded in Nashville: every single spot. Off and on, I was able to work an entire week or two there for Miller, for Burger King, for KFC, for McDonalds.

The Miller Beer recordings were a true eye-opener for me. I did the demos in Nashville for the J. Walter Thompson pitch that won the account. Then I insisted on recording all the final tracks there even though it would be more expensive. My gut told me the unique quality of the winning demos would be tricky to reproduce in New York.

I was right. A year later, I tried to do a quickie demo for Miller in Manhattan. I used the best studio musicians. It was a disaster, and I ending up flying down anyway. Nashville musicians have an innate instinct to play the fewest notes possible. New York musicians strive to play as many as possible. Every NY sideman wants to put his stamp on every performance; wants to come up with the great lick or fill that will be noticed by the *cognoscenti*. They really can't help themselves, and they think they are improving the track, but in fact, this is a foolproof way to destroy the straight-to-the-heart quality of country music.

I ran into this phenomenon again when I was hired to produce versions of the great Bob Marley song, "One Love," for a Foote, Cone and Belding pitch to land the Jamaica Tourism account. For the first time ever in NY, I decided not to work with an arranger. I knew exactly what I wanted, and there was no way any self-respecting NY arranger was going to go there. I didn't want to fight.

For the charts, I adopted the Nashville method, but wrote the changes in letters instead of numbers because we were using the original key of Marley's record. The guys all knew the song anyway. I kept the tempo as slow as possible. It had to be a little faster than the original, given that we were doing 60- and 30-second commercials instead of a minutes-long record. The groove suffered greatly with every notch-up on the click track machine. I stripped down the drum, bass and guitar parts to the barest minimum. I actually made the guitar player, John McCurry, play the bass part as well. He isn't the world's most technically proficient bass player, but he has great time and feel, and that was what I was after. Reggae music is all about downbeats; pop music is all about two-and-four. John understood completely — wasn't tempted to add anything fancy.

I was just as determined when it came to the singers — especially the background singers. I knew I had a great soloist in Babi Floyd, but the background parts had to be tonally perfect, too. I chose carefully: for the boys: Babi Floyd, Fonzie Thornton, and Gordon Grody; for the girls: Diva Gray, Robin Clark and Vivian Cherry. All African American (except for Gordon, who sounds more black than most blacks — and understands more about blend and feel than anyone else I know).

Their sound was instantly perfect; there was no need to conduct cut-offs, dynamics or anything else.

I've known for 40 years that as a producer, when you cast sessions correctly, the tough sledding is cut to a minimum. Hire the best talent and let them do their thing. Overall, in my style of music production, the fewer words said, the better.

Those Jamaica spots ran on the air without a change for more than 10 years. They won every award in the book. When the agency finally did change them, it didn't go well. They lost the intangible quality of authenticity we had worked hard to achieve, mostly because they sped up the tempo. It's encouraging that in the last year or so they've produced some new versions that are much better.

I learned much from my years in Nashville. They changed me, professionally and personally — for the better, I think. I have always burned hotter than most, and it's easy to see how that can come off as too forceful. Working and playing in Music City, USA taught me how to take some of that edge off. I began to relax more, calm down a little. I even started to speak a little slower and softer. I never did pick up the drawl, though.

OH BOY! THE SILVER FOX! We were all set to record the fabulous Charlie Rich in Nashville. It was a late morning start. The musicians were there; even Charlie's gun-carrying bodyguard was there.

Charlie never showed.

At the CMA awards the night before, while presenting a Best Male Vocal Award to John Denver, he was drunk enough to pull out a lighter and burn up the envelope.

Guess he didn't like the choice...

Chapter 40

Sins of the Father

————

I T WAS A DARK AND TERRIBLE TIME in the life of Marvin
Gaye, but I had no way of knowing that. In the late summer of
1980, Rob Mounsey and I boarded the Concorde to London. We
traveled there to record Marvin Gaye. His vocals were to be
overdubbed on a couple of brilliant tracks that Rob had arranged and
I had produced for Diet Dr Pepper. As always, a contract had been
signed with his management team before the session was scheduled.
We were both really looking forward to it. To work with Marvin Gaye
was any musician's dream assignment.

We arrived before noon at Air Studios, the recording facility
George Martin had built in downtown London. The studio felt like
familiar territory to me: no surprise, given all that time in New York
with Sir George. We took a tour of the studios, double-checked playback on our 24 track tape, set up a mike, and settled down to wait for
Mr. Gaye. He and his entourage showed up 30 hours later.

Needless to say, I'd spent the interim pulling my hair out. On the
phone constantly with everybody I could think of to call, I kept getting
assurances that Mr. Gaye was just running a little late and would be
there shortly. I came to learn later that he had pulled a similar stunt on
Princess Margaret. He had agreed to perform at her Royal Gala Char-
ity Show, but arrived so late that she and most of guests had already

left. I consoled myself with the thought that at least I was in noble company.

I had no idea that Marvin Gaye was then in a very bad place. In serious financial trouble and facing a dissolving second marriage, he was in the throes of heavy drug addiction, still struggling with deep depression over the 1970 death of Tammi Terrell, and fighting constantly with Berry Gordy and Motown. I'm not sure whether knowing all that would have changed what happened — probably not — but it certainly would have given me more clarity about why things went down the way they did.

Early in the evening of the second day, Marvin finally arrived. He looked healthy, chipper: was all smiles and charm. I didn't quite understand why he was accompanied by such a rag tag group. There were something like 18 of them (including the babies and children); all dressed in colorful African/hippie clothes. I didn't care; just breathed a sigh of relief that he was finally there. They happily encamped on the floors of the hallways outside the studio while Marvin and I chatted a bit. Then he asked to hear the track a couple of times in the control room.

As we played it, I could see his lips moving as he sang along in his head. As with all the celebrity talent who were set to perform to an existing track, we had sent cassette copies of the pre-recorded music in advance, with and without a scratch vocal. It was obvious that he was already quite familiar with it. I suggested we try a couple of run-throughs on the mike out in the studio to get levels, etc; and he nodded. He went in there and just wowed us all. His artistry, phrasing, tone, rhythmic authority and overall smoothness were mind-blowing. Rob and I were in heaven.

Why I hadn't instructed the engineer to press the record button just for the hell of it, I will never know, but that omission resulted in a huge loss forever.

I spoke to Marvin over the talkback. "Sounds absolutely fantastic! Are you ready to do a take or two now?"

He looked at me through the glass for a few long moments and then asked, "Can I talk to you inside? I have something I want to discuss."

Alarm bells began ringing in my head, but I stayed calm, "Why sure. No problem. Come on in."

In the booth he said to me, "I'd like to have this conversation in private, if you don't mind."

The alarm bells sounded a little louder. I asked the engineer for a private space, and he showed us into a cramped little room with a single couch, a chair and a table with a telephone.

"Susan, I just want to tell you how much I love this track. It's perfect. In fact it's so perfect, I would be interested in having you and Rob do some work with me on my songs."

Now, of course I was extremely flattered, but underneath the glow, common sense was warning me that I was being played by a pro. So I simply asked, "What did you have in mind?"

"Well, what I really have in mind is to be a true spokesman for Dr Pepper. I mean, I really love it, the taste and everything, and I do drink a lot of it. I want to be like Lou Rawls is for Budweiser. You know, on TV and everything."

True panic was starting to set in, but I tried to deflect the situation with, "Marvin, you have to understand. I have no authority at all for this kind of proposal. I'm just a music producer for Dr Pepper. I don't get involved in decisions like that. I'd be happy to pass on your interest to the powers that be, but that's about all I can do. So let's get this radio track done. I'm sure they will be totally thrilled by it, and then I can suggest what you have in mind. What do you think?"

For the first time, his expression changed. The mask slipped a bit, and a much less friendly Marvin Gaye looked at me coldly. "I guess *you* just don't understand. I love this track and product so much, I won't do your recording unless I get to be that guy for Dr Pepper. I have my heart set on it."

Okay: the threat had been made and received, and it seemed very real. All I could do was to promise to get on the phone with the Y&R and Dr Pepper people to convey the demand. Frankly, I didn't hold out much hope. I knew this was all going to end in tears.

I just didn't know that it would take so long.

I put in the first of many trans-Atlantic calls to the Y&R account people. Naturally, they became hysterical and yelled at me as if it were my fault. I had to remind them that, in this case, they had done all of the negotiations and sealed the deal with Marvin's manager. When I asked them what I should have done differently, they just said they would get in touch with the client and get back to me.

Marvin, the entourage and I sat on the corridor floor and waited (have I mentioned that I was more than five months pregnant with Alex?). Marvin and I passed the time philosophizing on a range of topics. Rob, on the other hand, had retreated, consoling himself by playing the beautiful grand piano in the now-deserted studio. While he talked to me, Marvin had one arm around a lovely young mother and the other around her 10-year-old daughter. He would occasionally lean over and kiss them on the cheek, nuzzle their necks, or gently caress their faces with his elegant long fingers. From time to time he'd reach over to rub my growing belly. He told me it gave him wonderful energy.

There was nothing overtly sexual about any of this, but it creeped me out, nonetheless. Especially when he went on at length about the morals clause he had noticed in the Dr Pepper contract. He told me it had to be deleted. He was crystal clear that he could never sign anything like that. It was an infringement on his freedom and his philosophy of love for all people. An insult to his way of life. *Blah, blah blah.* I kept my mouth shut and nodded my head. He began to act a little wild, a little unhinged, raising his voice louder and waving his arms about.

As the night wore on, I got sleepier and sleepier. I didn't dare leave, or let him leave. I knew I would probably never see him again.

Just before dawn, I had an idea about how to get us out of the mess. Also, I could see that Marvin was tiring and wanted to go home.

So I guided him back into the little horrible room to make a new proposal. I would get the Dr Pepper people in Texas to meet with him and listen to his ideas face-to-face if he would promise to do his vocal on the radio spots. He thought it over, agreed, and pledged to come back to the studio the next afternoon to record. But only if I got agreement from the Dr Pepper folks.

I thought it was a pretty good compromise, and gave it a 50/50 chance of at least getting the radio spots done. When I finally spoke directly to the lawyers at Dr Pepper, they shot it down: explained it was a very bad precedent to give into any threat. They said it was the kind of slippery slope that could only lead to more trouble.

As a music producer, I was crushed at the realization that no one would ever hear the perfect matchup of Rob's fantastic track with Marvin Gaye's vocals. But as a businesswoman and company president, I understood.

I let them give Marvin's manager the bad news, and went to sleep for a whole day. So much for planning a few pleasant days in London after a successful recording session...

I got over my pique — and was pleased a year or so later when Marvin Gaye went on to have a resurgence in his career and even greater success. Then devastated to learn of his death at the hands of his father. It was an accident: Marvin is said to have been intervening in an altercation between his mother and father over money. He was just trying to prevent violence, and he was shot and killed with a gun he'd given to his father.

Marvin Gaye Sr. was reputed to be a terrible man; a tyrant and dictator who physically and emotionally abused his children. All four were bedwetters; Marvin wrote that he was depressed all the time and believed he would end up as one of "those child statistics you read about in the paper." Mr. Gaye Sr. was an ordained minister, a supposed man of God gone horribly wrong. To me, it is not surprising that his sins were visited upon his son.

Marvin, the world still misses you a lot.

RICHIE HAVENS drove me crazy. I produced another Eastern Airlines soundtrack with him shortly after the John Barry experience.

With John, everything was cool, measured and professional. With Richie, it took hours and hours. Singing and playing his guitar at the same time, he would blow take after take. Looking up at me in the control room at National Recording Studios, he would shake his head, smile his toothless grin and apologize over and over again.

Both scores are masterpieces. But it's odd that Richie's track, when finished, had so much more soul and humanity.

Chapter 41

And Back to Haiti

I N EARLY 1982, ROB MOUNSEY AND I TRAVELED back to the island for Haitian Divorce 2.0. We were planning our wedding (number three for me); the legal stuff had to be worked out.

The country had changed quite a bit. Now, an underlying sense of fear and danger permeated the heavy, perfumed air. You could almost smell it. Last trip, it was jet fuel and decaying vegetation. This trip, palpable unrest.

The legal proceedings were the same (Dapper Dan greeted us at the airport, cane in hand). But the relaxed, laissez-faire attitude was gone.

We had booked into a luxurious hotel built into a palace that had once belonged to Pauline Napoleon, the Emperor's sister. Many of the elegant rooms, including a spacious bathroom, were open to the outside jungle...a jungle that definitely had invasion on its mind. I would awake in the morning to find two or three new feet of healthy vines creeping closer and closer to our bed. We slept under mosquito netting as the lizards and insects crawled across the worn stone floors. The tall, thick perimeter walls of the property were topped with triple strands of razor wire... The Haiti that I had loved just a few years before was gone.

Impending doom.

I could feel it.

On that second trip, Rob and I didn't travel around much — even though I had wanted to go and visit Cap-Haïtien, the birthplace of my treasured painting.

Once the divorce paperwork was delivered, I tucked it in my purse and we split. I couldn't wait to get off the island.

And within a very few years, there were no more tourists, no more nice hotels, no more sense of security at all. Haiti was slowly being crushed by the cruel, corrupt dictatorship of the Duvaliers — father and son. Yet even worse was in store for the guiltless people of Haiti.

Unbelievably tragic.

ON THE WAY BACK from one of my quickie divorce trips to Haiti, I went through customs at the San Juan Airport.

As the agent opened the cardboard tube that held the original Haitian primitive painting I had purchased in Port-au-Prince, I snootily informed him, "That's original art. It's not subject to duty charges."

Without a word, he motioned to a female agent, and I was led away to a humiliating strip search.

I learned a valuable life lesson: *Don't screw with little people in power.*

## Chapter 42

A Wonderful Day With Danny

———

I WAS PISSED, in a dreadful mood, as I sat down in the first class cabin of the American Airlines 747. I was on my way home to JFK from LAX. It was sometime in '83; I don't remember why I was in such a snit.

Thank God I had a junk novel with plenty of ridiculous sex scenes to get me through the flight. Unfortunately, my seat mate took off his shoes, and his feet stank. Worse yet, he wanted to make conversation.

As soon as the seat belt sign was turned off, I fled up the spiral staircase into the upstairs lounge. I positioned myself against the far corner of one of the horseshoe-shaped padded banquettes, and settled down to zone out with the stupid book.

Minutes later, I raised my head in time to notice a very strange-looking character who was entering the room. I looked down and away, but not before he'd made an indelible impression. He was wearing a pork pie hat, white terrycloth high water pants, and translucent, tangerine-colored walking sandals strapped in the back over ankle-high white socks.

He plunked down in the first banquette, the one closest to the door. I felt relieved and went back to my trash book.

Without warning (there was no turbulence), one of the conveniently placed crystal dishes filled with warm nuts slid across the surface linking the back of the banquettes, bounced off my shoulder, and dumped its contents in my lap. I jumped up and probably said, "What the *fuck*?"

In a nanosecond the weirdo leapt the distance between us, plopped down next to me and grabbed my book.

"Hi, what are you reading? Are there any dirty parts?" Somehow he immediately found one and started reading it aloud in overly dramatic fashion. At first I was mortified, but as he took sly little looks at me with twinkling eyes, I started to smile, then finally laugh.

We started to talk. He asked lots of questions, and I found myself opening up and telling all. It's that funny thing that sometimes happens on plane trips. Similar to when people find themselves confined together, waiting out a storm or some other disruption. Suddenly you realize that the total stranger next to you is actually a new-found soul mate. You exchange secrets that would normally be reserved for best friends. Maybe it's because you know you could crash and burn at any moment — or maybe you're just bored and want to make the time pass faster.

I'm pushing three million miles flown. And I've had some great chance encounters over the years. Once ended up sitting next to George Hamilton. (Yes, he was VERY tan). Imagine the confusion of the stewardesses (oops: 'flight attendants') as they assumed, given the same last name, we were a married couple.

Then there was a memorable flight sitting with Telly Savalas in row 1C & D: Kojak — in person! Blunt, funny, and totally real, he gave me useful insight into dealing with the business people of Hollywood.

And now, at some point in my heart-to-heart with the weirdo of the 747 lounge, he asked, "Do you know who I am?"

I was confused. "No, not a clue."

He said simply, "I'm Danny Kaye."

Unfortunately, that didn't mean very much to me. I'd grown up without any television, and rarely went to the movies. To make matters worse, I asked, "Aren't you the actor who could talk to Francis, the mule?"

With a slightly pained expression, he said, "No, that was Donald O'Connor."

I don't know exactly why, but he forgave me at once and we continued our discussion of life. The flight attendants visited a couple of times, but we shooed them away. We didn't want food or drink. We just wanted to be left alone. And we were. Oddly, no other passenger ever came up into the lounge.

We discovered we had many common interests. He was on his way up to Connecticut to hang out with Carl Sonheimer, owner of the Cuisinart company. Asked me to go with him, but I couldn't because I had sessions the next day. We both loved to cook. I took over Thanksgiving dinner when I was about seven because my mother and grandmother, albeit decent cooks, really didn't like all the work. I still prepare pretty much that same menu every year.

We talked about restaurants, equipment, ingredients, recipes, where to get what...everything. We both loved Italian. He loved Chinese, even told me about some complicated system he had installed in his San Francisco house involving extremely hot burners and a trough of ice water.

Then came music. I had no idea he was a famous conductor. I told him a bit of my history as a concert pianist. Found out we both had perfect pitch. I was a trained classical musician; he operated with his ear and his heart: couldn't even read music. It didn't seem to matter. As Dimitri Mitropoulos of the New York Philharmonic was once quoted, "He could get things out of my orchestra I never could!"

We got down to more personal matters. He was a great listener. It was more about me than him. I never did get many personal details from him, and only much later did I learn just how famous he was.

I told him about Rob Mounsey, father of my son Alex. I had just produced a whole pop album of Rob performing his own songs. It was a true labor of love; I sincerely believed in Rob's talent as an artist. It had recently been presented to John Kalodner, famous A&R man (Aerosmith and Geffen Records) and against all odds, he really liked it. The problem was that he wanted Rob to form a garage-type band, rehearse for live performances, and redo the record without Rob's extremely talented and competent studio musician friends. Rob turned the offer down immediately; just wasn't interested. Maybe this had been the reason for my dark mood as I got on the plane.

The discussion led to a conversation about what it took to become a face-famous person. Danny explained, "Susan, there are two criteria for becoming a face-famous person. One, you have to want it so much you'd be willing to give up a hand or a foot if it were necessary. Second is you can't be able to do anything else well, because if you can — that's what you should do with your life."

That made sense to me. I certainly understood it because I had never wanted to become face-famous at all. Although there had been a few articles written about me (*New York Magazine, L.A. Times*) and a segment on the TV show *20/20*, I stopped *Look Magazine* from publishing a long feature because they insisted on using photos that included Alex.

I loved my status as a big fish in the small pond of jingle production. Loved being important, but behind the scenes. Loved being able to go into Giorgio's on Rodeo Drive in ratty clothes, have the salespeople look down their noses at me, then drop a few grand. My, how the attitudes changed!

The fact was, I needed those designer outfits. More and more often, my presence was requested at high-level agency-client meetings up in the boardrooms. There, power dressing was important. I couldn't very well have a serious discussion with or make a vital presentation to the President of Citibank wearing rock and roll garb. Armani, Lagerfeld, or Nina Ricci, always with Manolo Blahniks, were what was called for.

Rob obviously didn't fit Danny's criteria for the face-famous, and I certainly understood Rob's 'my way or the highway' stance, but wow — it had cost an awful lot of time and money to learn Danny's simple lesson.

When we got to JFK, Danny insisted that we ride into the City together. He told the driver holding the placard with my name on it to get lost. As we stood at baggage claim to retrieve our luggage, a pushy old woman got right in his face saying, "I know you. You're somebody famous. Who are you? Are you Danny Kaye? I want to get your autograph!"

She grabbed hold of his coat sleeve and tried to force some kind of folded flyer into his hand. He jerked back.

"Get away! I'm not who you think I am and no, I won't give you an autograph. Go on now, scram!"

His response was understandably rough, but did seem a little out of proportion. I thought about this later. I had always assumed that celebrities needed and wanted all the attention the public gave them - to prove their worth, verify their fame. By the time we met, I guess he had put up with enough of it. I know I couldn't have endured that kind of harassment at all. It was a sobering moment, because he had been so warm, funny and truly simpatico with me (also a complete stranger).

The next day I received a phone call from both Danny and Carl. They wanted me to come up to Stamford and have dinner with them. Couldn't. Too bad.

A couple of days later, I did receive a Cuisinart 7 with all of the bells and whistles. I still have it downstairs in my pots and pans room, unopened. I'd purchased the professional-sized one a couple of years before, and still use it today. Kept the other one for — I don't know — must be sentimental reasons.

I FIRST MET CARLY SIMON in 1969 when Jake
Holmes brought her in to write for the company. She
wrote a few jingles for us and sang on a bunch of
sessions, then bowed out once her recording career
took off. In those early days, Carly looked and
dressed like a folk singer — a little bit shy and
vulnerable — but as her fame skyrocketed, she turned
into the stylish, strong, beautiful diva everyone knows.

Some years later (why, I can't remember), she and
then-husband James Taylor came into A&R to observe me producing a "Be All You Can Be" session for
the Army. Afterward, they took me aside, and James
told me I should be producing records. "You're so
damn efficient!" Of course I was pleased — but said I
was quite content with my day job....

I last saw Carly in the late '80s. I was headed into a
session and she was just leaving, tape in hand, to run
up to Clive Davis' apartment to play him the latest
'mix fix' on her new single. She was in gorgeous evening clothes, and though late for some event, still felt
the need to get his approval herself. I could see
something close to fear in her eyes...

Boy — what a powerful grip that man had on
everybody!

Chapter 43

Dino

———

ONE OF THE MOST IMPORTANT PEOPLE to know in Holly-wood was Dino, the evening maitre d' of the Polo Lounge in the Beverly Hills Hotel.

An Italian man in his fifties, Dino was always charming and formally dressed. He stood tall at the entryway of the famed cocktail bar in immaculate tux and tails. There he would greet, seat, and turn away his hopeful clientele. He could spot a hooker in an instant, no matter how well dressed. Even if he had missed her while showing others to their seats, she would soon be escorted out.

Once he met you, he remembered your name forever. "*Good Evening Miss Hamilton. So good to see you! And how is Master Alex, may I ask?*" He never inquired after my husbands.

The game that was always afoot was *where* he would seat you. When any show business mover and shaker would arrive at the door-way, his or her eyes would be inexorably drawn to the first booth to see who was there.

Booth Number One, with its big round table and red leather banquette (now a disappointing pea-soup green) was located across from the intimate Deco-styled bar. It was strategically situated in what you would have to call the Preferred Section. There were four booths (including Number One) across the back, and maybe four or five small tables between the booths and the bar.

To the right as you entered was the area I'll call Second Best. An alcove with perhaps three booths and another half dozen small tables and chairs. This was an okay place to be seated.

But God forbid you were ushered past those two sections to be placed in the long narrow alleyway parallel to the outdoor patio. We called it 'Siberia'. You would have to hang your head — become invisible — if you were ever led through the gauntlet to a seat in that sorry destination.

'Paging' was a big deal at the Beverly Hills Hotel in those days. At the pool, it was done over the loudspeakers. *Paging Mr. Davis. Mr. Clive Davis, you have a call.* If you raised your hand, the pool attendant would then bring the phone on a very long extension cord over to your chaise lounge. Clive never needed to identify himself. Being paged was such a symbol of prestige that some of the more needy folks would deliberately have friends call them for no other reason. One weekend I had been hanging out at the pool, chatting with a newfound acquaintance. From the first day, our conversations went from light and casual to intensely philosophical: one of those times when a total stranger turns out to be a kindred spirit. Late on Sunday afternoon, the loudspeaker crackled as the operator's voice rang out with, *Paging David Mamet, Mr. Mamet, please.* I was quite startled when my new friend raised his hand.

In the Polo Lounge, paging was done by Buddy. Buddy was a little person with an unnaturally high-pitched voice, permanently dressed in a light maroon bellman's suit with gold trim. His hat was a matching fez. He wandered through the tables, carrying a phone (once again on that long cord), announcing without expression, *Miss Hepburn, Miss Audrey Hepburn...* or *Mr. Lahr, Mr. Bert Lahr...*

I remember sitting at a table with Burt Bacharach and Carole Bayer Sager. They were arguing heatedly, but she was facing him, astride his lap.

I often lunched with good friends Steve and Linda Horn on the patio, surrounded by sweet-smelling flowering bushes and trees. He was a top commercial director, and she a senior editor at *Vogue*. Steve introduced me to one of the hotel's signature dishes: a Monte Cristo sandwich with a wonderful Cumberland sauce. If it is served that way anywhere else, I've never found it.

One night in the Hotel, I was awakened by alarms. It wasn't a fire. It was a major blackout. I fumbled around for my room key, threw on yesterday's clothes, and felt my way down to the Polo Lounge. I met up with David Wolfert, a colleague from NYC, a marvelous composer/songwriter and friend. We sat at a table by candlelight and shot the shit for a couple of hours. A piano player was performing softly — I guess to calm the patrons' nerves. David and I paid him $100 for his promise to never again play "Chariots of Fire."

I don't know why or how I became a favorite of Dino's. I certainly wasn't one of the Hollywood glitterati. Maybe because I was there so often by myself. Whenever he could, if I were with clients I wanted to impress, he would seat us in Booth Number One.

I would hold my head high and lord it over all of Creation.

I WALKED ALEX to his private school on Madison
Ave. every morning.

Unbeknownst to me, Jim Patterson, my friend
and most important client (Creative Director at
J Walter Thompson), spotted us as he passed in a
cab.

He phoned a day later and asked me many
questions about the security procedures at Alex's
school.

Months later, he told me that seeing us that
morning had provided him with part of the idea that
became *Along Came A Spider.*

Chapter 44

Nashville Bad Boys

———

THERE'S SOMETHING ABOUT SOUTHERN MEN that's irresistible, in a guilty pleasure kind of way. Think Dennis Quaid in *The Big Easy*. I don't know whether it's the drawl, the 'I don't give a shit' attitude, or just the extra dose of testosterone they seem to have. I fall for it every time, one way or another. I forget about qualities like sensitivity, the feminine side, intellectual dexterity, and casual sophistication in about a second. I want to hop on the back of his motorcycle or his horse and ride off into the sunset.

But of course I don't. Except once.

Teddy Irwin is a guitar player who worked a lot in Nashville, especially with Norbert Putnam, the successful producer and studio owner. But I first met Teddy in New York through Jake Holmes, a folk/pop artist in his own right. Teddy is a superbly talented guitarist in the Nashville sense: natural and intuitive, with great time and feel. He doesn't really read music, but he can make you cry with his licks and solos. And he is a bad boy. Impetuous and reckless, with a Wild West outlaw's mustache and a baby face. We got involved.

I was supposed to be in an "open relationship" with Walter Raim. This philosophy was quite popular with the NYC/East Hampton psychiatry set. At the time, Walter insisted I try a few sessions with his shrink, Dr. Ralph Klein. Although Ralph was extremely bright and had some keen insights, my therapy didn't advance after he suggested I take off my wet blouse following a rainstorm. Apparently, getting intimately involved with one's shrink was, if not *de rigueur*, at least acceptable. I wasn't going along with the plan.

Teddy and I went on a couple of wild automobile adventures. There was that earlier one in Spain, but this outing took place one fall weekend in the late 60's. I breezily announced to Walter that I was taking his Porsche 911 for a little road trip to Maryland with Teddy, and wished him good luck with whomever. I was following the Sullivanian rules by informing my Primary Partner where and with whom I was going to be. The '60s. Wow.

Teddy and I took off. He drove like a demon; we had liquor in the car, and he had some weed. They pulled us over in some small town, clocked at over 100 mph in a 35 zone. Teddy had me shove the open bottle under the seat and stuff the weed into my pocket.

But after he'd been arrested and hauled off to the local courthouse, I couldn't follow. The Porsche refused to even turn over. It needed some recovery time from too much *pedal to the metal* driving, I guess. I was left stranded on a side street with a dead car in a tiny town I didn't even know the name of — with no idea of how this was all going to turn out. I waited a couple of hours without a clue what my next move should be.

A squad car returned Teddy to the scene of the crime a half hour later. I was still sitting there. When Teddy tried it, the Porsche's engine became cooperative, and we were back on our way.

He explained his release with a grin. In the Courthouse, he'd been allowed to visit the men's room. At the urinals, he ran into the presiding judge, whom he happened to know. The judge was a good friend of Teddy's dad. He had watched Teddy grow up. So all he got was a slap on the wrist and an invitation to grab a beer together sometime. I believe this is typical luck for a lovable Irish bad boy from Nashville.

I met Vince Gill shortly after his move to Nashville in 1982. By that time, I was doing as much work as I could down there. I never regarded Vince as a natural-born country music artist. To me at that time, he was more of a rockabilly guy. He was a damn good guitar player in that genre: played and sang with the rhythmic authority of a young Elvis. I thought his voice seemed a little light and high-pitched to make it in country music. How wrong could I be?

In any case, we became friends. He wasn't really a bad boy, but you wouldn't know it from that twinkle in his eye. I adored and admired him and wanted to give him a leg up any time I had the chance. I knew he had just moved to town with a wife and young child, so I booked him on as many sessions as I could. A lot of Miller Beer, Burger King, etc. I remember one day he didn't show for a session that I knew would be particularly lucrative — spots that play often and for a long time can produce a steady stream of residuals for the singer. When he didn't show, I freaked. Somehow I managed to get hold of him on the phone. He was on the golf course. In my quiet deadly voice, I ordered him back to the studio. He complied. Many years later, I heard him tell this story on a radio interview, and thank me on the air. It made my day.

Then there was Dave Loggins. Wow, what a voice! I'd auditioned many singers for the male lead on the Miller Beer campaign based on "My Baby Is American Made." Loggins blew them all into the weeds. I didn't know who he was; I didn't know how famous he was. I just loved his voice. And as soon as I met and worked with him, I fell for his super cool attitude. He was actually better known in Nashville as a songwriter, having written many hits for other artists. But he was most famous for "Please Come to Boston" which he wrote and recorded as an artist. The single made it into the top five on multiple Billboard charts.

Dave Loggins is not the most polished of singers. He has an intangible 'everyman, regular guy' quality. You believe every word he sings; and somehow, you know he believes them with you. They come straight from the heart, but in an easy-going, effortless manner. There is a wistful, tug-at-your-heartstrings quality in his voice, too — most noticeable in his hit single, but it also came through in the happier, uptempo Miller Beer jingle. Once again, appropriate casting made my job easy, and that campaign lasted for years. I also used Loggins as a soloist for another successful J. Walter Thompson campaign, *This is a Burger King Town.*

Dave *was* a bad boy. Funny as hell and smart as a whip, he was an incorrigible flirt with any and all ladies. He could drink with the best of them and still maintain his razor-sharp repartee. The two of us did have quite a few one-on-one more serious conversations about life and relationships. He had a 'lone wolf' kind of aura: not exactly stand-offish — he just held his cards close to the vest. I never saw him with any one woman for long or even knew if he were married. I never pried; I sensed that was the way he wanted it.

Most evenings, after working in the studio all day, a bunch of us would hang out at our favorite bars until all hours, joking around and visiting with the local musicians, singers, songwriters, engineers and artists who'd stop by the table for a few minutes to shoot the shit. Most of the music people in Nashville seemed to spend all hours of day or night at their favorite watering holes. I wouldn't have been able to do it week in and week out — but I sure had a good time whenever I was there.

I have to count my good friend, Will Lee, as an honorary Nashville bad boy. He accompanied me on many trips down there from New York and fit in perfectly. He tagged along mostly for the work — Will was and is a *great* bass player who understood the Nashville style and never overplayed. He is also quite a singer. With our mutual friend Paul Shaffer as its leader, Will is a featured member of The CBS Orchestra (*The David Letterman Show*). Paul worked with me off and on in the late '70s and early '80s, but soon became unavailable most of the time...(I still remember his blistering performances on the B3 Hammond Organ).

I loved having Will on the Nashville scene. He got along with everybody, was often helpful in shaping the tracks and useful in charming and distracting any stray client who might show up for a session. I remember one time we were finishing up a spot for JWT, running late. Laurie Birnbaum (now Laurie Garnier), a client and friend, was with us. As we all got in the Hertz Lincoln Continental, she remembered something she needed, and ran back into the studio to get it. Will got out; he preferred to wait outside. After a few minutes, I jumped out to see what was taking so long. Just as I closed the door behind me, Laurie came back down the stairs. I had left the engine running. To my horror, I now heard the unmistakable sound of the car locking itself. One by one, all four doors and the trunk: *click, click, click, click, CLICK!*

We looked at each other with absolutely no idea what to do. We had to make that plane for all kinds of reasons. Couldn't call AAA — it would take much too long. By this point, Laurie was wringing her hands and bemoaning her fate. Will looked at me, then walked over to a nearby car, leaned in the open window, popped its trunk, and removed the tire iron.

His first hit bounced off the safety glass on the passenger side, but with the second (a big swing and smash), the pebbled glass rained down in a million pieces, most of it on the seat. No one uttered a word. Will hopped in the front, Laurie in the back and we sped off to Hertz.

There I filled out the paperwork and handed the clipboard over to the attendant. He looked at the non-existent window and glass-filled front seat, but *he* didn't say a word, either.

I wasn't charged for the damages. I can only deduce that this had happened a time or two before to other Lincoln Continentals...

My first, longest and closest bad boy friend in Nashville was David Briggs. I met David with Norbert Putnam when I first started recording and producing at their Quadrafonic Sound Studios. It was the happening place in town: lots of stars in and out all the time. I met David Foster there for the first time — watched him produce and arrange a session with a country group. I thought I was good; he was better. Little did I know how many odd ways ours paths would cross later.

I didn't get to know Norbert until much later, during that trip to London with Eliot. But Briggs was the keyboard player on all of my Nashville sessions, did a lot of my arrangements, and shepherded me around town, introducing me and entertaining me. We were drinking buddies. Our favorite hangout was a place called The Third Coast. It offered sofas and comfy chairs to lounge in, a riotous clientele, and a consummately wild bar scene. David used to tell me, "Susan, if you could lift up that big long bar, you'd be looking directly into the flames of Hell." There was ample reason to believe him.

Over the years, especially once I was allowed to produce my sessions at his own personal studio, House of David, I got to know him well. There were no secrets between us. We knew all the good, bad and ugly about each other. We tried two things together only once. One was sex; we both agreed there wasn't a whole lot of chemistry. We were much better off sticking to our brother-sister relationship. The other was coke. I had resisted trying it for years, but on one of our crazy nights, we made a mutual decision to do a line. It backfired on both of us. The drug wreaked havoc with David's sinuses (he was allergic to most plant life anyway). As for its effect on me, David remarked, "My God, girl. You've turned from Susan #2 back into Susan #1!" (#2 was mellow after a few drinks; #1 was Susan in the studio). In retrospect, maybe it was the coke that undermined that chemistry...

David is a big bear of a man, usually sporting a scraggly reddish beard. He always wore baggy jeans and rumpled work shirts, generally with a white t-shirt underneath. He lived and dressed as simply as he could. The word around town on David was that he was the tightest man in Nashville (he was a Scot, after all). He was also arguably one of the wealthiest and most powerful. He was respected and loved by all, and had his hand in almost everything. He was stingy with his money — he just didn't like spending it — but in equal measure, he was generous with his time and support. David helped many budding artists and writers get through tough times. The most famous of these was probably the revered lyricist and poet Will Jennings.

Will told me this story himself. Coming from a rough beginning in the oil fields of East Texas, he followed his talent as a poet. He told me how one day he left his teaching post at a university in Wisconsin, packed his meager belongings into his Volkswagen van, and headed straight to Nashville to become a lyricist. At first it was often a no go. I think he actually lived in the van for a while. But then he met David, who took him under his wing. From that day on, Will never had to look back, and his meteoric rise in the business is legendary. He paid David back by forming a publishing company with him. Needless to say, what flowed from that must have greatly warmed David's Scottish heart.

David was a friend and listening post through my three divorces. He in turn told me about his tumultuous relationship with Linda Thompson. He says he stole her from his good buddy, Elvis Presley. They were a natural: David was a Nashville bad boy; Linda was beautiful and hot. He told me he had built the back entrance to House of David because he didn't want anyone seeing her coming and going. He was terrified that Elvis was going to send someone into a session and shoot him. I didn't really believe he thought it would go that far; he could have been kidding around. In any case, he and Linda were together for a few years.

Now, Linda Thompson had long been smitten with Olympic Champion Bruce Jenner after she saw him on TV one night. She told Elvis she wanted to marry Bruce, and in 1981, five years or so later (after David), she did. They have two sons, Brandon and Brodie Jenner.

Now why is this worth recounting? Read on: I first met Linda after I moved to Malibu. I never mentioned my relationship with David Briggs. She had divorced Bruce Jenner by then, and married David Foster. They lived just down the road. My son Alex and I lived at the foot of a hiking trail, and often ran into Linda and her two Jenner boys. They and Alex had a couple of play dates. Two years later, after Michael and his four children moved in with me and Alex, we became friends with Rebecca Foster, David's second wife and their three daughters, Sara, Erin and Jordan Foster. At that point, Rebecca was married to Stuart Gross, founder of Harmony Pictures.

It gets more tangled. David Foster and Linda moved into a breathtaking mansion in an area of Malibu called Serra Retreat. Even for Malibu, "Casablanca" was a spectacular estate. So spectacular, we were thrilled when David let us use it as a location for a couple of kiddie video productions we did for Malibu High School. He was most generous, accommodating and interested in the project*. So at times during those years in Malibu, my five kids, the three Foster girls, the two Jenner boys and countless Kardashian girls were all hanging out at Casablanca. (Bruce Jenner, after divorcing Linda Thompson, married Robert Kardashian's widow). What a melange!

Off and on during our friendship, David Briggs would talk about Elvis. They spent 12 years together, from 1965 until Elvis's death. They first met when David was asked to sit in for a tardy keyboard player on an Elvis session. Elvis liked him, and that was that. David played on all his sessions, and went to Vegas with Elvis in 1975. They were close buddies, and Elvis treated him like a brother — even after the whole Linda Thompson affair.

In Vegas, David grew terribly homesick for Nashville. He threatened to leave many times, but Elvis would always find a way to stop him. David would make a plane reservation to fly home, but when he would go up to his hotel room after the show, he'd find irresistible temptation waiting for him in one form or another: either champagne, chocolates, strawberries, multiple beauties, or all the above. It worked. He told me how when Elvis would buy something for himself — a shirt or anything else — he would always buy an extra for David. They stayed together pretty much for the rest of Elvis's life.

After Elvis' death, David told me tales of his ghost's visits to the House of David. On more than several occasions, he would go into the tape storage room to find Elvis masters flung out of their places on the racks, lying in the middle of the floor. He swore it was true, and I believe him.

Tell Me No Lies was a full-length feature homage to Agatha Christie. The production used 66 kids from Malibu High (including one of David's daughters in a starring role), and had its premiere at Pepperdine University's 1,000-seat Smothers Theatre. It raised $10,000 that was eventually used to start a video department at the High School. I wrote it; Michael shot it, and we both directed it. Alex's gifted father, Rob Mounsey, composed the thrilling original score.

The most bizarre of David's Elvis tales, though, has to do with a possible contributing factor to his death. This is such a strange story, I have a hard time believing it's not real.

In the last few months of Elvis's life, the two of them were introduced (by Dr. John Harris, a local keyboard player) to a book about manipulating — even directing — the content of one's dreams. David explained it to me this way: *Say you're walking down the street and you see some hot chick walking toward you that you'd like to have sex with. Instead of having to make nice – take her out, buy her presents and then go through the hassle of having to tell her it's over – you just make her appear in your dreams, ready for anything you want. You can experience the act and the relationship as if it were real. All the good stuff and none of the bad!*

The concept wasn't limited to sex. You could hang out with whomever you wanted, famous or not, perform daring feats of heroism, win golf tournaments with the pros, swim with the dolphins — whatever. If your imagination could come up with the idea, you could make it happen in your dreams.

I tend to believe the story because the transference of something from real life into a dream happens frequently to me, and probably to most people. I can fall back asleep in the early hours while watching *Imus in the Morning,* and lo and behold — he and I will be having some kind of intellectually titillating confrontation. In my dreams, I've had similar encounters with all kinds of famous people. They all seem so real I'm disappointed when I wake up.

According to David, he and Elvis diligently worked through the book's training exercises and were amazed at the results. It started to work. In fact, it disturbed David so much that he quit immediately.

But Elvis loved it, and some nights couldn't wait to go to sleep. Sure, he was into drugs of all kinds, but they weren't enough to stop him from feeling increasingly fat, old, and unattractive. In his dreams, though, he was young and perfect again. I can't help but wonder if maybe (just maybe) the allure of the life he found in his dreams didn't weaken his will to guard against the danger that goes with drugs...until finally he'd used so many of them that he moved from Graceland to Dreamland.

THE PERP WAS A NOTORIOUS THIEF the NYPD had named *The Tile Man*. He targeted apartments up and down Park and Madison Avenues, gaining entrance by pretending to have been contracted to do tile work in the bathroom.

After he robbed my place, an off-duty homicide detective stopped by the apartment to discuss my part in the next day's sting operation. It was planned for the Diamond District.

Standing together in the kitchen, I offered him a Heineken. He said, "Sure."

I took a bottle from the fridge and turned to see him standing there, grinning, holding a pair of handcuffs.

My face paled and my eyes opened wide. When he saw my expression, he laughed.

"No, no, no!" he said. "I just use them for a bottle opener!"

Chapter 45

And For Next Season

———

THE CONVENTIONS WERE THE MOST FUN of all. Bottlers (beer and soda); Dealers (cars and trucks); Franchisees (fast food restaurants); and Affiliates (network TV stations).

At some, I would be a featured guest, presented as 'the face behind' the new jingle or musical campaign. Sometimes I was there to answer questions; sometimes just to schmooze.

But at others, I was there to oversee a live musical production, showcasing an extended version of the new theme song. Later ones — especially in the '80s and '90s — became huge, Broadway-show level production numbers requiring days to set up and rehearse. Most often, the conventions were held in resort destinations or magnet cities: any place likely to draw the most attendees. I certainly didn't complain when I had to go work in Aspen, California, Las Vegas or Hawaii.

The earliest convention I remember was the one where we introduced Dr Pepper's "Most Original Soft Drink Ever" campaign to the bottlers. This was in Waco, Texas, not far from where the drink was invented. I presented the documentary film we had produced for the event : a behind-the-scenes look at the making of our radio campaign featuring some of the 'most original' music artist of the time.

My first most vivid memory was of the wall clocks. The 10's, 2's, and 4's were all replaced with little Dr Pepper bottles. Some wacky medical researcher in the '50s claimed that most people have minor dips in energy around 10:30, 2:30, and 4:30. The ad agency jumped on it: these preventable misfortunes could be avoided by observing "Dr Pepper Time" at 10, 2, and 4.

The other indelible memory is of many large men in cowboy hats and bolo ties, pinkies raised, sipping steaming Dr Pepper out of glass cups, lemon slices floating on top...

The Kentucky Fried Chicken convention in New Orleans took place in the mid '70s. The production number for this one involved a gigantic wooden KFC box that sat onstage throughout the speeches and slide presentations. Then, at the finale, the box would suddenly open up to reveal a New Orleans band playing a jazzy version of our new jingle. My job was to rehearse the band and make sure our precious composition was being treated properly.

I wound up sticking around for the show. The director of the entire convention was an old college boyfriend, Christopher Shelton. We had even played Romeo and Juliet in a summer theater program following my graduation. When we first came face to face again, it was a bit of a shock for both of us (we hadn't parted on the best of terms). All was soon fine between us, though, and we were having a great time catching up...until the night of the dress rehearsal.

The run-through went smoothly until the grand finale. The box wouldn't open at all. That left 20 or so musicians trapped inside. The thing quickly heated up (in more ways than one: they wanted out!)

Big problem. It took chainsaws to free them, so the box had to be rebuilt overnight. Needless to say, we were nervous wrecks the next day. But in the end, all went well (even though we were missing a few players who refused to get back in their box).

More thorough immersion into the world of conventions began in 1977, starting with my first meeting with Steve Sohmer. I had no idea who he was when he called the office and brusquely demanded we meet. He turned out to be a mentor, a good friend, and a great client for more than 30 years.

The office where we met looked like it could have belonged to a harried newspaper editor. It was small, piles of papers were stacked everywhere, and the faint smell of cigar smoke hung in the air (I heard later he had worked in some capacity at *The Washington Post*). That day he was preparing to start a new job as advertising and promotion director for the CBS TV Network, whose ratings were currently in the toilet. In those days, that meant third place (out of three).

He told me he'd heard from good sources that I was the best, and that was enough for him.

Steve didn't waste any time. I quickly learned to keep my questions and comments short and to the point. He was unlike any other advertising client I'd ever had. He didn't delve into minutiae or background information, didn't seem interested. I sometimes suspected he had some form of ADD. If so, it would have been the good kind.

He wanted us to compose a theme song for the 1978 CBS promotion campaign. He had already written the line, copious lyrics, and was ready to discuss a musical direction. He didn't want to hear a bunch of demos from us, and he certainly didn't want any other company to compete. He wanted a hit song, and made it clear that it was my personal responsibility to provide him with one.

Together we did five campaigns in a row for CBS: network packages that involved weeks of work and were most lucrative. I produced many, many spots, starting with a two-minute song for a single airing on television, and an even longer version for the affiliates' convention. Many lengths, many styles, and for a few years, we did all of the customizations for local affiliates. I learned later to farm that part out — just too much work. *Turn Us On, We'll Turn You On; We're Comin' On; Reach for the Stars; Great Moments* are ones I remember for CBS. I was invited to some of the conventions, and was privileged to meet likeable Bill Paley and other biggies at the network. Steve always made me feel like a star, and introduced me that way.

The summer of 1982 was especially interesting. Steve had decided to switch over to NBC where he had been offered a better position. I think he was bored, anyway. After taking CBS back up to the Number One spot, he figured his job was done, and it was time to move on. The problem was that *both* networks wanted him to do their promotions for that fall's lineup — which meant that HEA would have to do both in addition to all our other jingle and scoring assignments.

Summer was always a busy season for us, anyway; many new campaigns were always kicking off in the fall (automobiles are a prime example). That summer I worked longer hours and through more weekends than ever before.

It paid off. NBC turned out to be a lot more fun. Magnetic, engaging Brandon Tartikoff was now in charge, and he gave Steve free rein to do whatever he wanted. Every year I got to go to Hawaii or Los Angeles for a week or more to put together a star-studded performance of the new song for the affiliates' convention.

One year the number ran longer than eight minutes. I worked closely with choreographer Anita Mann and her Solid Gold Dancers. Between the two us, we figured out the staging for the participating stars. I loved sitting on the floor of the dancers' rehearsal room, watching and listening as they stretched, readied for rehearsal, and gossiped about the night before. It was like having my own personal version of *A Chorus Line*.

For those shows it was also my job to teach the song, or certain parts of it, to the season's prime time stars. I would sit at an upright piano, play, sing, bang out rhythms on the wood — do anything and everything necessary to teach them their lines. There were frequent hilarious moments given the egos, tantrums, widely differing abilities — and sometimes, lack of willingness to participate at all.

Harry Anderson was the most talented of the bunch, and extraordinarily charming. Nell Carter was a pro. Phylicia Rashad courageously tried her best and Hasselhoff...well, was Hasselhoff. My son Alex, who always traveled with me, was over the moon about meeting Kit's owner. He was four or five.

Pierce Brosnan introduced himself with the 'don't I know you from somewhere' line and a 'piercing' look with those unbelievable blue eyes. Papa Cosby smiled over the proceedings from a distance, and Betty White outdid them all. I had the chance to sit next to her during a luncheon event. Exchanging nonstop uncensored observations behind the backs of our hands, we had a ball.

The songs for NBC got better and better. "Just Watch Us Now," written by David Buskin, won a CLIO and other awards; yet everyone's favorite (Steve included) was a bold, infectious, blood-stirring samba titled "Be There." Years before I had mentioned to Steve how much I loved samba music. He never forgot. One year he just said, "We're going to do a samba." Rob Mounsey wrote and arranged it. The produced track was astonishingly good and strangely emotionally uplifting. I do remember telling Steve as we finished the final mix of the two-minute spot, "You know, you are the only person I know who would have the guts to put a samba on the air."

It wouldn't happen in today's penny-pinching times, but I was given the money to fly 14 of New York's best musicians and singers with me and Rob from New York to the convention in Maui for a live presentation of the song. We partied in the aisles for the 13-hour flight and, come to think of it, never stopped until we had to leave the Island!

Steve left NBC (after raising it to Number One over CBS and ABC) to become President of Columbia Pictures for a couple of years. He then produced the mini-series *Favorite Son*, titled after his best-selling novel of the same name. When the TV series *Mancuso, FBI* followed, he hired me and Doug Katsaros to write the theme and make weekly trips to L.A. to score the episodes. The schedule went like this: on the plane first thing in the morning, 6-hour session in the afternoon, redeye back to NY. It took its toll for the summer; but oh boy! the frequent flyer miles...

I didn't hear much from Mr. Sohmer for a few years. Then, in November of 1998, I got a call from Steve's longtime secretary, Andrea. She said that Steve instructed her to tell me that if he were going to be dragged out of the retirement closet, I would have to be dragged with him. I was pretty happy about it. The children were leaving the nest; I had less to do. I was ready to jump back into the fray.

Off we went, this time to ABC. It was Steve's "threepeat." We didn't do the conventions, but we did do some outrageous promos for their shows, and a full orchestral *Saturday Night Movie* theme. Doug Katsaros and I made a quick trip to London to record a 60-piece live orchestra in the Sony studios (saving ABC lots of bucks on residuals).

We had pre-programmed the rhythm section in New York and planned to overdub the orchestra onto the 48-track tape. The London orchestra was quick and professional. Doug's creative rearrangement of the revived ABC theme was brilliant. I was having a wonderful time until Doug and I got back from lunch to listen to the engineer's first stab at the mix.

It was sheer disaster. Although I had carefully explained our concept of the mix as a predominant rhythm section with orchestral trappings, the guy didn't get it. In fact, he didn't have a clue. The whole thing sounded like mush (with some faint thumping in the background).

Doug had to catch a plane back, so I was left alone to clean up the mess. I succeeded, but it was an uphill battle at every step. I was forced to turn into an absolute bitch to get my way. The supercilious, misogynistic attitude of the snotty Brit classical music engineer got my dander up. I stuck forcefully to my guns, took no prisoners. Steve Sohmer was the client; the goods were going to be delivered. The ordeal did make me appreciate the genius of my favorite engineers back in the States.

The last joint Steve Sohmer-Susan Hamilton work romp started when he was hired by the PAX TV Network. The owner was Bud

Paxton, a Christian and family values advocate. His programming reflected his beliefs. His partnering with Steve and me may have made for strange bedfellows, but hey: we were guns for hire. We didn't have conventions to do, but we did have the May Sweeps conferences in midtown Manhattan.

The first big network song, "Share It With Someone You Love," was a little sappy and religious for my taste, but it worked for everyone else. The second year, however, Steve decided to do a gospel number with the theme, "Share The Wonder." He had no shame. He knew what would work. As with the samba piece for NBC, he was determined that it be authentic.

I knew in my bones that one secret to the sound and feel of the real thing was to use only black singers — the ones who had grown up in the church singing the hymns. I cast accordingly, making temporary enemies of my regulars. I didn't care.

After we had produced the instrumental tracks, I went out into the studio with my hand-picked choir. Steve had sent me a few hymns, and I played a couple of them to demonstrate what I wanted. Before they had heard more than a couple of bars, they joined in, singing along, filling in all of the harmony parts. The hairs on the back of my neck rose straight up. The sound, the blend, was perfection.

For the May Sweeps, we presented the finished piece live at the Sheraton on Seventh Ave. We had a pretty 10-year-old white girl come out to sing the a cappella introduction in a sweet, innocent, beautiful voice. Then the robed black choir on stage behind her exploded into the meat of the song. Their entrance was cued up to a prerecorded rockin' out rhythm track, featuring (of course) a B2 Hammond Organ. Behind them we projected the long version of the promo in sync, on a gigantic screen. Getting the timing right for the multiple elements was a bitch, but when it worked, it brought the house down.

My relationship with Steve continues today. We survived the various network wars, creative differences, all of his wives, all of my husbands, and long periods of being out of touch. Truly good friends are able to do that, with humor and mutual respect.

MOST COMPANIES KEEP their CLIOs on shelves in ritzy lighted glass cabinets.

When I moved back East again, I found a tall carton filled with the statuettes mixed in with a bunch of old HEA stuff. Most of them were rusted and broken, but in the true spirit of New England thriftiness, I was able to rescue six or seven.

They make very practical doorstops for a 1790 colonial house (though in the middle of the night they can be true toe-killers).

Chapter 46

The Genius

THE THIRD TIME'S THE CHARM. I kept repeating those words to myself as Rob and I prepped for our sophisticated Manhattan wedding ceremony and the all-out bash to follow. I was determined to make this one work! I had set the date on my parents' anniversary — their marriage had lasted forever, right? I vowed that we would have sex on our wedding night (I hadn't for the other two). Nevertheless, except for a single major exception, it turned out to be my biggest mistake of all...

A few months after the Eliot mess had calmed down, Rob and I started seeing each other regularly. I had tunnel vision. All I wanted was to get pregnant again. The work was still coming in fast, so we spent a lot of time in the studio — but also found time to have dinner and sex. Six months later, I got my wish.

The tone of this relationship was very different. I thought of us as living in a rarified, intellectual atmosphere. For a while, that part was a relief. Rob was brilliant: smarter than I (except in practical matters), but fastidious and hypercritical. I remember how he would cringe if I happened to eat an apple in his presence. He couldn't look at me; winced at every crunch. On the other hand, I certainly didn't have to worry about public displays of affection, anymore. There wasn't much affection at all. There was mutual respect and stimulating conversation. Rob was a classic ectomorph. Tall, thin — not at all athletic — he lived life almost exclusively in his brain.

Once I became pregnant, Rob moved into my 64th Street apartment — but also kept his Chelsea loft apartment and studio. He did a lot of his own record work there. I still worked every day and most nights at the office and in the studio...right up until the evening my water broke while we were dining at Le Veau D'Or.

Throughout the nine months of waiting, Rob had been attentive and conscientious. We were lucky: I sailed through an easy pregnancy. We shopped for baby things; he went to Lamaze classes with me. Nevertheless, I have to admit that I have very little memory of my personal life from the end of my relationship with Eliot to the birth of Alex. I do remember one December night when Rob and I lay in bed, watching TV, as the horrific events unfolded in the entryway of the Dakota.

Although the delivery was a nightmare, since both Alex and I came out of it just fine, that wasn't important.

Maybe it was the seriousness of becoming parents, I don't know — but there sure wasn't a lot of laughter or fun, except sometimes on a session with all of our musician and singer friends. Most weekends we drove to my Vermont house where we entertained colleagues from the City. We traveled several times to Europe and twice to Hawaii — but mostly for work. We did make time for three trips to Italy: *Lago di Como*, Verona and Venice by ourselves; then two to Sardinia with Alex and nanny: Calle di Volpe, and then Hotel Pitrizzia on the *Costa Smeralda* (still my favorite vacation spot in the world).

A presage of things to come: Rob was mortified one luncheon when a gleeful, naked three-year-old Alex escaped from his nanny and scampered through the elegant restaurant, ducking under tables and between the legs of the impeccably dressed guests. The Italians were delighted with the scene; later, Rob screamed furiously at me and the nanny.

We could not have been two more different people. I am an early morning extrovert who enjoys 'doing.' Rob loves to stay up until four a.m., smoke a little pot, then sleep until two. I enjoy sports, exercise, gardening, and throwing myself hard into everything. Rob reads, thinks, composes, and noodles on the piano. I wouldn't mind at all when baby Alex made a glorious mess while eating in his high chair. Rob would snap at me about Alex's lack of table manners. One of the worst moments came when I watched Rob slam the door to his office in Alex's face as the toddler begged to be picked up.

We did get married in the fall of '82. Alex was about to turn two — and I believed it would be better for him if we were husband and wife. I don't think either of us was that enthusiastic about the idea, but we made the best of it. First class all the way. We had a private, immediate-family-only ceremony in our apartment. Among the attendees was Steve Smith, a former boyfriend who was now married to Rob's sister Barbara. Rob and I pledged to work harder on accommodating each others' differences. Later, at the architecturally stunning Thread Building downtown, we threw a top-tier bash for more than 100 friends. Renny did the flowers and Glorious Foods catered. Once again, the impromptu musical performances went on into the night.

Despite our wedding vows, we grew further apart. Rob hated hanging out at my horse shows so I traveled to them with Alex and nanny only. Privately, I was relieved: it was a lot more fun without him. When we were by ourselves, we argued more; he criticized more. There were many nights when I stood in front of the apartment door, fighting knots in my stomach. The interpersonal tension didn't carry over into our work together, however. That continued to be exciting. But all the other areas of our life together were again — nightmarishly — falling apart.

Just before Alex's fourth birthday, we returned home from a trip to California. After settling Alex down in his room, I looked for Rob. He wasn't there. He had disappeared without a word. I called his loft and spoke to his friend Richard. Rob was there, but didn't want to speak to me.

I freaked for a few weeks. At my insistence, we saw a couples' therapist a few times. Stubbornly, despite all the evidence to the contrary, I was determined to make it work. I couldn't fail yet a third time, could I? Yes, I could. I remember in one therapy session, he whirled on me with his lips pressed in a thin, bloodless line, and snapped into my face, "You know the problem with you, Susan? You're just too god-damned good at everything." What could I say? I felt complimented. And perfectly miserable...

Rob had a kind of unspoken payback: a subtle way to keep the little woman down. He waged an effective campaign throughout our relationship to make me believe that I was not creative. Sure — maybe I was an excellent producer, moneymaker, manager; and I could edit other peoples' work — but after all, I created nothing from a blank page, did I?

I believed him, all the more when my father backed him up. I'll never forget one morning in my kitchen in Vermont when he answered a remark of Rob's with, "Well you're correct about that. Rollin was always the creative one of the three kids." (After I grew up, my father had gradually built up resentment as I became more and more successful).

Many years later, when I explained my creativity deficit to Michael, he burst out laughing. Then, when he saw that I was serious, sat me down and gave example after example to point out how ridiculous the notion was.

Later, it dawned on me that it was only after Rob and I split that I began to write some of my own little jingles, co-write songs with people like David Buskin and Gordon Grody, and come up with slogans and campaign ideas for pitches...

I gave up. Let Rob go. It was a huge defeat, but again, mixed with relief and a shade less guilt than I would have expected: I sensed that he had become quite infatuated with my secretary, Debbie. In her free time, she was working for him as a personal assistant on his record projects. Somehow, this added to my relief.

As usual, I turned the page quickly. Within six weeks, I was seeing other people and returning to a life with more fun in it. Even though he had certainly wanted out of the relationship, Rob brooded about the situation for a long time. He once told me that for a year, he would occasionally go to a bar, get very drunk, and think, "What happened? Where is my family? My wife, my child?"

But he ended up marrying Debbie, and they have two wonderful children. I once asked Debbie how she handled Rob's descents into depression, which could sometimes be accompanied by full-blown fetal-position paralysis. She told me, "I just laugh and joke him out of it." She turned out to be a better partner than I, that's for sure.

Rob and I continued working together for a while, but Rob couldn't stand it. Finally, both he and Debbie left HEA to work independently. I'm sure they did very well; his gifts are indisputable.

I still ask myself, *Why would you do it? Partner up with someone so incompatible? Deliberately try to muscle through such an obviously doomed relationship? Hang onto a situation that was incontrovertibly headed toward failure?*

Once again, my insightful eyewitness, Glenn Berger, supplies an outside view:

> *I remember the first time I heard a demo by Rob Mounsey. This was one of those rare life moments when you encounter a major fucking talent for the first time, a kind you heard maybe once in a decade. So, given my theory that Susan was more attracted to a*

talent-package than a good love-match, it didn't surprise me that she would trade up to Mounsey. Scheiner was not nearly as brilliant.

That nails it; nails me. I was so blinded by Rob's incredible intellect and talent that I refused to look any further. And suffered the consequences. Of course, the most unfortunate result of the breakup was the toll it took on Alex. To this day, he refuses to communicate with his father at all. For both their sakes and mine, I won't go into why.

MEL TORME TURNED TO ME after recording and said, "Young lady, you can produce me anytime!" Coming from him, it was the nicest compliment I'd ever had.

That session was perhaps the smoothest, most pleasurable of my career. David Buskin did a marvelous job of adapting his jingle for Mel; Dick Behrke's arrangement was perfect, but it was The Velvet Fog himself who knocked it out of the park.

Mel topped the experience off by taking us all to Michael's, where we listened in awe to his versions of Steely Dan and Donald Fagen songs.

Part IV

SOLO

Chapter 47

Dancin' on the Keys

────

FOLLOWING THE SUCCESSFUL RESOLUTION of the Elton John adventure in Boston, all was calm in Diet Coke land for a while. I assumed they were shooting, editing, and getting ready to put the spots on air. Then I got another call from Sue Read. A decision had been made to produce a duet version of the jingle featuring a yet-to-be named female artist.

Much discussion ensued. I campaigned for Gladys Knight: certainly one of the best female singers ever. Plus, I had recorded her and her Pips for another client some years before, and she had simply wowed me. Unbelievable style, a velvet tone, superb artistry and a completely professional attitude. There was talk of Aretha: another incredible talent. But Diet Coke rejected them both because of a weight issue. I was somewhat put off by the decision, but it was Sue Read who was thoroughly outraged when they settled on their final choice: Paula Abdul. She ranted and raved.

"She's a nothing. A zero. You call that a singer? She was a *cheerleader for the Lakers*, for god's sake. And dance? She's short and stumpy. Who wants to look at that? Not me. What were they thinking?!"

Part of what they were thinking was *Paula's just had a Number One, blow-out album with three Number One singles*. The clients didn't care how it was done — they just wanted to see Paula singing with Elton.

Given that all of the Elton footage had already been shot, the daunting task was to dream up some way to create a plausible duet commercial. And, despite her antipathy toward Paula, again it was Sue Read (with the help of director Steve Horn) who came up the plan: *Well, she **is** a good choreographer – she can sing and dance across giant piano keys while Elton is playing.* A clever idea, indeed.

I have always admired superstars who achieve mind-boggling success through sheer charisma, star-quality performance, chutzpah, intelligence, charm, and an understanding of the pulse of the audience. Even those who owe much of their success to outstanding producers and handlers. Those famous ones who succeed without the god-given, awe-inspiring musical talent of a Gladys Knight or a Ray Charles. Madonna, Britney, Lady Gaga, J Lo and Justin Timberlake have done exactly that, and yes: Paula also comes to mind. But not Amy Winehouse. Sorry naysayers, she was a Patsy, or a Janis — she had the goods. So does Beyoncé.

I was sitting one day with friend John McCurry, drinking at a bar in the East Village, watching cockroaches crawl across the railing. We were discussing the "real thing" in singers: who had it, who didn't. I was producing Michael Bolton at the time, and we were comparing him with John Waite, who I had recorded as lead singer of The Babys ("Missing You" is one of my all-time favorites). McCurry was Waite's friend and had worked with him a lot. He said, "If Bolton turns out to be the real thing, I'll suck my own cock, and I know I can't because I've tried." How right he was.

I looked forward to working with Paula — had confidence the concept would work. There was just one enormous roadblock. The Elton track we had already produced was totally wrong for the spot, most of all rhythmically. No one (except maybe German soldiers) could dance to it. I'm talking about men who would have never laid eyes on a black person. It had almost no syncopation, no anticipated downbeats, no pushes, no R&B groove in the drum or bass track. It was pretty much straight on-the-beat: 1, 2, 3, 4; 1, 2, 3, 4.

I thought long and hard. *Absolutely no chance of having Elton redo the track. Absolutely necessary to redo the track. Can't explain the problem to Sue and Lintas; they'll just give me blank stares. What to do? What to do? Have to tell someone. Will be liable for who-knows-what from Elton's people if we screw with the hallowed recording of his piano track?* Nightmares, I tell you; I had nightmares.

In the end, I bit the bullet and made my move. I recruited Doug Katsaros, Sammy Merendino (drum programmer supreme), and Rick Kerr, my engineer.

Ground Control was my recording studio on the ground floor of the HEA office building. We slipped into it in the middle of the night when no one would be around, and prepped for surgery. We muted almost everything except Elton's vocal and the click track; Sammy replaced the live drums brilliantly with a drum track that fairly forced your feet to move; we simplified the live bass track by surgically erasing some parts, replacing a few key notes with Dougie on a synthesizer.

Then, with my heart in my mouth, sooooooo carefully, we replaced the tiniest parts possible of Elton's piano tracks. We had no vacant tracks for backup; we had to go in on the original master tracks.

So we just did it. Had to.

At the end of the many hours in the operating theater, I called Mike Beindorff, the Coca-Cola client. He was at home (it was the middle of the night). I told him the deed was done. To this day, I can't believe that I had decided to confide in the client instead of the agency, but Mike was cool, and musically savvy. I had to tell somebody what we were doing. So I just made the call and stuck to it. I never told anyone else (except Sue, years later). It was another big risk that turned out to be worth it.

A bit more about Sue Read: she is one of the most amazing advertising writers I have ever worked with — and a good friend with a heart of gold. She actually taught me lot, all the while making me want to pull my hair out. She taught me to believe "never say never" and "anything is possible." Sue always said, "If someone can say no, he or she can also turn around and say yes!"

She is the only client who ever had to be locked in a closet during a shoot. (To be clear, it wasn't I who locked her in the closet — it was director Elbert Budin.) But she *never* held a grudge, and she always managed to get what she wanted in the end. So I guess (come to think of it) she won.

Sue Read created some of the most innovative work in an era of great advertising, including *Little Old Ladies* for Lipton Tea, *Colors* for Kodak Film, many Hallmark spots, "The Softer Side of Sears" and, of course, the Diet Coke stuff. However, she was consistently — take-it-to-the-bank reliably — maddening every time we worked together.

I don't think anyone really listened carefully to the doctored Elton tracks until it was time to record Paula in L.A. The shoot for the duet spot had been filmed to the newly manipulated music track with a

Paula scratch vocal, probably sung by Robin Beck. For playback, we dropped out Elton's vocal where necessary. Musically, everything went smoothly. No notice of the changes, no rumbles of discontent.

I did hear from Sue, however. The filming hadn't gone too well. Apparently Steve Horn, the director, took one look at Paula's outfit and said something like, "Honey, I think you better go take off that little skirt and put on some pants." Paula objected, but Steve prevailed with, "Listen to me. I can make you look beautiful in this spot, but not without the pants, so please go put them on." Paula acquiesced. Sue had been on the warpath for the whole shoot, made herself *persona non grata* with Paula and Paula's people. She could never get over her notion that a "second-rate talent" (in her mind) was being paired with her precious Elton — and on almost equal footing, no less! She and Paula were even worse than oil and water. Sue had no respect for Paula, and Paula hated Sue's guts. She let it be known.

Sue and I flew out to LA to record a radio version of Paula's vocals. Part of the deal. The experience was most unpleasant in every sense. Paula's management had insisted that we work with her record producers, so we drove up into the hills to a beautiful house with an absolutely gorgeous, full-service recording studio. I don't remember which of her producers were involved (many different people were credited on that first multi-platinum album), but there were two of them in the studio. They were both what I like to call 'Slick Willys.'

The track and the background vocals for Paula's solo radio version had already been recorded, but we were allowed to observe as they produced Paula. They treated her like crap. Insulting and making fun of her with the talkback mike off, and even with it on. At one point, Paula became really upset, threw her headphones to the floor, put the back of her hand over her mouth and rushed out of the room. I followed her into the bathroom, and found her throwing up in one of the stalls. Between sobs, she told me, "I'm not a singer. I'm a failure. I just can't do this." I talked her down and propped her up: told her truthfully how much I admired her — and we did get through it. Years later, I saw Paula do exactly the same thing on *American Idol*, reacting to some asshole who dropped his pants in front of the judges' table. This was no act. Despite her sassy public persona, Paula is truly sensitive: a softie, in fact.

The final recording was thrown out by Sue Read. The completed version was mechanical, flat, ground down into a pale copy of the cuts on her album. It was without even a tinge of soulfulness, or any of Paula's usual spark. I still have a copy. As an illustration of how these producers approached projects, the track was presented to us, with vocals, in four keys: A, A flat, G and G flat. All identical (except their machines had spat them out in different keys). I don't really know what the purpose was supposed to be.

At some later point, we did actually have to get Paula's voice onto the finished Elton/Paula duet spot. Back we went once more to some studio in L.A. This time, at her request, only Paula, an engineer and I were in attendance. Sue was actually hiding behind an interior door, occasionally making faces at me (she had been banished from Paula's sight forever). The job was done quickly; Paula was just fine, and — thank God — there was no drama.

I waited expectantly to see the spots on the air.

No luck.

Another phone call came from Lintas, this time from the account team. "Would you be willing to travel to LA to present the finished spots to both Elton and Paula for approval?" This was weird. Even for me, who often got involved with the advertising platform of a campaign. But...to represent the agency for final talent approval?

The account executive explained that Sue would be with me for Elton, but Paula's people had developed such antipathy toward the agency, the account team decided I should go alone to get clearance on the project.

My heart was in my mouth when we met with Elton in a huge screening room. We played the spots several times at deafening volume. I worried. But all was fine; he loved them; approved them. I really don't think he even noticed the changes we had made in the duet track. Now it was on to Paula.

I faced the creepy Paula people by myself. In a small office with a small TV and a video cassette player, we screened the spots together. Paula wasn't there. Just as well. There was one particular shot that everyone was worried about, including me. It was toward the middle, where she is squatting down with bent knees while singing. I coughed, and/or distracted them during those frames of the film both times we looked at it. Success! It passed inspection.

Fine. I'd done my job. I don't remember if they paid me, but I did get to fly on the corporate jet to Aspen and spend the long weekend attending some incomprehensible meetings with the Coca-Cola people and Sue Read. There were sumptuous dinners and late night drinks in fancy hotel bars. Moreover, I got to stay on afterwards for five days of spectacular skiing...

And Paula? Well, Paula has definitively proved her stature as more than a flash-in-the-pan, manufactured pop singer. Famous all over the world, she looked better than ever on *American Idol* and *Dancing With the Stars*. She is a survivor (and a strong one, at that).

THE LONGEST WEEK of my life in the studio was spent at Gotham Recording with the usually taciturn and patient engineer, Ed Rice.

We had to go through hour after hour of live Henny Youngman performances to edit together his best delivery of certain one liners that had been written into a bunch of radio spots. It took *five solid days!*

By the end, we'd almost killed each other.

Chapter 48

One of Those Nights

———

WHAT A FRIGGIN' NIGHT! I tell you... I got off the flight
from JFK at LAX and jumped into a cab to Melrose Avenue
and Lucy's El Adobe. I was going to be late for the dinner.

By the time I got there, they were already seated at the long rustic table. Well into their margaritas, judging from the volume of the
conversation and laughter. The table included a large group of clients
and one VIP guest.

Hunter Murtaugh, music director at Young & Rubicam, stood
up to make the introductions. I mumbled pleasantries and sat down.
Both Mark Hartley of the artist management firm Hartley and Fitzgerald, and Glenn Frey, formerly of the Eagles, now a solo artist, gave
me a thorough once-over. I had been expecting it. Being late had
forced me to face the situation earlier than I would have wished. Made
me face it rumpled, disheveled, fresh off the plane. In New York black.
With boots and coat. When it was a beautiful 75 degrees in L.A., and
everyone was dressed for afternoon shopping on Rodeo Drive.

My uneasiness had to do with the divorce from Eliot a few years
before. He was a client of Hartley's firm — and a very good friend and
working associate of Glenn's. The divorce hadn't been pretty; Eliot
had been quite upset. I expected a certain degree of hostility.

In fact, I got none. Mark was most diplomatic, and from the twinkle in Glenn's eye, I think he was slightly amused at my obvious discomfort.

We had all gathered to work on a radio campaign for Old Style Beer. It was a Midwestern beer. I had never heard of it, but these clients had a lot of money and were deadly serious about launching a first class, national-level campaign. Their agency of record was Y&R Chicago, but they had drafted Hunter of Y&R NY to handle the music business negotiations and production.

The backstory goes like this: they were first determined to buy the John Cougar Mellencamp song, "Small Town." Hunter was authorized to offer an obscene amount of money for the advertising rights, and actually made the offer to the manager while Mellencamp was on the other line. He turned them down flat. At the time he was very much involved with Farm Aid, and spoke out loudly against greed and the corporate world. He had publicly announced that no corporation would ever use one of *his* songs for commercial gain.

When Hunter relayed the bad news to the clients, they answered, "Offer him double." According to Hunter, he almost fell off his chair: by this point, they were up in the millions — an unheard-of sum at the time. Mellencamp turned them down again. He had planted his flag and was going to stand by it. (That position didn't last forever, though: his songs have since been prominently featured in ads. Given the number and quality of top-tier celebrities involved in corporate advertising today, that's hardly a surprise).

Hunter's next move was to hold a jingle competition for the campaign, which my company won. The line was *I've Got A Dream. (What can I say?...[sigh])*. The commercials were pure Americana, and Jake Holmes wrote a fabulous song, as usual. Hunter then succeeded in negotiating for Glenn Frey to sing the spots. I was hired to produce. Glenn did get a very large, well-deserved sum. Against the norm, he charged the agency more because he DIDN'T write the song. Also, as I learned much later, he was going through a nasty divorce at the time, so the extra cash probably came in handy. That could be part of why he never gave me a hard time about Eliot.

Okay, back to Lucy's:

After dinner, Hunter, Glenn and I ditched all the beer clients and the Chicago account people, climbed into the white stretch limo and motored west on Sunset Blvd. to the *Hotel California* (aka the Beverly Hills Hotel) to drop off my luggage.

I had begged Hunter to be allowed to retreat to my room for the evening, but he was adamant that part of my job was to participate in all activities. I had no idea where we were going so I didn't even bother to insist on changing my clothes. While driving all over in the limo, we did get to hear some of the new album Glenn was working on, and that was great fun. But I didn't much enjoy the cloud of familiar fragrant smoke that engulfed the whole passenger area.

The first stop was the Palomino Club in North Hollywood to catch a set of Delbert McClinton and his band. Blood-pumping, raw, gutsy, tight blues/rock with a rowdy crowd and sawdust on the floor. What a pro. But it was three hours later for me, and despite being thoroughly exhausted and thoroughly pissed at Hunter, I succumbed to a WTF moment. I joined them in shot after shot of truly fine tequila, whooped it up with the audience, and just went along for the ride.

If I thought we were done for the night, I was wrong. Off we went, ending up somewhere near Downtown. A funny, semi-deserted industrial area. It didn't seem appropriate for the hottest, most exclusive disco/dance club in L.A., but there we were: at Helena's. Whisked through the VIP entrance and shown to a round table next to the dance floor.

One look around and I was completely horrified. I felt like I was under a spotlight in a Fellini nightmare. Gorgeous beauties, dressed to kill, shimmered and glittered across the dance floor, rubbing up against their well-muscled partners, all dressed in all black. Towering over everyone was Brigitte Nielsen, notorious super-model, actress, and at that time, rising Hollywood star. She had a helmet of slicked-down ash blond hair. Her very low-cut, one-piece sheath fashioned from some silvery metallic material was so short it revealed at least two inches of perfectly toned, golden-tanned butt cheeks.

I sobered up in a hurry. I had never felt so unprepared, so out of place, so *trapped* in all my life. Remember, I was dressed in dark, rumpled, cold weather clothes. I fled to the powder room to collect my wits, but the scene I ran into there made things worse. I was the only one under 5'8" tall; I felt like a five-year-old girl trying to make my way through a crowded Miss America dressing room. My face came into near-collision with more fake boobs than I care to remember. I was also the only one over 40.

I slunk back to the table. Glenn waved me over to sit next to him. I didn't even put up a fight. I sat huddled there, trying to see if I could force all 5'3" of me to disappear into the cushions. I couldn't. I kept my eyes down and my mouth shut.

Bob Seger, then George Michael came over to the table to chat up Glenn. He, of course, made a big deal out of introducing me and Hunter. Sure. Why not?

It got worse.

Some young good-looking guy came up to the table and asked me to dance. I refused with some idiotic excuse, but Glenn jumped up, grabbed my arm and pushed me onto the floor saying, "Oh no. Don't be an idiot! Go and dance with the guy, for Christ's sake!" I did, and survived a couple of tracks just fine (I do like to dance), but I suspected it was a setup of some kind.

Much later (by then, well past dawn in the East), I had a remarkable, comforting, elucidating conversation with Glenn. My guard was down; so I explained to him how small I felt in this star-studded arena.

He smiled at me and said something I'll never forget. "Susan, you just don't get it. I'm not at all interested in any of these women. These days, I'm mostly interested in the woman who's going to make me cinnamon toast in the morning, sit across the breakfast table from me without makeup, and ask me how my day went. Do you know how to make cinnamon toast, by any chance?"

I laughed; the dark mood lifted, and I began to realize what a kind man this guy was.

The next day, we started work in the studio fairly late for me. No wonder, after the night before. The pace was leisurely. We were doing everything in *the Eagles' Luxury Way* (as Hunter used to call it). I loved it. If there were such a thing as a music producer's spa, this was it. No checking the clock. No worrying about overtime on anything. We had a whole week to get done what I would normally be able to finish in one very long day, if pushed.

Glenn had personally picked and booked the musicians. I believe they were basically his band: the guys who were playing on his current album. I specifically remember Waddy Wachtel's great guitar playing, but all of them were terrific.

As always, I kept my mouth shut as they started to run down the tracks. There wasn't an arranger *per se*; they read from a simple chord chart. But Glenn was right in the studio with them, walking around and giving direction. The tune Jake had written was harmonically simple, but tricky in structure.

I eventually wandered out of the control booth and into the studio. I stood against the wall until enough confusion had developed... it was Susan time: time for me to speak up.

I spoke quietly and concisely, but with enough musical specificity to raise some eyebrows. It took a few of these interruptions before Glenn stopped the band and announced with a smile, "Well guys, she obviously knows what she's talking about, guess we should listen." He gave me a slight nod, so I went back into the control room, and from then on was comfortable using the talkback.

I should mention the engineer. Bill Szymczyk is a legend. He was behind the board, quietly doing his thing. It's really strange and embarrassing that I remember so little about him. Hunter recently reminded me that he was our engineer — and obviously the reason why the finished product sounded so damn good. The engineer and producer of *Hotel California* — one of my top five favorite albums of all time — was there in the studio with me, recording a beer jingle for the Midwest. Pinch me, please...

Hunter didn't spend a lot of time in the booth. Instead, he paced up and down in the waiting room, talking on the phone and wheeling and dealing for Young & Rubicam. He had become quite the executive, and often left our project for meetings and power lunches. Of course he checked in to make sure things were going well, but he didn't seem to want to get involved in the nitty-gritty. This was quite a departure from our first encounters (and a relief).

Years before, when Hunter had first been hired by Y&R, we became instant enemies. Screaming and fighting enemies. I'd been used to a great deal of autonomy in the studio and he wanted to establish authority by delving into minutiae on every session. I remember a meeting with just the two of us and Manny Perez, head of production at the Agency. Manny sat us down and told us that Y&R needed both of us and we were going to have to play nice. Over the next 10 years or so our relationship evolved into mutual respect and eventually, of course, we became best of friends.

We finished up the backing tracks in two days and then started on vocals. Working with Glenn was a delight. I am a huge Eagles fan, so I experienced a frisson of pure excitement as he opened his mouth and sang on mike *right in front of me!* I did a bunch of takes, then gave him a break while I started comping together a performance. He stayed, listened and watched for a long time without saying a word. My respect for him grew some more. Eventually he said, "Okay, you certainly know your stuff — but I think I can teach you a few things about comping."

And boy, did he! What followed was a Masters' level tutorial in subtlety and technique. He showed me how to put together different pieces of takes I would have considered impossible. Right down to single syllables from different performances. It was fascinating. I immediately started experimenting with what he taught me, and it worked perfectly in many cases.

And then he admitted, "I learned it all from Don. He's the true master of this stuff." I don't know if they were even speaking to each other at this point in the feud/breakup, but he certainly still respected Mr. Henley, and didn't hesitate to give him credit where credit was due. Retrospect tells me that having Bill Szymczyk there to execute all my attempts to apply what I'd learned was really like cheating on an exam. He was an experienced master also, maybe *the* master (I mean — who taught Don?).

The rest of the sessions were a snap. There was one little wrinkle when Jake flew in from New York to participate in the background vocals. Glenn's voice and his just didn't blend well together. We all knew it, and everyone was gracious about it. Jake understood, so Glenn ended up doing the BG's with Tim Schmit (a former Eagles member).

The final mixes were also a joy. Pretty much Bill did them by himself with just a few suggestions thrown in by Glenn and me. Even Hunter didn't find much to grumble about. He did come in to ask Glenn if he were satisfied with his vocals and with the whole project. Glenn tilted his head in my direction and answered, "I don't know. Ask my producer." He said it lightly with a wink, and Hunter didn't mind — but it sure made me feel good.

One last adventure on that trip. On my last day in L.A., I was hanging out at the Beverly Hills Hotel pool when I was paged. It was Hunter. He sounded slightly annoyed. He told me he wanted to have dinner with Glenn that evening to thank him for everything, but Glenn told him he wouldn't go unless I was there, too.

We dined at Dan Tana's, the West Hollywood landmark and celebrity hangout close to the Troubadour. They served their good, traditional Italian: no *haute cuisine*, simple presentation, 100% delicious. We were led to the best table, one with dark red leather upholstery and a foot-deep wooden ledge behind it. We discussed all kinds of things (except beer commercials). Glenn and Hunter talked old cars; both were fanatics. Glenn told us about his ongoing health regime: no smokes, no drugs, no alcohol, workouts at 5am with a personal trainer, etc. He did look great and very fit. Since Hunter and I were drinking Absolutely perfect vodka martinis, he did promise to have a shot of ice-cold vodka with me after dinner (I forget exactly why; I think I may have teased him into it). Glenn and I also talked about Aspen, a favorite haunt for us both. He gave me his numbers in both L.A. and Snow-mass, and told me to call next time I was planning to visit Aspen.

We were finishing our coffee when a strange expression came across Glenn's face, and he stared intently past my left shoulder at the potted plant on the ledge behind me.

His brow furrowed. "What's that behind you?"

I turned around and spotted a little wrapped package hidden under the leaves.

He said, "Go ahead, pick it up. I think it's for you."

It was a large bottle of Joy perfume with a plain white card that read "It was a 'Joy' to work with you. Glenn" in his bold black writing. I was floored. This, after all of my trepidation at the beginning.

And we did do those shots.

HERBIE HANCOCK is probably the smartest composer I ever worked with.

I was in L.A. while he and Bernie were back in our offices in NYC, trying to figure out how to make Herbie's underscore composition fit with the cuts and actions of the 30-second film they had up on the Moviola.

I explained our complicated system that used the 'sacred' blue book of numerical tables. It coordinated click track tempos and beat numbers with feet and frames of film.

Normally, it required multiple sessions and a couple of days to teach it to a composer. It took Herbie about 15 minutes over the phone to learn it perfectly.

Chapter 49

Bolton

————

*S*USAN WON'T HAVE VERY NICE THINGS TO SAY *about me*, said Michael Bolton to my new friend, Brooke Shields. He was right. Before I sat down to write this book, I promised myself to stay away from outright negativity. And up to this point, I've done my best. But restraint has its limits! The truth will out...

One of my favorite advantages as owner of a jingle company was to be free to discover people with extraordinary talent and then provide them with the exposure that would lead to financial success. Once I started to use a singer frequently, the word would get out, not only to my competitors, but also to the advertising agency producers and music directors. Everyone in the industry always wanted to use the 'new kid on the block,' and it became well known that I often found them first. People in the business were obsessed — sometimes to their detriment — with 'different' and 'new.' The movers and shakers were always too quick to throw out the old and valuable.

My good friend Will Lee benefitted from this phenomenon. I introduced two of his girlfriends (not at the same time) — Robin Beck and Kaz Silver — to the business. Each was superbly talented, and each became the new 'darling' of the ad music people.

This phenomenon wasn't limited to singers; it could and did happen with writers, arrangers, musicians, studios and engineers. But the results were far more dramatic with singers. My number one partner in this quest was always Gordon Grody. A fantastic singer in his own right as well as a very close friend, Gordon would tell me about new talent, bring me tapes of them or even march them unannounced up to my office and demand that they sing live for me right then. Most of the time his discoveries were singers, but he also steered me toward gifted engineers and musicians.

Another friend and colleague, John McCurry, also introduced me to exciting new talent, but Gordon made it a priority. One day (years after I left New York), he sat me down on the sofa in his living room where he was coaching a somewhat plain, brown-haired girl named Stefani. Dressed in jeans and a tee shirt, she stood by the piano.

"You gotta listen to her and her material. I tell you, she's got something."

I was annoyed with Gordon; I had just dropped by to say hello and had a million things to do that day in the City, but I sat there and listened, and as usual, Gordon had a point. The girl accompanied herself on the piano with great presence and a sassy spark. Her songs were pop and catchy. Gordon introduced her as Stefani Germanotta, but she later changed her name to Lady Gaga.

One of the people Gordon brought to my attention was Pattie Darcy. I fell in love with her voice instantly. Not only its smoky quality, but the emotional punch — the believability — and her incredible technique. I started to hire her immediately and frequently. Pattie went from making eight grand a year to $80K the next year, then to $800K and more.

I introduced her to Michael Bolton; he introduced her to Cher. She made the decision to leave the 'velvet trap' of the jingle business to become Cher's back-up singer, confidante and alter ego for years.

Gordon also introduced me to Vicki Sue Robinson ("Turn the Beat Around"). A distinctive and strong singer with unbelievable r&b chops, she was pulling herself up out of some rough times. I helped. Soon other music companies followed my lead. Then came Joe Lynn Turner ("Deep Purple"), Louie Merlino, and Marc Cohn ("Walking in Memphis").

It occurs to me that right around that time (late '70s/early '80s), a sea change was starting to happen in the world of jingle singers. The stars of the business were no longer unidentifiable, flawless, perky voices. This new group had character, even distinguishable flaws.

But Michael didn't come from Gordon. He came through Louis Levin, his manager, who sent me a demo tape and set up a meeting. I recognized his value immediately. On the other hand, Gordon didn't like him at all, although later he admitted that I had been right about his appeal.

With Michael, it was the sound of his voice, the tone. For women of any age, it conjured up the best, pure, unadulterated sex scenarios they could imagine. It was amazing.

I once explained, "When Michael would step up to the microphone and open his mouth, it would take only a couple of notes. The knees of the women clients in the booth would buckle; they would practically swoon onto the floor. He never failed me." Other less couth individuals in the room (typically the assistant engineers) would mutter, "Lotta wet panties in here..."

He did a lot of work for me. Other music houses caught on, and he was hugely successful in the biz in no time. We became pals and hung out a lot. We shared the ability to find humor in the ironies of life's twists and turns. He was a struggling rock and roller, conflicted about his probable divorce from his wife, the mother of his three daughters. I never bought the rock and roll part (he seemed more r&b to me) but hey, if that's how he wanted to see himself, so be it.

We had our catch phrases: "the RTD bus" and "take the two bedroom." To Michael, the symbol of his former poverty was having to take the RTD to get around. I told him it would soon be limos. When he had to get an apartment in the City, my advice was, "Go for it: take the two bedroom. You'll be able to afford it." I was right about the apartment — and of course he never did ride the RTD again.

Our friendship blossomed and his career soared. In the studios, we couldn't look at each other without cracking up as the women fawned all over him.

I was very careful about the jobs I chose for him. Stylistically, he had a limited range; but within those parameters, he was easy to produce. I made a giant mistake once when I hired him to sing the Stevie Winwood song, "Back In The High Life Again" for Miller Beer. The whole chorus of the song requires singing on the upbeats, which Michael couldn't do at all. He just couldn't hear the difference between *on* the beat and *between* the beats. I've run into a few other very soulful singers with the same problem.

He became more and more attentive, almost courting me in a non-sexual way. He would press a little piece of paper in my hand as he left the studio with '*thinking of you*' written on it. When it turned out we were both going to be in L.A. at the same time, he threatened me with, "If you don't get in touch with me while you're there, I'll hire detectives to hunt you down." We palled around at least a couple of times on that trip.

One day he came for a visit to my office. He told me he was doing an album for Columbia Records, and wanted me to produce a track on it. I was flattered, but had my misgivings. I remembered my decision not to accept a position as a staff producer at Columbia many years before, and the reasons for it. Too much time invested for what so often turns out to be such a small return.

He persisted. Because we were such good friends, I finally relented. The tracking sessions went well; we followed with a lot of vocal work in my studio, Ground Control. It took many late nights. The song was titled "Walk Away," written by Michael and über-famous Diane Warren. To me, the song was obviously about his failing marriage. So one night, after we had wasted too much time getting nowhere, I pushed every button I could think of: goaded him into talking about Maureen and his daughters. He grew increasingly angry and upset — and I got the performance I needed.

That Michael Bolton album, *The Hunger*, did fairly well, and achieved some critical acclaim. I got full producer's credit on the cut.

In the midst of production on the next album, *Soul Provider*, Michael came to me again. This time he asked me to produce "Georgia On My Mind."

I told him flat-out that he was crazy. "Listen Michael, you got away with "Sittin' On the Dock of the Bay" on the last one, but Otis Redding is dead — and as far as I know, Ray Charles is still very much alive! "

He told me to look at it as a challenge; to at least think about it. He knew how to push my buttons, too.

I had a talk with Richard Tee, my favorite piano player in the world. I knew I couldn't do the track without him. He thought about it for a while, then said, "I remember once hearing the intro done in 4/4 time. I think we should do it that way." I was hooked and agreed to the project.

Michael informed me casually that he was going to take half the producer's credit. He said it was just the way things were done when artists became stars.

This time around, we fought tooth and nail. I put my foot down and won all of my battles. I got my Richard Tee intro. I got Rick Kerr, *my* engineer. I got Chris Parker on drums — Michael didn't think he was a famous enough name; I knew he was perfect. I made Michael drop the key a full whole step from the one he wanted. I insisted he start the performance quietly, in his lower register, and not really let loose until the second chorus. He generally wasn't happy unless he was singing full volume in the upper stratosphere. This time I made him wait.

I also forced him to sing live with the band while we were recording the track. Over and over again from the little booth. I really wanted one complete band take. I didn't want to have to replace anything with an overdub, and I certainly didn't want to paste and edit two or three different performances. We were working without the omnipresent click track. Eventually, I was quite pleased with the final take, and so was Michael.

With "Georgia," I worked for days and days comping his vocals. The task was much harder than with "Walk Away" — a different kind of song altogether. "Walk Away" is a pop song. We were doing "Georgia" as an R&B classic — much looser rhythmically, much more difficult to successfully match any two vocal takes.

In the beginning, Michael was there, watching me every second. But as his trust in my judgment grew, so did his boredom with the tedious process. As time went on, he would just check in occasionally. He had important schmoozing and wheeling and dealing to handle.

We needed an instrumental solo in the middle of the song; I had created the space for it in my arrangement. Not an electric guitar for sure; no, I wanted the darker, sexier tone of a tenor saxophone. I wanted Michael Brecker.

I knew both of the Brecker brothers quite well. Randy, the trumpet player, was the older brother, the more flamboyant and outgoing one. Michael was quieter, gentler, and an absolute master of his instrument. I had a crush on him for years. Both of them played on my sessions as often as I could get them.

Michael Brecker readily agreed to play on the cut; we had a mutual respect thing happening. The session was quick and an absolute delight. He nailed it effortlessly. It gave me goosebumps. Even Mr. Bolton didn't have any comments.

The first single to be released from "Soul Provider" was the title tune. It did all right, but not great. I was busy with my regular day and night job and didn't pay much attention. Then one afternoon I got a phone call from Michael in L.A. He told me Columbia was ready to release "How Am I Supposed To Live Without You" as the second single. He lowered his voice, said he wasn't totally happy with the existing cut on the album. He felt something wasn't quite right with it, that it needed something more. He said he had been racking his brain over the problem, but hadn't come up with answers. He wanted to fly back to NY immediately and sit down with me in a studio to listen to the master multi-track.

He made me come to the studio around midnight. Time was of the essence. He believed I could figure out what to do.

I had ideas instantly. Yes, the track needed to be beefed up with heavy-duty rock guitar power chords in the choruses, but more importantly, the vocals had to be redone. They lacked passion.

We went into the studio, and John McCurry added the electric guitar parts. His characteristic raw sound helped the chorus sound more rock and roll and less pussy 'adult contemporary.' That part was easy. Redoing the vocals on a song he had written long ago — a song that was so ingrained that he automatically sang it in a certain way — proved to be a lot more difficult.

We worked on the verses first. The changes we made were subtle but important for what would happen later in the choruses. I coaxed more underlying sadness and bleak hopelessness into his performance. By the time my comping was done, I'd replaced about half of the lines of the verses. I explained to Michael that the quiet, down verses would set up the explosion of raw emotion in the choruses.

The major chorus change was one of emphasis. Instead of singing the hook line in his usual linear fashion without much dynamic range, I wanted "*HOW* am I supposed to live without you?!" *Lots* of aspirated '*h*' sound. I made him throw both hands up in the air as he sang that word. Also, when the line repeated in the chorus, I had him sing, "*HOW* am I supposed to *LIVE* without you?!" holding the note on 'live' to the last nanosecond possible.

We finally got a performance we both liked; then it was off to L.A. to mix the single version. I don't remember where we mixed it; I don't remember the name of the engineer — only that he was somewhat uncooperative. I do remember Michael was there with Cyndy Garvey, and that they spent most of their time on the couch making out like two teenagers. I didn't give a damn, but it was most distracting (especially the cooing noises). I gritted my teeth, tried not to look, and beat up the engineer until I got what I wanted.

The single came out and hit Number One on the Billboard Hot 100 charts. It also won a Grammy for Best Male Pop Vocal. I watched the show, fully expecting a 'thank you' from Michael, but it wasn't there. When I confronted him about it, he told he had just forgotten and would make it up to me. He had his chance on some other big show, but I wasn't mentioned.

In retrospect, I have to believe that he didn't want to admit to needing my help. Also, when, after the fact, I asked (boy, was I dumb about the record business in those days) for some kind of credit or participation for getting him his Number One single and his Grammy, he told me there was no way. Everything had already been allotted. I was paid $4,000 for my contribution.

Together we went to a CBS party at Black Rock in celebration of his success. I just remember Donnie Ienner, President of Columbia Records, putting me into a chokehold as he instructed, "Just keep making him sing, Susan. That's all I ask. You're doing a terrific job!"

The next debacle came with the proposed single release and video of "Georgia." Michael Bolton came up with the bright idea of replacing Michael Brecker's superb sax solo with one by his new golfing buddy, Kenny G. He said it would be good for the video and good for sales. I was horrified, but what could I do? Michael flew me out to L.A. for the umpteenth time. He loved it out there. Why wouldn't he?

This became the session from Hell, the nightmare of all time. We started early in the evening; we finished after dawn. All for a 30 or 40 second solo. Kenny G was a nice enough fellow, although I bristled at his asides about his wife. I think he actually called her, 'my barbie.'

I learned that Kenny G couldn't put together a serious jazz solo to save his life. I know, I know, I know. He's among the two or three top album-selling instrumentalists in the world; but I'm telling you, that night he was completely over his head. I don't really blame him. Michael Bolton had miscast him. Kenny G was trying to emulate the incomparable Michael Brecker, and I was stuck holding the bag. It was so bad that I couldn't even comp anything out of the hundred takes. I finally had to *notate* on music paper some phrases that I cobbled together from his ramblings. But it got done. I washed my hands of the whole thing, and went back to New York, absolutely disgusted. "Georgia" as a single had only moderate success, but did do well enough to get Bolton another Grammy nomination.

Still, I just hadn't learned my lesson. Stupid, stupid, stupid Susan.

Michael was now a big star and ready to do his next album, *Time, Love & Tenderness*. He offered me the bone of co-producing "When A Man Loves A Woman" with him, but in the meantime, had me comping vocals on all the other songs he had already recorded with another producer. I spent day after day working at The Hit Factory, doing song after song — maybe six altogether. Michael would check in every so often to hear the finished product. He had a few nits here and there, but nothing major.

For "When A Man Loves a Woman," we agreed to record in L.A. He trusted me. We decided on a date, and I booked the studio, engineer, and players. I also chose the key. In the meantime, I wanted to find out what my participation on the album would be for all the work I had been doing. Michael was overtly angry that I even dared to ask. We started fighting, and the fighting continued and escalated.

On the night before our scheduled session for "When a Man...," I was having dinner with friends at the Musso & Frank Grill in Hollywood. I spent over an hour in the phone booth across from the coatroom, screaming at him. It didn't end well. He absolutely refused to give me even a half a point for producing all the vocals on the album. I believed his vocals *were* his records and that I'd earned participation in the royalties. He believed I was just a technician who should be well paid — maybe $2500 a track — but once again, the pie had already been divvied up, and there was none left in the pan.

The next day we did the "When a Man..." session anyway. Our interaction would have had to warm up to reach 'frigid.' We were barely on speaking terms. The track, on the other hand, was a triumph for me. I had done the arrangement by myself. I knew exactly how it should sound, how it should build, and where the payoffs should be. I just gave the guys a chord sheet and explained what I wanted. Jeff Porcaro gave us one of the best drum fills of all time. Michael Thompson played guitar. He was relatively new on the scene (I had to browbeat Bolton to use him), but he came through brilliantly. The well-respected John Beasley played the piano. I didn't know him personally, but he was recommended highly and performed perfectly.

I made Michael sing live in a booth, as I had with "Georgia." The track had been custom crafted by me for him, and eventually we got amazing performances from everybody, including him. But the chill in the air between us was thick enough to cut with a knife, and we parted on icy terms.

The next day I got a phone call from Michael's personal assistant telling me that our relationship was terminated as of that day. I was not to contact him further.

I explored legal action, but unfortunately my lawyer was his lawyer. There was a conflict of interest. Obviously, my lawyer abandoned me and stayed with the bigger client. I didn't blame him, but it was game over. I didn't have the powerhouse lawyer and I wasn't willing to spend the bucks. I licked my wounds and went back to my day job, which I vastly preferred anyway.

"When A Man Loves A Woman" gave Michael his second Number One spot on the Billboard 100 and a second Grammy for Best Male Pop Vocal. They used my track (except for replacing the bass player with Randy Jackson). In fact, I had told Michael at the ill-fated session that only the bass part should be replaced. I have no idea how much of the live vocal track they used. I do know that the ar-rangement and production I did on the song was perfectly suited to Michael. I guess I was proved right with the single's success.

I received no mention or credit for anything I did —including all the vocal comping for the album's other tracks. Because I had no pre-vious written agreement with Michael, I was properly screwed. His people even stonewalled me on the fact that it was my arrangement and production on the track for "When a Man." I didn't have the heart to pursue it; just didn't need the negativity in my life. I had believed he was my friend, but I was wrong: life lesson learned the hard way.

But, then again...karma is a bitch that can come around and bite you. In his entire fabulous career, he's had only two Number One Bill-board Top 100 hits and two Grammy wins. I played a major role in the creation of all of them. After we parted ways, there were no more to be had.

There is a kicker. At some point before our blowup, I negotiated a deal with J. Walter Thompson for Michael to do a version of the song, "Daddy's Little Girl" for a 60-second Kodak commercial. He ab-solutely killed it, as only he could. When my eldest daughter was married a couple of years ago; we played that track for the father/daughter dance. I can't imagine a more perfect version of the song for that moment.

Ah, Michael: what might have been...

PETER CETERA has a distinctive, pure, clear voice. In L.A. I produced a vocal session with him for a Kentucky Fried Chicken campaign.

He was quick, professional and carefully doubled every word of his vocal to get his 'sound.' I did notice that he couldn't pass a mirror without stopping to examine the image and smooth his hair.

But the thing that sticks in my mind the most is the picture of him grabbing his crotch every time he went for a high note.

## Chapter 50

Elton, Part *Deux*

———

IT WAS SO UNFAIR. I shouldn't have been the one who got to go
on the trip. But Elton had made it part of his new deal with Coca-
Cola, so there was nothing anyone could do about it.

In the summer of '91, just as Alex and I were relocating from the
Palisades to Malibu, Lintas held another competition for a Diet Coke
song to go with their new campaign. It was a remarkably innovative
campaign that integrated Elton with clips of famous old movie stars
like Humphrey Bogart and Louis Armstrong. We lost the jingle competition to Crushing (another large music production company). I
think one of the Alessi brothers and Joey Levine were the composers.
David Wolfert was the arranger. All of them are tremendous talents.
Their song was great; it deserved to win.

As with the *Just For The Taste Of It* campaign, the tracks were to
be recorded in the U.S. without Elton. But the vocals were scheduled
to be done in London at the Townhouse recording studios. And some
of the spots would have to be recorded in five or six different languages!

The London session was planned to last a whole week, and it
took every bit. What a drag for the Crushing guys: one minute ready to
take the working trip of a lifetime; the next, completely out of the picture. Life's not fair sometimes.

I understood, though. A few years before, Elton had been at a very low point in his life, yet we'd managed to make it through that first Diet Coke campaign with flying colors. He knew and trusted me. He didn't know the other guys. End of discussion.

Of course the agency agreed to his terms, and I was hired to first produce the tracks in L.A., then fly to London in early October to work with Elton.

Recording in sunny Southern California is a unique experience—nothing like the airless, windowless studios in tall buildings in the cities where I was more accustomed to work. I remember the sessions at United Western Recorders with fondness. Way down at the eastern end of Sunset Blvd., it was a lovely complex of studios in that not-so-great section of town. Come to think of it, I can't think of any studios in L.A. located in upscale neighborhoods, except maybe funky Shangri La in Malibu (the one that was designed by Bob Dylan and The Band).

Anyway, studios in L.A. are generally just one story tall, so their exits are right at ground level. Step outside for a breath of fresh air and you will be greeted with sunshine, the smell of flowers, the sight of palm trees and the chirping of birds. Even in the not-so-great sections. That's L.A.: deceptively beautiful. I was once driving down a residential street off Olympic Blvd. on my way to work when the bullets started flying. It was a beautiful early morning, all seemingly quiet and serene. Other cars were not yet filling the side streets as I took my usual shortcut from Malibu to West L.A.

And yet, there were the unsettling *pop, pop, pop* sounds of real trouble. I ducked way down and kept the car moving ahead slowly. As I peered over the bottom edge of the driver side window, I could see a body lying in a pool of blood in the middle of the quiet little street. The cops moving in with guns drawn. Strange. The yards were all well-kept, as were the houses. Neat. Painted in pastel colors. Not even a barking pit bull. Nothing like where trouble was likely to happen in NYC, or any other metropolises I know. There, the scene would include the appropriate grime, debris, broken glass, abandoned buildings, graffiti — all the traditional symbols of broken dreams. But not in L.A...

The Diet Coke tracking sessions for Elton at Western were easygoing, fun, uneventful. The L.A. musicians were professional and very competent, even if they lacked a bit of the grease and soul of New York musicians. One stark exception was Jeff Porcaro: my favorite

rock drummer of all time. But I had Doug Katsaros as leader and stand
-in pianist for Elton; he wrote out charts for the band using the Crushing demo recording. It was easily duplicated (I added a few touches
here and there — couldn't help myself). Ringo Starr was recording an
album in the studio next door with a lot of our other west coast musician friends. On breaks, we would all hang outside and shoot the shit,
Ringo included. Once or twice we went out to the Formosa for drinks
after work: the whole scene was more like Nashville than L.A. There
were no agency folks to cause trouble, so it was a blast.

A month passed before I took the polar flight from LAX to
London and checked into the 11 Cadogan Gardens Hotel. It's right off
Sloane Street, near Knightsbridge and Belgravia. A bonus is the short
walk to Harrod's, the greatest department store in the world.

The hotel is incorporated into a couple of brownstones straight
out of the Victorian era. Stepping inside is like stepping back in time:
dark carved wood antiques and plush fabrics, velvet curtains with gold-
en tassels, all lit by lamplight so dim it reminds you of gaslight. I
suppose it would be listed in a directory as an elegant boutique hotel,
but it also bears more than a slight resemblance to the hotel and personnel from the BBC's *Fawlty Towers*. Everyone on the staff was a
charming but crazy character, the guests were as bizarre as they were
interesting to talk with, and the rooms, although quite elegant in appearance, were falling apart. At least mine was. There was the little
surprise that would greet me every time I sat on the toilet. The big
heavy mahogany facing on the bathtub would crash to the floor, only
an inch or two from my bare feet. I learned to be quick and alert.

That week I came to know the owners: a young couple with two
boisterous children who regularly rampaged up and down the narrow
stairs. The "butler" was actually more of an all-around handyman. He
came to fix the problem in the bathroom, and eventually left with a
'*live with it*' shrug of the shoulders.

One tradition at the Cadogan Gardens was late afternoon and
late evening cocktails in the parlor. There was an honor bar with a few
hors d'oeuvres for the guests who would congregate to converse. They
were an odd enough group for me to feel like an extra in an Agatha
Christie movie.

The agency had hired a foreign language coach for Elton. The
first day we spent a few hours with her at the Townhouse. She was, I'm
sure, excellent in her field, but neither Elton nor I took to her. She was
stiff, humorless, and a pure academic with no understanding of music.
In short, impossible.

We decided we could fend for ourselves and fired her. After all, I spoke fluent Italian and French, and could get along well enough in both Spanish and German. The fifth foreign language was Japanese, and although I couldn't speak it, I knew enough to understand that, like Italian, it was totally phonetic and would be passable if no undue emphasis was placed on any syllable. In the end, we muddled through and heard no complaints from any of the participating countries.

Elton was a completely different person from the Elton I had worked with in Boston. He looked healthy, was upbeat, jocular, and professionally focused on the business at hand. He told me he had quit all of his previous bad habits, and felt great. When I asked him what had led him to live in Atlanta, Georgia, of all places, he simply said, "I met someone, and that's where he lives."

We kept chipping away at the workload in good humor. We worked hard on pronunciation, and had fun trying to sing in German or Japanese. Day after day, late morning to early evening, we plowed on until it was done.

In the middle of the week, a delivery was made to the control room. It happened to be my birthday, but I didn't think anyone there knew it. Apparently Elton did. The delivery consisted of a bower/tower of perfect white hybrid tea roses on a heavy wooden frame. The apparatus was as tall as I am, and attached to it was a note of appreciation from Elton. I was floored — and touched. He really is (in addition to everything else) a terrific and sensitive guy.

Throughout that week of sessions, we talked a lot about music during frequent tea/coffee/biscuit breaks. Elton explained how he approached writing his songs, and how he intended to do his next album. Basically, he put the band in the room, the page of typewritten lyrics (usually from Bernie Taupin) on the grand piano's music stand, and started writing with his hands, his voice and his heart. He gave them free rein. The band joined in when possible and gradually the whole song came together. It reminded me of what I had seen in Boston: how both his keyboard and vocal performances fell into place. Measure by measure, phrase by phrase. Inexplicable. Magical.

I had other fish to fry after the session on birthday night. I said goodnight to Elton around 6 pm and, with the help of the driver, stuffed the roses into the trunk of the studio car and drove back to 11 Cadogan. We squeezed the bower into the hotel, and I told the astonished staff to distribute the roses to all of the rooms for everyone to enjoy.

After a tolerable dinner at the hotel, I changed into rock and roll wear (tight jeans, tall boots, black turtleneck and Harley jacket) and took off in a cab for an address in some district. It turned out to be laced with canals. Already past 10 pm, the neighborhood was dark, dank and scary. The area between the strips of murky water was lined with ancient, crumbling buildings barely lit by dim street and stoop lights. My publishing company had set me up to meet with someone named Frankie Miller. As I looked around, I became more than a little nervous, and kicked myself for agreeing to meet at his apartment. But I had to follow through. I climbed the three flights of wooden stairs up to his flat. The venue was less than inviting.

I didn't know it, but Frankie Miller is a legend. I hadn't the slightest inkling of how well-known and universally respected he is. Frankie is one of those artists who had the talent, personality and guts to do it all, yet never made it to the top. Should have, but didn't. From the 60's on, he wrote great song after great song, many of them covered by big artists; put together fantastic bands with himself and musicians from super groups, (the most famous was The Stoics); worked with record label after record label; tried Nashville; tried New York; London; Edinburgh; Glasgow; etc. Over the years, he explored a lot of styles, all of them done well: hard rock, r & b, country — you name it. But no combination ever really clicked, and by the time I met him, his career was at a low.

We hit it off instantly. Frankie is my favorite kind of guy, a bad boy to the bone. Sure, we listened to some of each other's music and songs, but the night was mostly spent drinking Scotch neat out of jelly glasses, smoking cigarettes, and gabbing until very late in his crowded, dilapidated apartment with its crappy furniture and out-of-tune upright piano.

At some point I said to him, "You know, what with your accent and attitude, you remind me of my Scottish friend, Ian." He looked at me quizzically and asked, "Ian who?"

"Ian Clews, but you wouldn't know him. He's from Malibu."

Frankie's face turned ashen. He clutched at his heart with one hand and grabbed my arm with the other. "Ian fuckin' Clews? *Ian Fuckin' Clews*? You know *Ian Clews*?!!! I thought he was fuckin' dead! You just about gave me a heart attack. Nobody's seen or heard from him for over 20 years. He just disappeared one day, *bam*, and that was it! We all thought for sure he'd bought the farm somewhere!"

It was my turn to be dazed and confused. How was it possible that Ian, my very close friend in Malibu — skilled horseman, survivalist, vegetarian wild man, gun collector and Scottish ballet dancer — knew this stone rocker?

So I guess I didn't know that much about Ian, after all. Had a secret mysterious past, did he? AND it involved the music business: *my* business! I was shocked and a little pissed off.

But I also couldn't wipe the smile from my face. I couldn't wait to get back home and blow his cover to smithereens...

WHAT MAKES AN INTERESTING STORY? I asked myself that question when selecting the tales that should be included in this book. Certain celebrities made the decision process difficult — they were the superb professionals whose sessions in the studio were performed gracefully, flawlessly, and (sad to say) without drama. No story there!

That group would have to include Leontyne Price, B.B. King, Bo Diddley, Was (Not Was), Tony Bennett, Chaka Khan and Rufus, Donna Summer, Al Jarreau, The Allman Bros, Tom T. Hall, the Mills Brothers, Tanya Tucker, the Temptations, Richard Page of Mr. Mister, Alabama, and the Oak Ridge Boys. Dedicated professionals, masters of their art, it only *seems* that these stars perform without effort.

It's too bad, but true: the most memorable sessions are always the ones filled with *sturm und drang...*

Chapter 51

Clewsy

———

IAN CLEWS AND HIS BAND, The Pathfinders, burst onto the music scene in Edinburg, Scotland, one Saturday night in 1964 with a debut performance at McGoos that blew the top off the place. This Scottish beat group from Glasgow soon ruled at the famous club. The crowds adored them, especially the lead singer, "Clewsy" (as they called him). His other nickname, "Cludgie," was reserved for times when he got flushed, grumpy and dark. A journalist/fan wrote:

"The first thing that struck me was that Clews, the lead singer, looked a bit of a jessie - hands on hips and long manicured nails. But what a great voice. From the off they played some of the most incredible music we had ever heard or never heard!"

Beat music, or Merseybeat (so named for the bands who played at The Cavern Club in Liverpool, near the Mersey River) is a musical genre that sprang up in England and Scotland in the early 60's. A fusion of rock and roll, doo wop, skiffle, R&B and soul, its defining characteristic was a driving beat — not just on the backbeats of two and four from rock and R&B — but frequently on all four beats of the measure. The beat movement also gave rise to a band line-up that became standard for most acts: lead, rhythm and bass guitars plus drums. Both verses and choruses were often sung in tight harmonies, kind of like doo wop groups, with nonsense syllables sometimes showing up in the background vocals.

Beat bands were strongly influenced by the American music scene. The Beatles came up with their name in part because they considered themselves a "beat" group and liked the obvious pun, but also out of their admiration for Buddy Holly and the Crickets. Crickets, beetles, beat music...

A complete picture of the emerging music scene in the British Isles should include a mention of skiffle. When the popularity of jazz began to decline in the '50s, a new craze took hold. 'Skiffle' was improvised jazz combined with elements of the hillbilly sound. Instrumentation often included guitars, washboard, jugs and single-string bass: cheap instruments that even teenagers could afford. Although skiffle disappeared almost as fast as it appeared, its echoes can be heard in many big name artists of the era. Three of the Beatles played in skiffle bands like the Quarrymen Skiffle Group (John and Paul), and the Eddie Clayton Skiffle Group (Ringo).

For about three years, The Pathfinders enjoyed tremendous success in Scotland. (Once outed, Ian eventually gave in and told me all about it).

He was a bloody star and he loved it. Most of all, he enjoyed the theatrics — that's what he loves to talk about. Not about his phenomenal singing voice, which was everyone else's focus. No, it was his showmanship, his ability to electrify crowds and get them roaring just by marching up and down the front of the stage. He was an incredible dancer, the result of years of professional study in both Highland dancing and classical ballet.

One of his innovations was the use of two drummers simultaneously. Now it is quite common; in those days, revolutionary. The blood-pumping synchronized rhythm at twice the volume drove the audiences to a frenzy. In other performances, he would change the pace by putting a grouping of upholstered furniture on the stage and dimming the lights. He would then lounge on the sofas, talking and singing in an intimate fashion. The people swooned.

Ian loved outrageous costumes. One day he was an American gun-slinging cowboy, the next an English fop. That explains the critic's "a bit of a jessie" comment, but I can assure you, there is nothing effeminate about Ian. Hetero all the way, and I'm sure the trail of broken-hearted women stretches from across the pond and the North American continent to Malibu. He isn't a big man, maybe 5' 8", slim, toned to perfection, with the grace, flexibility and speed of an Abyssinian cat. Much later when I got to know him, he almost always wore tight-fitting jodhpurs with tall riding boots. Probably to show off his perfect dancer's arse.

Out of the blue, the club McGoo's closed its doors. Some said it was due to gangster pressure: the Italian owner chose to get out instead of paying up. Another club called The Place quickly picked up both the talent and the customers. Many liked it better because the stage was set low and the audience could get closer to the acts. Another loyal fan wrote:

"...here the Pathfinders were kings. Clewsy was master and commander. They introduced us to unheard soul gems, R & B masterpieces, as well as new beat tracks. They were the complete band and I can honestly say I never missed a performance at The Place by The Pathfinders. Then one Saturday night Clewsy told a packed crowd that the band was signing for Apple Records and leaving Scotland. You could have heard a pin drop as well as my jaw hitting the floor. I knew they would move on to bigger things but we were just not prepared for it. They did a final gig. When the band came on to say farewell and played 'I'm Gonna Miss You,' I swear Clews ran off stage in tears. I wish I could contact him today to tell him that he and his band were worshipped in Edinburgh."

Things went downhill after that, slowly and painfully throughout the early 70's. Apple Records was brand new. They really didn't have it together. One bright spot Ian told me about was being given the chance to sing the first serious demo of the song "The Long and Winding Road."

But as a whole, the big move to stardom was a disaster. The band's name was changed to Jason's Flock, then changed back. Apple Records renamed them White Trash, then just Trash, and finally, at the depths, when they performed as a backing band for some female singer, The Trashcans.

Marketing strategy was not a strength of Apple Records.

Band members left and were replaced. Managers were fired and replaced. Different styles were tried and rejected. Money was hard to come by, since all four Beatles had to approve everything. One member quit and returned to Scotland to became a tailor. In all, a few sides were released, but basically, it came to nothing. Sad — very sad.

In my opinion, the biggest problem was that The Pathfinders were a cover band. There wasn't a real songwriter among them, and the time for successful cover bands was quickly waning. It's too bad they were never hooked up with great writers, because with Ian's sense of style and ear for what people wanted to hear, I'm sure things would have worked out differently, and famously so.

When I quizzed him about his mysterious sudden disappearance, he explained, "Susan, I was left with a fancy car, a bunch of equipment, a really bad heroin habit and nothing else. I was going to end up dead on the streets, and I knew it. So I split, period."

It's no wonder no one ever found him. Ian escaped to Africa and hired on to work on a huge farm owned by some Scottish relatives. Leftovers, I imagine, from the British colonization of Africa. I don't know how long it took, or exactly how it happened, but he eventually became a mercenary soldier for hire.

Ian began telling his gruesome tales almost as soon as we met in Malibu. (Never a word about the music business, though). Alex, my impressionable 10-year-old, and I were educated about terms such as "pink mist" (the visual effect of someone's head being blown away by a high powered rifle) and "hunting for tigers": riding through the jungle with spotlights trained on the trees above. We were given a blow-by-blow of how he and a few of his mates cleared out an airport that had been overrun by rebel bad guys. I don't remember what the body count was, but Alex, a video game lover, was certainly impressed.

Ian was and is a master horseman. He was definitely an early version of the horse whisperer. He has uncanny communication with the beautiful beasts. When I saw him ride or train, I was always struck by his ramrod posture and absolute grace. Apparently, he had also done quite a bit of training and showing hunter/jumpers somewhere, sometime. He would talk about waking up in the "grey motel" (the hospital).

On many occasions, I rode with him over the Malibu hills and through the canyons. One time we were in a state park up at the top of Kanaan Dume Road when the mare I was riding bolted. I pulled and pulled on the reins to no avail. Ian kept pace with us and shouted for me to pull harder with a jerk. I did; she stopped on a dime. I went flying.

When I came to, Ian was kneeling next to me, pressing a wet kerchief on the back of my neck. He got me back on the horse, back to the stables and eventually back to my house in the Palisades. In light of the liability situation, we agreed to spare the owners of the mare news about what had happened.

I could barely move for the next week or so but gradually recovered. Many years later in Aspen, I had to have X-rays after a slip on some sidewalk ice. The doctor told me, "There's nothing broken on your right side, probably just sprained muscles...but what the heck happened on your upper left side? You have four healed fractures in your upper ribcage. Were you in a car accident?"

At least I didn't have to wake up in Ian's 'grey motel'...

Guns were an important part of Ian's life. He had always loved them, starting as a kid watching American westerns on TV. Rumors circulated in Malibu that he had amassed a stellar collection of firearms stashed out in the desert somewhere. The cache was supposed to be worth a fortune and included everything from AK 47's to muskets from the Revolutionary War. He told me it was his legacy: the inheritance for his child.

When I first met Ian, he was pretty much a rolling stone, moving from friend's house to friend's house, with no visible means of support, but always informally contributing something, helping with odd chores or solving problems around the property. He was reliably entertaining and frequently the life of the party. Never had a dime to his name, but always had something to offer.

We hit it off from the beginning, but I still don't quite understand why he didn't tell me anything about his musical past. He was aware of what I did, but never expressed much interest until, of course, I blew his cover. Then the floodgates opened and we talked about music and the music business often. He even came to the studio with me a few times.

Alex and I were living alone in my house in Malibu when the L.A. riots sparked by the Rodney King affair broke out. The morning after the first night, Ian showed up and presented me with a beautiful .357 Magnum. I still have it. He took me to a range and showed me how to use it. Under his watchful supervision, he even let Alex fire it.

Another time, he was in our backyard. It backed up against a vast expanse of protected land. He was furious at his shoes, a pair of Uggs he had spent good money on, worn day after day for months, but which had now developed holes. Alex and I watched in fascination as he whirled in a shotputter's circle, kicked one boot high in the air, and shot it full of holes before it hit the ground.

"Awesome," said Alex after he'd watched Ian finish off the second one.

Ian stayed for a while at Judy Maura's tumbledown horse farm in Malibu. This was before she moved with her mother up to the not-falling-apart horse farm in Encinal Canyon. That first house was full of gaps and holes — barely livable. Ian told us he would spend his evenings just sitting in a chair in the kitchen, shooting rats with a .22 as they ran for their lives across the floor. Most nights would end with quite a pile.

There was also the time he got so mad at something he saw on TV that he took the set up the hillside behind the house, set it on the ground, and shot it to pieces from 200 yards away. "Good target practice." was his observation. In fact, he liked the experience so much, he would look around for discarded sets, arrange them in a row on the hill, and send them off to eternity in a blaze of gunfire. It was always fun to watch.

The craziest, stupidest and most dangerous experience, however, took place at the Wrigley Mansion in Phoenix. It was our fault, Michael's and mine. I don't know what we were thinking...

We were videotaping the end of the climactic chase scene for the movie *Tell Me No Lies*. We had been working on the movie for more than a year; this was the project for Malibu's public High School.

I had rewritten an end scene in which the cunning murderess shoots at the canny detective. Somehow we let Ian convince us to let him shoot LIVE ammunition at Alex (the detective) on the garden terraces in the back of the Mansion. The flower pot he was aiming at appeared to be only a foot or two from Alex's head (actually it was a good eight feet away). It all went fine. Only one take was needed, but the reaction from Alex as the pot behind him exploded was certainly convincingly real. Ian said, "I told you I couldn't miss."

Clewsy was intense, fanatical and meticulous in everything he did. From his tea to his food to his weed (he never touched alcohol). He was also the ultimate survivor. If Armageddon ever came, and I decided I actually wanted to continue living, he would be the person I'd want at my side.

I am delighted to report that he is safe in the hills of Malibu, enjoying life with a wonderful woman and a bunch of horses. Recently, I even received a recording of an excellent new song he just wrote. Who knows what the future will bring?

FOUR DAYS WITH SQUEEZE in some little British town, a whole day with Bonnie Tyler in Manchester, and a perfect afternoon/evening in a London studio with Petula Clark. All in one week in the late '70s. My own mini-tour of the British Isles.

Glenn and Chris were painstakingly meticulous (reminded me of Donald and Walter). Bonnie's voice was truly unique (very American rock'n roll style, reminded me of Rod Stewart). Petula was a total pro who sang brilliantly and behaved elegantly (reminded me of English royalty).

All the same, I never did get used to rushing out in the middle of a session to get a last pint at the local pub. Smelly, grimy, smoke-filled places — good cheer or not. I have never drunk more light ale, golden ale, brown ale, dark ale, strong ale, old ale, porter, bitters, mead, stout or beer in my life.

Chapter 52

Pattie and Phoebe

——

WE SAT IN MY ROOM AT THE Beverly Hills Hotel. Hunter
Murtaugh, music director at Y&R and I were meeting with
Nelson Riddle. Mr. Riddle was a household name: the leg-
endary orchestrator/arranger who had contributed greatly to the suc-
cess of other household names like Frank Sinatra, Ella Fitzgerald and
Nat King Cole.

We had a plum of an assignment for him. Valentine's Day was
coming up, and Hallmark Cards had agreed to produce a full 60-
second commercial using the Gershwin song, "Love Is Here To Stay."
Sixty-second ads were rare in those days. Mr. Riddle had been selected
to do the arrangement, and Hunter had also successfully negotiated
with distinctive artist Phoebe Snow for the vocal. A dream team for
sure. I was honored to be asked to produce the session.

Nelson didn't say much during the meeting. Hunter and I got
into a lengthy discussion regarding details: studio, engineer, configur-
ation of the orchestra, scheduling, etc. We also had to agree on a singer to record a scratch track for the agency, client and Phoebe. Her concert schedule wasn't going to allow her to make the recording session
in L.A.

At some point Hunter and I both stopped talking and just
looked at each other. We realized we hadn't heard a word from Mr.
Riddle in quite a while. We both turned in our chairs to check his reac-

tion. He was sound asleep with his chin resting on his chest. I guess he had already decided that at least *he* knew exactly what had to be done, and there was no point in blabbing on and on about it.

The session was a real treat. The entire orchestra was recorded all at once on the Warner Bros. soundstage in Burbank. No click track, no editing, no overdubbing, no close miking of anything. Nelson had a wonderful sense of timing. He brought the track in close to 59 seconds for every take. The scene was a throwback to the great days of studio recording in the '40s and '50s. I imagined seeing Frank, Ella or Dean on mike in the room. Both Hunter and I wished we had 10 tunes to do that day.

Robin Beck sang the scratch vocal after we recorded the orchestra, and did a perfect job. It was a treat for her, too. Accurate, in tune, but not overly stylized. Bringing personal style to the track was Phoebe's job. The final vocal session was done in New York a couple of weeks later and Phoebe slayed it, as expected.

A few years later I worked with Phoebe on another memorable project. Chevrolet was introducing the Geo car and Campbell Ewald, their Detroit based advertising agency, had somehow bought the rights to Rodgers and Hammerstein's "Getting to Know You" from *The King and I.* HEA did many arrangements of the song, both instrumental and vocal, but at some point we decided to produce a duet version. We chose Dr. John and Phoebe Snow.

Once again, Phoebe wasn't available for the original session; we had to record the vocals separately. Not my choice of how to get the best out of a duet, but in this case, the finished track became one of my all-time favorites.

Dr. John, born Mac Rebennack in New Orleans, is a devotee of voodoo and an altogether colorful character. At the beginning of his career, he mounted theatrical stage shows, often dressed in elaborate costumes with gigantic headdresses and all of the voodoo accoutrements: sticks, shakers, beads, etc. His early music was peppered with voodoo rhythms and chants, but evolved into a mixture of traditional New Orleans R&B, funk, psychedelic rock, blues and boogie-woogie. He has been — and continues to be — a living force in the music business.

I worried as I watched Dr. John slowly shuffle into the studio, wearing slippers and leaning heavily on a stout walking stick. He was a large man, at least 250 pounds, and he didn't look healthy. I knew he was an acknowledged heroin user and saw evidence when he pushed back a sleeve as he sang. His eyes were closed and he swayed back and forth...but sing he did!

It was classic Dr. John. I didn't know if he were in one of his voodoo trances or just high; I only hoped he didn't fall over. After he gave us a few performances of the whole song, I knew I had enough to comp his part in the duet.

Phoebe came in later. First she sang a couple of complete solo performances. She then listened to his track while singing so she could match his phrasing on the lines that were written for them to sing together. The final product made me proud.

I worked with Phoebe one last time in '02. David Buskin phoned one day when Michael and I were in the midst of our move from Malibu to Hudson, NY. We were actually going to be in a kind of limbo. We needed to leave California sooner than expected because Flea (yes, it was *that* Flea of the Red Hot Chili Peppers who bought our house) insisted on moving in early. Because our new place wouldn't be ready in time, we had to spend two weeks at a friend's house in Vermont. With our four displaced dogs.

David told me he wanted to collaborate on the writing of a new theme song for Tufts University in Boston. Once approved, we would then go into a studio and I would produce it. I tried hard to wriggle out of the project, but he wouldn't let me. He was oddly insistent.

David explained he had become good friends with a Tufts alumna who wanted to commission the song for her alma mater, pay for it, and then donate it as a benefactress. I didn't know until much later just how 'good friends' they were. It was a tangled web to be sure. Risa de Ravel was a powerful woman who owned her own very successful communications company. She was pushy, overbearing and wanted to be included in every step of the creative process. This didn't go over too well, and she ran into my emphatic "*No!*" often. She complained and whined to David to no avail.

I produced a full-blown demo of "The Light On The Hill" after Risa approved the music and lyrics. She had always wanted a celebrity to perform 'her' song, and David suggested Phoebe. I had some misgivings as I had heard that Phoebe was dealing with some health problems, but David told me that Buskin and Batteau (his brilliant and funny two-man act with Robin Batteau) had performed with her recently, and she was fine.

Well, she wasn't. During the Tufts session, it was obvious to everyone that she was suffering ill health. By the time we were ready for her to sing, the results were quite strange. She would stand in front of the mike, wait for her musical entrance, but never get started. She would hold up her hand to stop the playback, then say she had to go to the ladies room. She also kept ordering food into the studio: plate after plate. It was just odd. I knew that Phoebe's whole life was tragically focused on the care of her severely disabled daughter. This behavior in the studio, though, seemed to hint at health problems of her own.

It took hours, but I finally cobbled together a fairly weak performance by Phoebe. I knew it wouldn't fly (and so did David). We had Pattie Darcy replace Phoebe the next day. By good luck, she happened to be in town.

When Risa wanted a live performer to introduce the new song at the annual alumni festivities that year, Pattie flew in with her husband Courtney and gave an energetic, stellar performance. By the end of the song, she had clusters of Tufts students joining in on the choruses. It was a thunderous hit, and the birth of a new musical tradition for a fine University.

The next year, the song was to be performed by Keith Lockhart and the Boston Pops Orchestra for "Tufts Night At The Pops," Risa was still holding out for Phoebe: she was the bigger name. I knew in my gut that this would be courting disaster. I creatively fudged some information about Phoebe's availability, and, at the last possible moment, worked through the logistical nightmare of flying Pattie in and out of Boston. She was in the middle of the all-but-perpetual Cher farewell tour, and had only one night off per week. It happened to be the night we needed her — but we had only hours to spare on either leg of the trip.

Andree of Singers Express, who represented Pattie, came up from New York, bringing a gown and makeup. I rehearsed the piece with the rhythm section and the Pops arranger. Just before the live concert, Pattie did one run through with Keith Lockhart and the whole orchestra. Once again, she came through for me, performed brilliantly, and earned a standing ovation from the packed crowd. Keith was quite impressed with her, and took Pattie up to his dressing room to discuss future projects.

Pattie was a close friend: fair to say, just about as close a friend as any I've had in the music business. She and her husband Courtney Jones lived with me for a few months in the Pacific Palisades, just after Alex and I moved to California. Even when starring in the Broadway show *Smokey Joe's Cafe* or touring with Cher, whenever she could, she made it her business to do any job for me, big or little. We would hang out afterwards and catch up on what love and life had brought us.

Pattie was unique. Always funny and sunny, she brought tremendous positive energy to every situation, social or professional. I never once saw her down. There were a few phone calls in which she poured her heart out, but never in person. She was a dynamo who brought creativity into the studio and light and laughter into her friends' lives. Too often I have a bad habit of turning the page on friendships, letting them suffer neglect when time and distance intervene, but Pattie was one of the few exceptions. We stayed in touch.

Pattie went back to her original profession of hairdresser after she came off one of Cher's farewell tours. She and Courtney lived in Jersey, close to where she grew up. She worked out of a crappy little shop. She certainly didn't need the money, but she always had to be *doing* something. In this case, she was giving back to her old town and old friends.

A year or two later, Cher called again to tell her they were going out on tour one more time, and to get ready for rehearsals in a month. At the same time, Pattie and Courtney were preparing to climb on their motorcycles for an epic ride out to Colorado to buy some land. They wanted to build a house and try life in a different part of the country. They never made it.

One day, after they had been painting a deck and having a few beers, Courtney went into the next room for a nap. When he woke up, he looked for Pattie. She was lying dead on the floor in the next room.

Pattie's cause of death was declared to be from natural causes, but there was no autopsy, no specifics. The lack of more definitive information has always bothered me: she had been given a clean bill of health from her doctor only a few days before. For me, the news was devastating. I was physically ill for days. I was still recovering from the deaths of Kacey Cisyk and Vicki Sue Robinson, two other fantastic girl singers — friends I'd worked with closely for years. It didn't seem possible; it didn't seem fair. Three very talented women who had contributed so much to our business were gone. Way too soon.

Michael and I drove the long hours to get down to New Jersey to attend the wake her friends and family were holding to celebrate Pattie. It was at the local bikers' bar where she had been entertaining regularly. More than 100 people were there, but other than the two of us, nobody — not one person out of all the friends she had in the business — had bothered to come across the Hudson River. One unfortunate truth about the jingle world has always been "outta sight, outta

mind," and Pattie had been away from the studio scene for a few years.
But I was glad I was there. I got to tell her mother and sister how much
she meant to me.

JOHN MCCURRY, DOUG and I were in Ground Control, working on an underscore for a tampon commercial. The two young female clients were most irritating. We had just wasted a half hour trying to come up with a musical sound effect for the cut to the beauty shot of the product.

John said, "How 'bout this one?" as he put his index finger into one cheek and pulled it out with a loud "pop." The clients were not amused.

Chapter 53

A Dog and Pony Show

———

ON THE TARMAC AT THE RALEIGH DURHAM AIRPORT, John McCurry answered the outraged orange jump-suited worker with, "Well, then I guess a crack pipe is out of the question?"

John had just been screamed at by the guy after he lit up a cigarette as we walked toward our puddle-jumper. It was waiting to fly us to the golf resort where the ad conference was being held. I yanked him by the sleeve of his jacket and practically threw him up the portable metal steps into the small plane. I'd had enough of his antics already that morning.

We'd started the trip early at LaGuardia. David Buskin, Doug Katsaros, Robin Batteau, John McCurry and I were on our way to speak and perform at an advertising conference in North Carolina. It was being hosted by our good friends and clients at ad agency N.W. Ayer. I sat next to John. He wasn't in great shape, probably hung over. He went into a full-blown panic attack as soon as they sealed the hatch. I had to hold him down; talk him down. It was the first close call of the day.

At the stopover, we had decided to get out to stretch our legs. We browsed in the gift shop. The southern locals didn't seem to appreciate our group. John sported a coiffed and pouffed rock and roll hairdo: quite a picture, given his flaming red hair. He was dressed in tight black skinny jeans, black leather jacket, sunglasses and Beatle Boots. Doug had on one of his typical tie-dyed florescent hippie outfits, crowned by a genuine mullet. Robin and David, more conservatively dressed, actually looked like undercover FBI agents. I probably wore a full-length mink coat, a Gianfranco Ferre dress and 3½" Manolo Blahnik heels (my signature shoes).

As we wandered through the little store, I noticed that certain onlookers and people in uniform were gathering outside to peer in. Someone had evidently sounded the alarm. *Aliens invade local Airport!!* In fact we were rounded up by security people and asked to get back on our plane. McCurry put the icing on the cake with his remark to the airport worker.

Back to the gig at hand. Sometime during the 80's, the group of us put together a little two-part show about the role of music in commercials. In the first half, I spoke about general principles and screened examples of current ads, both good and bad. In the second half, the rest of the 'band' joined me on stage to create jingles on the spot.

Similar to an improv comedy troupe, we would first ask the audience to give us a product, two positive attributes, two adjectives and two musical styles. For instance: Green Giant frozen peas; 'tastes like fresh' and 'saves time;' 'bright green' and 'sweet;' 'classical' and 'blues.'

We would brainstorm for a minute or two, throwing ideas, lines and specific words around at each other. Then Dougie would sit down at an electric keyboard; Robin would pull out his violin; John would strap on his electric guitar, and David would pick up his acoustic. Doug would lay out a chord progression and rhythmic feel in one of the two musical styles as an intro. Four or eight bars later, the other instruments would join in, then someone would start to sing a line or two based on what we had come up with in our initial huddle. Eventually, a chorus with a memorable hook would appear. Everyone would zoom in on it and repeat it. After a minute or so, Dougie would abruptly jump to the second musical style, and the rest would make the necessary adjustments to perform it that way. We would always finish with a big ending flourish. *Ta dah!*

I would stand on the side and kibitz, comment, and suggest whatever came to mind. But it was the funny, brilliant, super-creative guys on the stage who did most of the work.

How the crowd loved it! We would do three or four of these improvs in a row, but they would always beg for another and another, making up ever more outlandish guidelines. I remember one we had to create for colored condoms in a Gregorian Chant — followed by Jamaican Reggae. In reality, the creative process we were demonstrating wasn't that different from how we would approach a real jingle assignment or a real pop song collaboration.

After the show we had the expected fancy lunch with the Ayer people and their guests. Pat Cunningham, Ayer's creative director, divvied the group up, seating us at different tables. I was a little worried when he placed John McCurry next to the President of AT&T. But McCurry was in a charming and funny mood, so all went well, and the bigwig was delighted to rub elbows with a real rock and roll musician. He said he couldn't wait to get home and tell his children.

We had time to kill before the plane ride back. It prompted a decision to take a stroll around the golf course. I changed into flats. We were quite a sight amidst the golfers in their colorful clothes with little animals and objects printed on pants and skirts.

We paused at a large pond to argue about whether the crocodile head we could see about 15 feet from shore was real or not. Doug and John went down to the edge to get a closer view. While they were still arguing, the head disappeared. They weren't looking when all of a sudden the huge, very real monster sprang up out of the water, jaws snapping and moving faster than I ever could have imagined. It chased them right up the bank onto the lawn. We were screaming; they were running for their lives.

I'd never seen anyone actually sprint in Beatle boots. And thank God, Doug was a former stuntman.

I tell you, it was a close call.

DURING MY ADVERTISING YEARS, my third and most important mentor was Jim Patterson, then creative director of J. Walter Thompson.

He saw to it that I was awarded many jobs. He brought me in early to participate in discussions about long-term campaigns and pitches. He challenged me to be bold, and demanded original thinking from me and his creatives by hanging a *Startle Me* sign on his door. His own imagination was limitless — as wild as it gets — much better suited to fiction, free from the constraints of the advertising world.

Not the easiest person in the world to communicate with, I was aware that many of his staff were afraid of him. It took me a while, but I broke through. We became friends.

Frequent drinking buddies in those times, we had a lot of laughs. I also sat with him as he grieved about the death of the love of his life.

I respect him greatly, and am deeply satisfied by all of his well-deserved success. He taught me a lot — and he is the one who first encouraged me to write this book.

Chapter 54

The China Club

I T WAS THE PLACE TO BE SEEN in the mid-'80s through early '90s. Music people, record executives, movie stars, sports stars: they were all there with their entourages. At least on weeknights. Weekends were generally overrun by the B and T crowd. The glitterati avoided associating with them. 'B and T' translates as 'bridge and tunnel': people who needed to come by bridge or tunnel to reach midtown Manhattan from Jersey, Brooklyn, Queens, the Bronx, or Staten Island.

It was a wild scene over there at 75th and Broadway. The entrance was a single unmarked door on Broadway, right next to the Beacon Theater. The door opened onto a cramped, dingy landing. If you could get past the hulking bouncers, you went down a black staircase that opened into the main underground room. I never arrived before eleven or midnight; nothing happened until then. For most, the party went on until two in the morning, regular closing hours in NYC. But for a special few, the China Club could last until past four, leaving me just enough time for a few hours of sleep before getting to the office at 9:30 or so. I didn't go every night (I would be dead if I had), but through the last half of the 80's, I was there a couple of times a week.

The noise inside was eardrum-shattering, what with the pumped-up dance music and the screaming crowd trying to hear one another. This was not an atmosphere conducive to intimate conver-

sation. It was also rowdy — people pushing and shoving in fun; play-
fighting — often leading to real fighting. Someone was always getting
thrown out.

There was a good-sized dance floor, always full. To the left as you
came in, there was a raised platform area with round tables of differing sizes. Maybe 10 to 12 of them. The people swarming around them
seemed to dart from table to table, but maybe that was just the effect
of the strobe lights. This was the VIP area, and you had to be someone
famous to be welcome up there. There was no other place to sit in the
Club, so lesser lights had to just stand around, drink in hand, collect-
ing glimpses of the celebrities and their antics.

Oddly enough, even though I certainly wasn't face-famous to
the general public, I always had a VIP table waiting for me. Why is a
somewhat disturbing tale.

I had been working at the Nashville studio House of David fairly
frequently, and had grown friendly with a new assistant for David
Briggs, the owner. We'll call him Anthony.

More than anything, Anthony wanted to move to New York City.
He was a sweet kid, eager to please, so I helped him get an entry-level
position at one of the recording studios. His seemingly charming
father, who was always hanging around David's place in Nashville, fell
all over himself with gratitude. I managed to make excuses for not being able to accept his invitations to dinner in Nashville, but he was so
persistent back in New York that I finally gave in. I had dinner with the
whole family.

The mother was very old-style Italian, dressed in shapeless black
clothes. The daughter was attractive and friendly, but wore a trashy, in-
your-face outfit (probably just to spite her parents). The father was a
snappy dresser, always in pointedly expensive suits. At that family dinner, he spent all of his time focused on me, asking a thousand questions.

I surrendered as little information as possible, but he seemed to
know a lot about me anyway. In the next few weeks, I fended off more
of his nearly daily invitations for drinks, dinner, whatever — but he
wouldn't quit.

I finally agreed to meet him for a cocktail to tell him it had to stop.
We met fairly early in the evening, and I happened to mention I was
going to the China Club later. He paid the tab and insisted we go up to
the Club immediately.

He marched in with me without even a question from the door guards, sat me at one of the VIP tables, and told me to wait. When he returned, it was with two men; he introduced them as owner and manager. He carefully explained to them that I was a very important person in the music business, and that he expected me to be seated immediately at a VIP table every time I came in. They nodded, introduced themselves, and told me if I ever had any problem getting what I wanted at the China Club, I was to ask for either of them.

I was simultaneously freaked out and impressed. I started to get it. His son had told me his father owned a business in New Jersey — something to do with pouring cement for foundations.

Whatever he said to the China Club people worked. Whenever I walked in, I was greeted by name and seated quickly.

I wasn't as impressed in a good way when Anthony's father showed up unannounced at my country farm in Putnam County. He explained that he was just in the neighborhood and wanted to visit. His sudden appearance at what I considered my private, unknown-to-the-public sanctuary deeply spooked me. I screamed at him and ordered him off my property.

And then I got a letter. He explained in it that he just wanted to help, and would set up a co-owned publishing company for me and him that would make us both a lot of money. He offered a sizable advance. I responded that if he ever contacted me again, he would hear not only from my lawyers, but also from the authorities. I had seen *The Godfather* several times. Thankfully, I never heard from him again.

Nevertheless, my buddies at the Club were most impressed with my ascendancy to the elevated stage with its coveted tables, though I never did tell them how I'd attained my new status. Usually, I would arrive with musician friends who had access to them anyway — most often with funnyman and talented guitarist John McCurry. His best friend, Julian Lennon, would often be there already, hanging with up-and-coming actor Christian Slater or others. I had a kind of unspoken empathy with Julian — still do. We became friends.

Some random memories describe the time, but I think the Club-goers had best remain unnamed... Once I saw a certain famous rock star at a nearby table, accompanied by a coterie of gorgeous, scantily clad women, proudly pull out his naked 'rod' and show it off to all around. It reminded me of children in 9th grade.

Many patrons would make frequent trips to the back room in pursuit of private recreational activities. Another very well known actor insisted on having the back room completely cleared when he chose to visit it. He would come into the Club dressed for all the world like a Maytag repairman from the suburbs: high-water khaki pants, light blue polyester short-sleeved shirt over a white tee: missing only the pocket protector. He kept mostly to himself. I was told that he was completely obsessed with Whitney Houston — had been sending her bunches of white roses every day for more than a year.

There were always a few tables of headliner basketball and baseball players who only seemed interested in getting wasted and horsing around with each other. A raucous and raunchy bunch. Most of the fights came from their tables.

I spent a lot of time on the dance floor, blowing off steam. None of my famous companions would ever be seen out on the dance floor with the riffraff, but I loved it. I'd dance with anyone who asked me.

For me, this was a recent change of behavior. Up until a couple of years before, you would never have caught me dancing. I was afraid of looking like a geek. Yes, I had studied ballet, but that had nothing to do with looking cool or making the latest stylin' moves. In my summer of upheaval (1985), I'd spent a few weekends with my GBFF (that's gay best friend forever), Gordon Grody and his gorgeous Canadian lover, Andre, at their equally gorgeous beach house in East Hampton.

One late night they literally dragged me out onto a dance floor in some club, then held me there until I started dancing with them. I was drunk enough to give in and start moving to the beat. Throughout that summer, I proceeded to shed all of my inhibitions about dancing. It's fair to say I became a wild woman on the floor.

The China Club nights in Manhattan ended when I moved to California. I did go to the one in L.A. with McCurry and Julian, but just once. It was a riot. The comedian Sam Kinison was there with his Moroccan girlfriend, Maliki. I remember she had on a tight flowered sheath dress and sported a Carmen Miranda hat with several kinds of fruit attached. She paraded around the club with tray after tray of 'Sex on the Beach' shots held high on one hand while Sam screamed and ad-libbed until we screamed with laughter. It grew very late.

I had way too many of those deadly sweet drinks, and when John stopped to get gas on our way back to the Palisades, I barely got the passenger door open fast enough to puke onto the asphalt. I've never been able to look at that drink again. In a way, it was a fitting close to a relatively dark period in my life.

Yeats told us things fall apart; the centre cannot hold. That's what was happening to me as I left New York. Maybe I was slouching toward

Bethlehem — or maybe I was just skulking away from New York. Whatever. I couldn't keep it together anymore. My mother — my champion — had died. The business was morphing into something unrecognizable. Alex's father had split; we were alone now. And I was hanging out at the China Club.

To prove what? That I was still young, hip and attractive? How far can you fall from grace? At least I had the sense to pick up the pieces and move...

THREE QUESTIONS FROM a six-year-old:

"Mom, when you were born, where was I?"

"Mom, would you rather be suddenly deaf or suddenly blind?"

When told by a well-meaning friend, "Alex, do you know what the one thing is that the more you give, the more you get back? It's love, Alex!"

To which Alex asked, "What about pain?"

Part V

REINVENTION

Chapter 55

Swan Song

———

BOMBS WERE DROPPING on Baghdad as we started the first of many recording sessions for what was being called "the pitch of the century."

The client is one of a handful of companies whose name and products are catchwords on nearly every street corner in the world. Now they had shocked the advertising industry by putting their entire ad budget up for grabs: hundreds of millions worth, winner take all. I'd been tapped by one of their smaller foreign agencies for whom we had previously created two highly successful jingles (one so popular that we recorded a pop single version which sold 50,000 copies). As a result, although it was completely unheard of, HEA — a lowly *music* company – would wind up shaping their entry and winning the day.

I put together a team that produced a full complement of scripts, songs, radio spots, even a philosophical positioning essay — along the way, transforming the proposed 'line' into the slogan that ultimately beat out all the others. In English and dozens of foreign languages, it's still being used ten years later. From my point of view, it made for a particularly gratifying swan song.

The advertising agency stakes were so high that it took an unusually long time before an amicable settlement was reached — and if you're wondering why the names of the agencies and corporate giant are mysteriously missing from this fable, let's just say that sometimes it's the lawyers who get the last word!

ASHTON KUTCHER, playing Walden, sang our Dr Pepper jingle on an episode of *Two And A Half Men*.

Walden first sings a few of Charlie's complicated, non-melodic jingles, ends with "I'm a Pepper/He's a Pepper/She's a Pepper/We're a Pepper/Wouldn't you like to be a Pepper too?" and asks Alan if Charlie wrote that one also.

When Alan says no, Walden shrugs and says, "Not that catchy anyway..."

Chapter 56

Escape to L.A.

AFTER 25 YEARS IN NEW YORK CITY, I packed a couple of suitcases, told Alex, "We're outta here!" and moved west. I'd heard the rule, 'In L.A., make sure you live west of Barrington,' so I rented a fully furnished house in the Pacific Palisades. I thought, *nice community, good place for Alex, close enough to the recording studios.* I was mistaken.

My decision was influenced by the fact that I'd been doing a lot of music production on the West Coast. Many of the people I was working with convinced me that life in "La-La Land" was beautiful. Well it was, for a while.

Alex was always begging me to go out and 'bag some kids.' So when I saw a man walking his two children down the street past our new house, I rushed out, introduced myself, and asked if his boy and girl would like a new playmate. He turned out to be Frank Langella, and two good things happened: Alex got some new friends, and *I* got to hang out with some fascinating people in Frank's circle: Dom DeLuise, Mel Brooks and Anne Bancroft among others.

Still, from the beginning, I did have an uneasy feeling about the rest of the Palisades. The women I saw shopping in the big fancy Gelson's market or playing with their perfect-looking children in the parks, too often reminded me of *The Stepford Wives.* My neighbors peeked through the fence or hedges; I even caught people across the canyon spying on us through binoculars. Granted, I was a single mom, employed a gorgeous young male nanny/houseboy, and long-haired, tattooed musicians and singers were coming in and out of the house for meetings and writing sessions at all hours. Alex and I were not a good fit with the town. We lasted barely a year.

Gus, the houseman, was way too good-looking. I suspected he was gay, but he went on and on about his girlfriend. Although quite competent at everything he did for me, it all unraveled by the end of the year. One night as we were driving home from Malibu, Alex asked me a question.

"Mom. Do you think Gus is gay?"

I remained calm. "What gives you that idea, Alex?"

"Because I saw him making out with George on the bed in his room."

George, famous chef from Aspen, currently working at a top L.A. restaurant, had been around the house a little, but hey — I sort of recalled a wife and daughter in Aspen. Yet Alex never lied. It was one of the best things about him.

One day when Gus was on vacation, I found my Mercedes dead in the garage, so I had to borrow his Jeep to pick up someone at the airport. As I rummaged through his top drawer looking for the keys, I found a necklace of mine next to a bottle of my signature perfume, Cabochard. *Uh-oh.* When confronted, Gus said he had "borrowed" them because he admired me so much. He loved to wear both of them and fantasize.

Great.

Then, shortly after Alex and I came home from a trip, the local police paid a visit. They said complaints had been filed about naked men playfully chasing each other around in my backyard (*those damn binocular freaks*). I had to let Gus go. Fortunately, the lease was almost up.

Alex's schooling presented another problem. I enrolled him in the local elementary school. In my childhood, I had done fine going through the Los Angeles public school system and after all, this was a sophisticated, wealthy community. I didn't know, however, that hundreds of non-English-speaking children from central L.A. were bussed into the school every day.

Alex lasted a little more than a week. He had come from a highly rated French private school in Manhattan, and the differences were too much to take. The language problem alone meant that most of his school day was spent copying sections from a children's book over and over again. Also, his teacher, Mrs. Chen, constantly screamed at the class in broken English.

So one day, mid-morning, my nine-year-old strolled into the Palisades kitchen to inform me that he had climbed the chain link fence during recess and walked home. Convincingly and calmly, he stated his case, finishing with the fact that he was never going back there. I scrambled; found a private school up Topanga Canyon (the Calmont School). Things went much better there.

It was during that wretched Year of Dislocation that I was introduced to Malibu. In those days, it was still quiet, rustic, and not overpopulated. I couldn't wait to move us there. I found a terrific house at the end of a *cul de sac*. Totally private, with a great yard and lots of Spanish Colonial character, it backed up onto State Conservancy land. A trail led to a spectacular waterfall. I committed, sent for my furniture from New York, and we settled in.

All along I was still doing quite a lot of jingle work, but I was freed from the grind of running a big company with its 16-hour days. I had much more time for myself. At first, I just worked out of the big L.A. studios, but eventually set up my own little operation 30 miles to the south in West L.A. I also built a tiny recording room in that first Malibu house.

I produced two entire albums — one for Robin Beck, and one for the European artist Dan Lucas. I found new and interesting engineers, musicians, writers and singers for a number of projects, and wrote songs with a variety of creative people. I got to hang out with legendary Desmond Child at his museum-like home in Santa Monica. I helped him out by doing some comping and clean-up work on several of his projects, including producing song demos with Brooke Shields. Desmond deserted the area after the Northridge earthquake, fleeing cross-country to South Beach. He and his longtime partner, Curtis Shaw, have now moved to Nashville, where they are raising their two sons (Desmond is the biological father).

I loved Malibu, and those two years at the end of Via Escondido were action-packed. The house was great for entertaining, and

I did a lot of it. Dinner parties almost every week; the kitchen was ideal for my style of cooking for an audience, and perfect for just hanging out. Guests like Ridley Scott, Richard Gitlin, Ray Liotta, and Jake Busey would show up. Many a night was consumed by endless conversations with John McCurry and his best buddy, Julian Lennon. I was invited to the hippest Malibu parties with the Simpson/Bruckheimer movie crowd, and wrote songs with Eric Carmen, Stephen Bishop, Lisa Dalbello, Jeff Lorber, Aimee Mann, Kane Roberts, and John McCurry. I got to see Fred Couples play at Riviera, and Bjorn Borg compete in a private exhibition match. It was party, party, party. And empty, empty, empty. With the exception of John and Julian, none of the relationships lasted more than a couple of months.

Alex and I would take off for Aspen whenever possible, sometimes bringing my new best friends from Malibu along: my assistant, Gail Esposito, Angela Best (George Best's ex-wife and my personal trainer), her son Calum (Alex's best friend), Scott Humphrey — a great programmer and keyboardist who did a lot of work with me — and my collaborator, friend, and partner in crime, Richard Benoit.

Richard is a brilliant and creative engineer/producer; also a wild man and lady-killer. We tore it up many nights in bars and at parties from Malibu and Beverly Hills to Mammoth and Aspen. He was *Buddy Bad* and I was *Betty Rake* (as in 'rake 'em in and rake 'em out').

One time, the two of us spent the entire month of November in Hamburg, Germany, mixing the Dan Lucas album, *2000*. We spent seven grueling days a week cooped up in the all-inclusive studio (personal chef included — which meant we couldn't even escape for lunch). When finally liberated, more often than not we'd flee to one of the local bars. Richard drank two of them out of their entire stock of Guinness. We are close still.

The fact is, after three failed marriages, I'd decided that I wasn't cut out for long-lasting, serious relationships. The men who came through my revolving door then were younger, good looking and — I have to admit — uniformly shallow. It was better that way. However, the never-ending, going-nowhere whirlwind of social activities and meaningless flings started to wear thin.

I joined the Malibu Tennis and Riding Club to devote some time to healthier pursuits. After playing in a pickup doubles game one day, Sharon, a tall, wholesome-looking woman with long, straight blond hair, suggested we have lunch. She mentioned her four children and husband, but was mostly interested in hearing about my life. She was fascinated, but I thought a bit envious. We became friends, sort of — and I invited her over to the Via Escondido house. She visited frequently, usually just parking herself to observe my tumultuous single life. She liked what she saw, more than once telling me, "I wish I were you!" I kept my mouth shut...

I was forever in search of friends for Alex, so I brought him over to her house on Point Dume for a playdate. Preferring my more interesting house, well-stocked pantry and unlimited access to a giant TV and video games, Sharon's children began to visit Alex regularly — coming up with ever more creative excuses for staying overnight. I believe this had a lot to do with food...

"Really? We can have a whole peach? Not just half? And how many cherries, each?"

"As many as you like. Fruit's good for kids."

I would frequently find one or two of them in the big pantry closet with the door closed. Hands in cereal boxes or cookie packages, looking guilty. "Sorry, Susan." "Sorry, Susan."

"Leave the door open," I would say. "You can have whatever you want."

Sharon and I remained friendly, but not close. I did invite her and her husband Michael to one of my dinner parties. There were 12 guests, mostly high-powered showbiz types. I recently ran across a photograph taken at that dinner...it is oddly prophetic. In it, posed before the dining room table, all the guests are smiling for the camera. Michael and I are standing next to each other in front of the group, looking for all the world like the host and hostess...

I believe I was deliberately set up by Sharon to take over the raising of her children. I don't think her husband was meant to be part of the package. But that's how it worked out. Shortly after we met, she asked me out of the blue to be their 'godparent' if anything were to happen to her and Michael. It was a strange moment.

Unbeknownst to me, it turned out that Sharon had set her eye on a soap opera actor whom she had been following around Malibu for a year or two. They'd recently begun a relationship. Sharon, thrilled with the drama of it all, decided it was time to get rid of Michael. She told him she wanted him to leave. Stunned (he had been oblivious to what was going on), he refused. Sharon asked me to deal with him on her behalf, saying that he wouldn't listen to her. Despite four children and 14 years together, it seemed that Michael and Sharon were even less compatible than Rob and I had been.

I personally negotiated a different living arrangement for them, and they separated quickly. Immediately thereafter, I remember sitting with her at the bar at the Tennis Club. The truth had just come out about the boyfriend.

"What the fuck is going on?" I asked. "You're leaving me with your kids and your husband while you ride off into the sunset with Beau!"

Incredibly, she replied with a self-satisfied smile, "Yep, that's the idea."

The kids were thrilled with the new situation. Alex was relieved to have my laser-like attention diluted by four other beings. Michael and I were kindred spirits. A plainspoken psychiatrist had once told me, "Susan, some people are just not cut out for marriage." Apparently, he was correct: my technically unmarried relationship with Michael has lasted for 20 years. Go figure.

After a couple of rocky months, we assumed full custody of the children — so my family went from a unit of two to a flock of seven. In my mid 40's, I plunged gleefully into a whole new life, the kind most people have in their 20's or 30's. I was suddenly raising five children: Dexter 6, Scott 8, Joscelyne, 10 and Darcy 12 (Alex was 11).

It was new; it was challenging, and it was a blast (most of the time). I did have a pet bugaboo: I insisted on knowing where they were and who they were with at all times. One phone call was my nightmare come true:

"Mrs. Hamilton? This is Officer Tolin with the Malibu Police Department. We have a...Dexter Alkus in our squad car? He says you're his mother? We found him at Hughes Market, sitting with his friend Morgan in the back of a car with expired plates that's registered to a felon? We'll bring him on home, but is there anything you'd like to say to him?"

"You can tell him he's grounded for a month."

It turned out to be a pretty innocent mistake. The two boys had hopped a ride into town with a guy who rented a cottage from Morgan's mother. They just wanted to go to Blockbuster, but had no way of knowing they were dealing with a brother-sister team of grifters. Dexter did know, however, that he needed permission...

Unfortunately, grounding any of the boys (there were now three) had little effect. They were perfectly happy to hang out at home, playing video games.

A few rules were necessary: just a few. I often think parents get into trouble with their kids by arguing about too many little things. I learned to pick my fights carefully; to try to have them only over big issues.

My first rule: no hitting. Also, no slapping, no hair-pulling, no punching, biting or kicking. Ever. They could never understand why they were allowed to spit and name-call, but couldn't whack each other over the head with a toy piano or whatever else might be handy. It took patience, but the violence stopped.

I told them they could ask questions about anything, and I would answer them as best I could. I promised never to lie to them. (The only exception turned out to be about money: I wouldn't tell them how much money I made or how much certain things cost, or were worth — I thought that focus was inappropriate). Of course, sex and drugs were Popular Subjects One and Two.

I also told them they were allowed to use swear words around me and their siblings, but had to cool it a bit around their father, and never, ever, use them in public or when we had company. Alex held his head in his hands as the other four marched around the house, chanting "Fuck fuck, shit, shit, piss piss..." They got bored soon enough.

Of course there were some rough patches while everyone adjusted, but I suspect fewer than in many blended families. The kids regarded me more as a fairy godmother than the wicked stepmother. In the blink of an eye, I'd turned into Florence Henderson.

Although for the next few years I continued sporadic jingle and record work, more and more of the time I found myself applying my production skills in new ways. I produced unique vacation experiences in Costa Rica, Hawaii and Aspen; a point system for chores and homework; and turned my lifelong fascination with cooking into nightly gourmet dinners for the family — which more often than not included any number of kid friends who happened to be around. One of the children once remarked, "Around here, it's like having Thanksgiving dinner every day!"

As the years ticked by, one by one the children turned into insufferable teenagers. I'd been warned about this.

"You can't! You just can't call Shannon's parents to find out if they're going to be there during the party! It's not cool you're embarrassing me. And I'm going anyway!"

"No, Joscelyne, you're not. I have to call. It's my job." (Most of the time, the parents were going to be there anyway).

"Darcy, right back upstairs, please. You're not wearing that to school."

"But *WHY*? It's what everyone else wears."

"Don't care. You look like a prostitute; go change."

(Answered by the slitted-eyes stare, the shoulder shrug, the big sigh, then, muttering what might have been *bitch*, a flounce upstairs...)

As the numbers mounted against me, I found myself searching out new strategies. High on the list: the need for surveillance. I'd decided the most foolproof way to keep track of them was to volunteer at the school. I was able to cover most subjects, and soon, what started as occasional classroom help turned into the school's request that I get a substitute teaching credential. To the consternation of my musical colleagues, I started teaching at least two days a week at Malibu High School.

So the kids couldn't get away with much. I knew all of their teachers, all of their assignments, and all of their friends. As hoped, this proved to be a teen's nightmare (for the girls, especially).

Ms. Pallathena, the guidance counselor, called toward the end of the school year: "Susan, we'd like you to chaperone the Senior Prom" (an all-night, lockdown affair).

"Sorry, Nancy. I just don't have the time."

Ms. Palathena (now whining a bit): "Susan — you know all of them...and you know what they're up to."

A big sigh, then, "Okay, fine."

During those riotous years, my work in the music business ceased almost completely. I had decided that being responsible for raising five human beings was a full time job — and ultimately more important. I missed the excitement of working with the zany creatives, the electricity in the studio, and making the big money. But this new life seemed just as rewarding.

We spent nine years together as a complete, tight-knit family unit. We had a lot of laughs, not so many tears, and plenty of adventures. We survived the 6.7 Northridge Earthquake and fought two dangerous brush fires that came right up to our house. The house later burned to the ground while Flea owned it (he didn't get to the roof-mounted sprinkler system in time).

Finally, in 2002, the family scattered. Michael and I moved back East to Wolfeboro, New Hampshire; Darcy and Alex were in colleges on opposite coasts, Scott and Joscelyne were in Aspen, and Dexter stayed behind in Malibu with the Noltes.

I have to say, my time with all of those kids represented the longest and the most carefree chapter of my life.

I know, I know — those who have raised a bunch of teenagers will probably call me nuts for saying that. But I'd had a lot of prep. After years of dealing with ad people, musicians and singers (many, children themselves), it was more like skiing down a blue trail instead of the double black diamonds I'd contended with for so many years.

WE RAISED CHICKENS during all our years at the Malibu house. The fresh eggs were delicious; when the hens grew too old, they were passed off to our Guatemalan housekeepers.

One morning I sent Alex and Dexter up to the chicken house at the top of the property to collect eggs for breakfast. They rushed back, out of breath and eyes wide, telling a tale of carnage. Michael didn't believe it, and accompanied them back up the hill.

There was only one hen left of the nine. She was running around the pen, squawking, panting and terrified. In a dark corner lay a neatly stacked, gruesome pile of eight headless corpses. There was no logical explanation.

Later that day, Enrique, our gardener, nodded his head knowingly and announced, "Chupacabra." We almost believed him: the apocryphal blood-sucking monsters are said to roam Puerto Rico, northern Mexico, and Southern California. The creature supposedly resembles a small bear with a row of spines down its back.

Nobody slept well that night.

Chapter 57

Scott

THE LAS VEGAS VACATION to the new Wynn Hotel had been planned for a few months, but we never thought it would be spent grieving over the loss of our son, Scott.

We received the call from the Clark County coroner's investigator one dreary January afternoon in New Hampshire. Scott's body had been found lying between cars in the parking lot of a cheesy hotel/condo complex about five miles off of the Strip. He had fallen from a balcony.

In shock and totally confused, we made frantic phone calls to the rest of the children on the West Coast. We hadn't even known Scott was in Vegas. We were terrified that his younger brother Dexter had been with him and was missing. Gradually, the disturbing story unfolded.

Scott had just been accepted into the Astrophysics program at UC Santa Cruz as a junior. He was to start classes in September. We were thrilled for him.

He, all the rest of the children, and a couple of their friends had just converged on New Hampshire to spend Thanksgiving weekend with us at our new home in Wolfeboro. It had been a picture-perfect family gathering in the New England late fall. We told funny stories and laughed a lot.

We knew Scott and Dexter had driven down from Santa Cruz to Malibu to visit their old haunts and friends after the Christmas holidays.

We eventually discovered that Dexter was holed up at a buddy's house in Malibu, where he had been all week. He knew nothing about what had befallen his brother. Scott, apparently, had been hanging out with a bunch of casual but not close friends, and those guys had convinced him to accompany them on a short road trip to Vegas, where the objective would be to crash an Adult Entertainment Convention.

We learned after the fact that Scott had been an off-and-on user of cocaine and ketamine. We were shocked; we'd had no idea. Over Thanksgiving, he hadn't even drunk any champagne. We had never seen him stoned.

On the last night of their trip, Scott had been with the disreputable group at the condo complex and had become extremely high. He announced to them he was going out on the balcony to get some fresh air. He never came back in.

They didn't notice for hours, and when they did, as soon as they figured out what had happened, they ran like the rats they were. They didn't call anyone; they didn't even check on him. We were shown a security video of them running down the back staircases, pulling on their shirts and jackets as they went. They left his duffel bag in the apartment. Cowards. Low-lifes. Snakes.

For Michael and me, those five days in Vegas were like a Fellini nightmare. We were staying in the most luxurious new hotel, but spending hours in the worst section of the underbelly of the city.

The funeral parlor we were sent to by the Coroner's office was a house of horrors. Just a mile or two from the hotel, it couldn't have been further away by any other measure. A grim little bungalow sitting practically under the freeway, surrounded by the constant loud whine of traffic. Gravel paths lined with plastic flowers stuck in the dirt. Chain-link fence around the perimeter. A cur, tied-up and barking next door. The cheap, crappy interior with more fake flowers and plastic religious icons. On our way in, we passed a carelessly left open door: on display inside, a corpse. Someone's father, probably. Hard to miss.

We were shown into the office of the Director to make our grim choices. She was a ghoul. An aging Latin showgirl type, showing too much cleavage and sporting long, fake fingernails with chipped black polish. She pretended to be sympathetic as she told us how much extra we would have to pay to retrieve the *cremains*, and suggested the most expensive urn. We'd need to pay extra to expedite the process, if we wanted to leave town as soon as possible.

I was a wreck. Despite a resolve not to show emotion in front of this vulture, I cried through the whole thing. My eyes turned extremely dry and sensitive. By the next day, I couldn't open them in any kind of light for more than a few seconds.

We left Las Vegas and flew to Malibu for a weekend of remembering and celebrating Scott. I rented a house overlooking the ocean. Lots of Scott's friends came; some from far away. We all visited, spoke, laughed, cried and wrote in a journal.

Everyone has his or her own way of dealing with grief. I mostly cooked tacos, rice and guacamole for everyone, as I had done so many times as the children and their friends grew up.

I think of Scott most days. Even now, seven years later. Right after the event, I kept having dreams in which I would discover that he was actually alive! I would wake up ecstatic, and then have to start crying all over again. That same experience has happened to me before with loved ones I have lost suddenly. I guess it must be part of the grieving process.

In a garden close to the house, I have a big stone planter in the shape of a beautiful frog with soulful eyes. I plant it every year with white petunias. Frogs were Scott's favorite.

MY GORGEOUS GIANT SCHNAUZER, Blackjack, is a television addict. He guards the sets at all hours and attacks whenever an enemy appears. His fangs will hit the screen as we yell, "*NO!* Blackjack!"

At first it was just other dogs. He eventually expanded his hate list to all animals, violent humans, and anything that looks like a weapon.

The worst thing, though, is that he recognizes every enemy's commercial after just a note or two of music or a word or two of dialogue. He can be sound asleep in the next room, but it takes only seconds before he comes flying through the air to bite the TV.

Do you have any idea how many ads have animals in them?

Chapter 58

Postscript

————

THE '60s, '70s, AND '80s WERE THE GLORY DAYS of the jingle business. The best work was done, we all made lots of money — and we loved what we did for a living. Then it all changed dramatically. Sure, there had been signs of erosion in the preceding years, but the plunge in the '90s was spectacular.

Some of the causes can be blamed on technology. Synthesizers went a long way toward eliminating string sections. At first, at least for a while, I insisted on mixing a few real players in with the synthesized sound. But that didn't last long: the machines got better and better. It eventually got to the point that you could create a reasonable facsimile of a complete track without a single real-life player (except for the programmer, of course)! Then all you needed were singers. The remarkable onslaught of home computers followed soon after. And by that point, any teenager in his garage could whip up a demo.

These bursts of technological advancement had a disastrous ripple effect on the business; most especially on our relationship with our advertising agency clients. Competitions between numerous participants became the norm. The philosophy behind that practice seems to be that if you can throw enough pieces of tape in the air, maybe one will stick. Personal relationships that had been built on trust through years of working together gradually faded away, replaced by ever more powerful music directors who named the contestants. Successful arrangers and composers chose to retire. Jingle houses became schmooze centers - *who had the best vodka and the purest coke?* For most of us, it just wasn't much fun any more...

Other events conspired against us as well. Downturns in the economy resulted in a shift of power within the advertising agencies — away from the creatives and toward management, bean counters, and account people. Demands for compliance with every whim and notion of their clients, no matter how ridiculous, trickled down from above. After all, they were the actual advertisers, the people with the money, *so bend over and let them have their way with you; just keep them on the balance sheet, for God's sake!* Account people actually started showing up at our sessions. Unheard of in previous times, it was more than just a symptom. It was something that wasn't going to get better any time soon.

The good times were over, at least for the time being. Besides cookie-cutter type jingles and underscores, much music for advertising these days relies on what I call "borrowed interest": just pay the big bucks for some existing hit song, come up with a cockamamie idea that connects it to your product, and hope the fans will turn into consumers and buy your stuff.

I am an eternal optimist, however, and do believe that ultimately there will be a renaissance.

During the years at HEA, my biggest reward always came from spotting the tiny spark in someone, being able to nurture it, then standing back to watch it catch fire. This wasn't limited to the talented people who made music; many others moved on to great success. Kathy Brega and Glenn Berger went back to school and became shrinks. Kevin Halpin continues his successful career as a leading New York engineer. Sherry Reaser Clark has a booming business as a Vermont florist. Jake, Bernie and Nick formed their own company with my friend David Lucas, and had a good run for a number of years. Connie Boylan has a great job as a music contractor at Disney. Gerard heads a department at McCann. Debbie DeMeo married Rob Mounsey. Rachel Margulies Smit has her own song-writing company in NYC: *Your Songs Created.* Jewelle Gomez is a celebrated poet and writer. David and Robin are performing again as Buskin and Batteau to rave reviews and sold-out concerts. Doug Katsaros is tearing it up on Broadway and much of the rest of the planet.

And I went on to raise those five children and teach at Malibu High School. I thought my time in the biz was over. But it wasn't. I was rewarded with two more Steve Sohmer network gigs. And the most satisfying swan song of all.

And after that, who knows? I have a feeling the book's not finished...

SITTING IN A ST. GERMAIN CAFE, Michael and I were doing some final proofreading of this book. We were inside because it was pouring.

The gentleman at the next table was curious. I explained (as best I could in French) who I was and what we were doing.

With no warning at all, he pulled a heavy, ornate cross out of his pocket and slammed it down — first on my open page, then quickly on Michael's. With a shooing-away motion and intense expression, he declared himself a prelate and the book *exorcised*: the devils were gone!

I hope he's right...

INDEX

CPSIA information can be obtained at www.ICGtesting.com
Printed in the USA
LVOW08*0603081113

360375LV00002B/21/P